The Eater's Guide to Chinese Characters

The Eater's Guide
to Chinese Characters

James D. McCawley

The University of Chicago Press
Chicago and London

James D. McCawley is professor of linguistics at the University of Chicago and an authority on Oriental cooking, food, and restaurants.

Title page calligraphy by Masami Kawahira

The University of Chicago Press, Chicago 60637
The University of Chicago Press, Ltd., London

© 1984 by The University of Chicago
All rights reserved. Published 1984
Composed by Asco Trade Typesetting Ltd., Hong Kong
Printed in the United States of America
91 90 89 88 87 86 85 84   1 2 3 4 5

Library of Congress Cataloging in Publication Data

McCawley, James D.
  The eater's guide to Chinese characters.

  1. Cookery, Chinese—Terminology. 2. Chinese language—
Word formation. 3. Chinese language—Conversation and phrase
books. I. Title.
TX350.M3 1984   495.1′83421   83-14535
ISBN 0-226-55590-9
ISBN 0-226-55591-7 (pbk.)

Contents

Acknowledgments

The suggestions and encouragement that started me on the protracted research project that has resulted in this book came from George Lakoff, who I thank for having led me to undertake the most enjoyable research that I am likely ever to do. In the more than ten years I have worked intermittently on this subject, I have received valuable information and suggestions from a far greater number of persons than I can possibly acknowledge, but I must at least mention a few who have been particularly kind and helpful to me: George Chao, Calvin Lang, Sandra Thompson, and especially Anthony Yu, whose detailed comments on an earlier version of the manuscript enabled me to fill many serious gaps and purge it of much misinformation.

Introduction

The purpose of this book is to enable non-Chinese who enjoy Chinese food to better exploit Chinese restaurants. There are a number of reasons why it is useful to a patron of a Chinese restaurant to know the Chinese characters for the various dishes. First, in many Chinese restaurants, either there is a separate Chinese-language menu that bears little relation to the English-language menu (for example, the Chinese-language menu in many restaurants in Chicago Chinatown lists three times as many dishes as the English-language menu) or there is a Chinese-language supplement to the menu (perhaps in the form of slips of paper bearing Chinese characters, taped to the wall) listing the day's special offerings. Second, even when the menu is fully bilingual, the Chinese names of many of the dishes may be more informative than the English names, since the Chinese names are relatively uniform, while the English names follow the proprietor's whim and his often faulty command of English. And third, writing out your order in Chinese characters may assist you in the battle that one must often fight with waiters for treatment befitting a normal human being.

1

Some General Remarks about Chinese Characters

There is a widespread misconception that all Chinese characters are some kind of picture of the meanings that they stand for. While many characters in fact originated as pictures, not all of them did, by any means, and the writing system has evolved in such a way as to pretty well obliterate the pictorial origins of those characters that are basically pictorial. The following ancient and modern forms illustrate the development of some characters from a pictorial form to something much less obviously pictorial:[1]

日	女	水	鹿
rì sun	*nǚ* woman	*shuǐ* water	*lù* deer

A certain number of characters are indirectly pictorial in that they are composed of pieces that are pictorial in origin and whose meanings are related (perhaps metaphorically or fancifully) to the meaning of the whole character, for example:

---

1. The pronunciations corresponding to the characters are given in PINYIN, the official spelling system of the People's Republic of China. Popular spellings are used in this book only in the definitions, for example, 天津 *tiān jīng* is translated as "Tientsin." Otherwise the pinyin system is adhered to, since it gives an accurate rendition of the sounds of Mandarin and since any effort that you spend in learning it will be repaid in the facility that it will give you in pronouncing Chinese names that you see in current newspapers and magazines. The reader should consult chapter 11 for an explanation of what sounds correspond to the various letters in the pinyin system of spelling.

林 *lín* woods (composed of "tree" plus "tree")

森 *sēn* forest (composed of "tree" plus "tree" plus "tree")

好 *hǎo* good (composed of "woman" plus "child")

囚 *qiú* prisoner ("man" inside box)

尖 *jiān* pointed ("small" on top, "large" on bottom)

However, most characters are not pictorial at all but are compounds of two characters, one (the RADICAL) which gives a clue as to the general area in which the character's meaning lies, and one (the PHONETIC) which rhymes with the word that the character represents.[2] For example, the character 火 *huǒ* "fire" is the radical of many characters that denote methods of cooking, as in the following characters, which are given along with their phonetics:

炒 *chǎo* to stir-fry; 少 *shǎo* few

炸 *zhá* to deep-fry; 乍 *zhà* at first

烤 *kǎo* to dry-roast; 考 *kǎo* to examine

燒 *shāo* to roast with sauce; 堯 *yáo* name of an early Chinese emperor

The character 食 *shí* (one of several characters that can be translated as "to eat") is the radical of a number of characters that refer to food and eating, such as the following, given with their phonetics:

飯 *fàn* cooked rice; 反 *fǎn* wrong way round, to revolt

餅 *bǐng* pancake, biscuit; 并 *bìng* to combine

餐 *cān* dinner; 殘 *cán* remnant

---

2. This description is inaccurate in two respects. First, the system of radicals and phonetics originated in ancient Chinese, and thus it is not rhymes in modern Mandarin (or in any other modern dialect) that are directly relevant to the system but rather rhymes in ancient Chinese. Second, I am using "rhyme" here in a somewhat odd sense, namely, that for things to rhyme, they must have not only the same vowel and the same final consonant (if any) but also "similar" initial consonants, for example, *pai* rhymes with *bai* and *mai*, but not with *dai, kai,* or *sai*.

飽 *bǎo* full (after eating); 包 *bāo* to wrap
餃 *jiǎo* ravioli; 交 *jiāo* to deliver

The character for "dinner" illustrates two sources of difficulty in learning the system or radicals and phonetics. First, the radical is not always at the left; indeed, it is often not at all obvious what part of a given character is its radical. Second, neither the radical nor the phonetic need have the same shape that it has when it is an independent character. These points can be illustrated also by the following characters, in which the "fire" radical appears at the bottom of the character and has the form of a row of dots rather than its full form 火:

煎 *jiān* to pan-fry slowly
熏 *xūn* to smoke (fish, etc.)
煮 *zhǔ* to boil
蒸 *zhēng* to steam

Just by looking at the last character, one cannot tell whether the crossed horizontal line at the top or the row of dots at the bottom is the radical—both those elements are in fact common radicals.

In what follows, I will largely ignore the system of radicals and phonetics. However, one of the foundations of the system nevertheless looms large in this book, namely, the fact that most characters consist of components that occur elsewhere, both as independent characters and as components of other characters. The task of learning characters will be greatly simplified if one learns to recognize the pieces of which a complex character consists. You will find it easier, for example, to remember the characters 煮 *zhǔ* "to boil" and 猪 *zhū* "pig" if you observe that they share the element 者, combined in the one case with 灬 (which is in fact the "fire" radical, though you don't need to know that in order to recognize

it as a component of the character) and in the other case with 犭 (which is the "animal" radical).

2
How You Slice It

In this chapter we will begin learning some characters that appear frequently in names of Chinese dishes. While the name of a Chinese dish sometimes involves a fanciful metaphor or a play on words, more often it is a quite straightforward indication of the central ingredient(s) and the mode of preparation. One aspect of the preparation that is very often mentioned in the name of the dish is the way in which the ingredient is cut. Thus, the following characters appear in the names of many dishes:

丁 *dīng* to cube, diced
片 *piàn* thin slice
絲 *sī* shred (i.e., julienne-cut piece)
塊 *kuài* chunk (especially for poultry on the bone, cut into bite-size pieces)
球 *qiú* curl, ball (not like "meatball," but a small strip that curls as it fries, e.g., half a shelled shrimp)

These characters may be combined with names of ingredients, as in

肉片 *ròu piàn* meat slices (actually, pork slices: unless another meat is specified, pork is understood, just as for us "egg" means chicken's egg unless another bird is specified)
牛肉絲 *niú ròu sī* beef shreds
魚片 *yú piàn* fish slices
鷄丁 *jī dīng* chicken cubes

蝦球 *xiā qiú* shrimp curls
鷄塊 *jī kuài* chicken pieces
三絲 *sān sī* shredded three ingredients
肉丁 *ròu dīng* pork cubes

By adding to these combinations the character for a method of cooking, one gets names of real Chinese dishes:

炒肉片 *chǎo ròu piàn* stir-fried pork slices
炸牛肉絲 *zhá niú ròu sī* deep-fried beef shreds
煎魚片 *jiān yú piàn* pan-fried fish slices
炸鷄丁 *zhá jī dīng* deep-fried chicken cubes
炒蝦球 *chǎo xiā qiú* stir-fried shrimp curls
炸鷄塊 *zhá jī kuài* deep-fried chicken pieces
涼拌三絲 *liáng bàn sān sī* cold "salad" of three
    shredded ingredients
炒肉丁 *chǎo ròu dīng* stir-fried pork cubes

Exercise 1. Translate the following into English.

1. 蝦片   6. 炒三絲
2. 鷄絲   7. 炒鷄丁
3. 炒牛肉片   8. 蒸魚片
4. 炸魚片   9. 涼拌蝦
5. 煎鷄球   10. 蒸牛肉塊

Answers to this and other exercises are in chapter 12; you should compare your answers with those given to see how well you did.

3
The Basic Stuff

The names of many ingredients contain the characters 肉 *ròu* "meat," 魚 *yú* "fish," and 菜 *cài* "vegetable," for example:

牛肉 *niú ròu* beef (literally, "cow meat")

羊肉 *yáng ròu* lamb (lit., "sheep meat")

墨魚 *mò yú* squid (lit., "ink fish")

鮑魚 *bào yú* abalone (鮑 by itself means "abalone," but it is generally combined with 魚 anyway)

鯉魚 *lǐ yú* carp

白菜 *bái cài* Chinese cabbage (lit., "white vegetable")

榨菜 *zhà cài* a kind of pickled kohlrabi (lit., "squeezed vegetable")

泡菜 *pào cài* another kind of pickle (lit., "steeped vegetable")

芹菜 *qín cài* celery

雪菜 *xuě cài* a kind of pickled greens (lit., "snow vegetable," also called "red-in-snow")

Exercise 1. Translate the following into English.

1. 炒白菜
2. 炒牛肉片
3. 炸鯉魚
4. 炒墨魚
5. 涼拌芹菜
6. 炒鮑魚片
7. 蒸鯉魚
8. 煎牛肉片

In the names of many dishes, two ingredients are mentioned:

白菜炒肉片 *bái cài chǎo ròu piàn* pork slices stir-fried with Chinese cabbage

芹菜炒墨魚 *qín cài chǎo mò yú* squid stir-fried with celery

This is especially common with rice and noodle dishes:

鷄片炒飯 *jī piàn chǎo fàn* fried rice with chicken slices

肉絲炒麵 *ròu sī chǎo miàn* fried noodles with pork shreds

Exercise 2. Translate the following into English.

1. 白菜炒鮑魚片
2. 榨菜炒肉絲
3. 魚片炒飯
4. 牛肉片炒麵
5. 鷄絲雪菜炒麵
6. 芹菜炒肉片

4

Looking Up Characters

By now you have been exposed to quite a few characters, undoubtedly more than you can be expected to remember at this point. If you are going to get anything out of the rest of the book, it will be necessary for you to supplement your memory with a systematic glossary in which you can look up characters that you either don't remember or don't know at all. This raises an interesting question: how can Chinese characters be arranged so that one can know where to look to find a particular character?

A number of systems for the arrangement of characters in a dictionary have been used. In the traditional "radical system," characters are arranged according to their radicals. The radicals in turn are arranged according to number of strokes: first the one-stroke radicals such as 一 and 丨, then the two-stroke radicals such as 力 and 刀, then the three-stroke radicals such as 口 and 宀, and so on. Characters with the same radical are arranged by number of strokes: in the section for the radical 日, the character 日 comes first, then characters such as 旦 in which there is one extra stroke, then characters such as 早 in which there are two extra strokes, then characters such as 旱 in which there are three extra strokes, and so forth. In the more recently devised "stroke-count system," characters are arranged by number of strokes: first the one-stroke characters such as 一, then the two-stroke characters such as 十, then the three-stroke characters such as 千. Characters with the same number of strokes are arranged by their first stroke as they are written in

traditional calligraphy, for example, the characters that "begin" with a horizontal line come first, then those that begin with a vertical line, and so on. Note that under the radical system, the characters 計 and 詩 might well be on the same page of the dictionary, since they have the same radical, whereas under the stroke-count system they would be on widely separated pages, since the one has nine strokes and the other thirteen. There is also the "four-corner system," in which each character is assigned a four-digit number, each digit corresponding to the stroke that appears in each of the four corners of the character.

A book such as this, which is not written for specialists in Chinese, calls for a system of arrangement that allows a person to find a character rapidly without detailed knowledge about the Chinese writing system. None of the standard systems fills this bill. It is often very hard to tell what part of a character is its radical. Both the radical and the stroke-count system require that one know odd conventions regarding what counts as a stroke (would you have guessed that 司 counts as five strokes?); and if you get the stroke count wrong, you are likely to search in vain several pages away from where you should be looking. The four-corner system requires some fairly arcane knowledge about how one identifies strokes. The stroke-count system requires you to know enough about traditional Chinese calligraphy to tell which stroke is the first stroke (would you have guessed that in 少 the vertical stroke in the middle is the first stroke?).

I have chosen to adopt a variant of what I will dub the "division system," which was introduced in Koop and Inada, *Japanese Names and How to Read Them* (Eastern Press, 1923; Routledge and Kegan Paul, 1963), and is also used in O'Neill, *Japanese Names* (Weatherhill, 1973). The

Glossary lists first those characters that break down into a left half and a right half (e.g., 汕, 炒), then those that divide into a top and a bottom (e.g., 京, 芋), then the characters that are divisible into an enclosure and an enclosed (e.g., 回, 風), and finally the characters that do not divide into two separate parts. The left halves, tops, and enclosures are arranged according to the number of strokes, using a simplified system of counting strokes that is explained below. For any given left half, top, or enclosure, the characters containing it are arranged according to the number of strokes in the remainder of the character. The indivisible characters are simply arranged according to the number of strokes. To illustrate this on some specific characters:

鯉 consists of the left half 魚 and the right half 里. The left half contains thirteen strokes according to the stroke-counting system used in this book (it would be eleven according to the traditional system of counting strokes). The character is thus found in section L13: the part of the Glossary where characters with thirteen-stroke left halves are listed. The thirteen-stroke left halves are named L13a, L13b, and so on, and 魚 happens to be L13a. (One can find 魚 in the index of left halves given at the beginning of the Glossary.) Since 鯉 has an eight-stroke remainder, one looks for it under L13a.8 and finds it listed as L13a.8a (the other characters having 魚 as left half and an eight-stroke right half are listed as L13a.8b, L13a.8c, etc.). Names such as L13a.8f are used in cross-references, as when the character that you have looked up is a variant form of another character.

蘭 consists of the top ⁺⁺ and the bottom 闌. The top consists of four strokes and thus can be found under T4: the section of the Glossary where characters with four-stroke tops are listed. It is in fact the first of the four-

stroke tops, so the character will be listed under **T4a**. Since the bottom consists of nineteen strokes, one looks for T4a.19 and finds the character there, listed as T4a.19a. A major advantage of the division system over the stroke-count system becomes apparent here. One can easily make an error in counting the strokes in something as complicated as this nineteen-stroke bottom part. In a dictionary where characters are arranged according to their total number of strokes, such an error throws you completely off the track—you will be searching many pages away from the page you really want. With the division system, even a rough estimate of the number of strokes in the remainder will usually be enough to enable you to find the character: if you have found the top or the left half and know within a couple of strokes how many strokes are in the remainder, you have narrowed the search down to perhaps half a page; and since the Glossary is restricted to characters related to Chinese cooking, the area that you will have to search is reduced even more than it would be in a general-purpose dictionary that was arranged according to the division system.

鳳 consists of the three-stroke enclosure 几 and the fourteen-stroke remainder 鳥. It is found in the Glossary listed as E3b.14. (In cases like this, where there is only one character in the Glossary with a given top, left half, or enclosure and a given number of strokes in the remainder, there is no letter at the end of the name of the character; if there were more than one character listed that consisted of 几 and a fourteen-stroke remainder, they would be called E3b.14a, E3b.14b, etc.)

Where only one character having a given left half, top, or enclosure is listed, it is grouped under miscellaneous four-stroke left halves or miscellaneous seven-stroke tops or miscellaneous five-stroke enclosures, and so forth. The

characters in each miscellaneous group are arranged according to the number of strokes in the remainder and are given numbers like L6*13, the number for 鴨 *yā* "duck," which has a six-stroke left half and a thirteen-stroke right half and is listed under miscellaneous six-stroke left halves because no other character with that left half is listed in the Glossary.

Finally, there are indivisible characters such as 果. Since it contains nine strokes, it will be listed in section U9: nine-stroke indivisible characters. (It is listed as U9c: it is the third of the nine-stroke indivisible characters listed in the Glossary).

We will regard a character as divisible into a right and a left half (or a top and bottom, or an enclosure and an enclosed) only if it is normal to leave a space between the two parts. Thus, 古 will be treated as an indivisible six-stroke character rather than as consisting of a two-stroke top and a four-stroke bottom, since the two parts are normally run together. Since there is a certain amount of freedom as to whether a space is left between certain parts of a character, you should be prepared to imagine spaces or to ignore spaces in some cases where a character isn't where you looked for it in the Glossary. In several cases where it is not obvious that a character is divisible, it is listed here both ways, for example, 美 is listed both as U9i and as T6d.3.

Sometimes there is more than one way in which a character can be divided. For example, 意 might be regarded either as dividing into a five-stroke top and a nine-stroke bottom or into a ten-stroke top and a four-stroke bottom, depending on whether the middle part is regarded as belonging to the top or not. In such cases I have arbitrarily imposed the policy of assigning as little of the character as I can to the top or to the left half; thus 意 will be found

under T5 rather than under T10 and 湖 will be found under L3 rather than under L9. I have followed this policy even when it produces ludicrous results, for example, that 三 is to be counted as having a one-stroke top and a two-stroke bottom.

In the method of counting strokes employed here, each "corner" within the character initiates a new stroke. Thus, 日 is taken here as having five strokes. Traditionally it is counted as having only four strokes, since the horizontal line at the top and the vertical line at the right are written with a single movement of the brush or pen. In the method adopted here, you don't have to know how the hand moves in writing the character the traditional way: the printed shape will give you enough information to find the character. In the traditional method of counting strokes, a tiny "hook" at the end of a stroke counts itself as a separate stroke; here, however, "hooks" will be ignored in the stroke count, for example, ⌡ and ⎸ will both count as one stroke, not as two and one respectively. Thus, 丁 is counted here as two strokes, not three, and 糸 is counted as seven strokes, not eight.

There are several cases in which alternative ways of writing the same element involve different numbers of strokes. For example, the "vegetable" radical traditionally consists of two crosses and is counted as four strokes: ⺾; however, the horizontal strokes of the two crosses are often joined: ⺿, in which case there are only three strokes, as counted here. When alternative ways of writing a left half, a top, or an enclosure exist, all are listed in the Glossary, each under its own stroke count; the characters involving that element will all be listed under one particular variant of the element, and the entries for the other variants will direct you to that variant.

Exercise 1. Find the following characters in the Glossary.

1.	肝	6.	回	11.	北	16.	滷	21.	雜
2.	清	7.	豆	12.	蠔	17.	麻	22.	餛
3.	豬	8.	蕃	13.	皮	18.	乾	23.	蘿
4.	糕	9.	腐	14.	鴨	19.	醋	24.	鶉
5.	馬	10.	油	15.	家	20.	砂	25.	圓

Once you have gotten used to the way the Glossary is organized, you may find it useful to learn the numbers of strokes in various frequently encountered elements, for example, 隹 in item 21 of the above exercise counts for eight strokes. Knowing some of the stroke counts will reduce the time it takes you to look characters up.

5

Let's Decipher Some Menus

Now that you have learned a number of important characters and know how to look up characters in a dictionary, you are in a position to start deciphering menus. In this chapter I will give examples and exercises involving relatively simple made-up menus (menus much shorter than most Chinese restaurants would have); in chapters 6 and 7, examples will be given of full sections of menus from real Chinese restaurants.

Consider the following menu:

冷盤類		猪肉類		豆腐類	
拼盤	3.50	回鍋肉	2.75	家常豆腐	2.25
棒棒鷄	2.45	家常肉片	2.95	麻婆豆腐	2.25
五香牛肉	2.25	榨菜肉絲	2.45	紅燒豆腐	2.15
燻魚	2.45	魚香肉絲	2.95	冬菇豆腐	2.50
		家常腰花	2.75	砂鍋豆腐	4.50
湯類		木須肉	2.75		
榨菜肉絲湯	1.40			蔬菜類	
白菜豆腐湯	1.20	海鮮類		火腿菜心	2.25
酸辣湯	1.20	紅燒鯉魚	3.95	鷄油菜心	2.05
		糖醋全魚	4.25	魚香茄子	2.35
鷄鴨類		乾燒明蝦	3.45	炒雙冬	2.55
宮保鷄丁	2.95	茄汁明蝦	3.45		
醬爆鷄丁	2.75	宮保蝦仁	3.15	麵類	
油淋子鷄	2.95	豆豉蝦仁	3.15	炸醬麵	1.25
炸八塊	3.25	紅燒海參	3.75	担担麵	1.25
香酥鴨	4.00	蝦仁鍋巴	3.95	肉絲涼麵	1.25
北京烤鴨	12.00			麻醬涼麵	1.00

The menu is divided into sections, each having a heading that ends with the character 類 *lèi* "category." Reading from top to bottom in each column, the first section, *lěng pán lèi* "cold plates," translates into English as follows (with pronunciations added, for the benefit of the interested reader):

pīn pán assorted appetizer plate
bàng bàng jī bang bang chicken (shredded boilded chicken with spicy sesame sauce)
wǔ xiāng niú ròu five-spice beef
xūn yú smoked fish

This section contains one new character worth memorizing: 香 *xiāng* "fragrance."

The next section, *tāng lèi* "soups," lists the following items:

zhà cài ròu sī tāng pickled kohlrabi and shredded pork
soup
bái cài dòu fu tāng Chinese cabbage and bean curd soup
suān là tāng hot and sour soup

The new characters in this section which you should
memorize are 湯 *tāng* "soup," 豆 *dòu* "bean"; 豆腐 *dòu fu*
"bean curd"; 辣 *là* "hot" (spicy).

The dishes of the next section, *jī yā lèi* "chicken and
duck," are

gōng bǎo jī dīng chicken cubes stir-fried with chili
peppers and peanuts
jiàng bào jī dīng chicken cubes quick-fried with bean-
paste sauce
yóu lín zǐ jī oil-dripped chicken
zhá bā kuài Peking-style deep-fried chicken pieces
(lit., "fried eight pieces")
xiāng sū yā aromatic crisp deep-fried duck
běi jīng kǎo yā Peking roast duck

Important new characters: 醬 *jiàng* "sauce"; 油 *yóu*
"oil"; 子 *zǐ* "child"; 鴨 *yā* "duck." 子 is often used as a
diminutive, for example, 鴨子 really means the same as
鴨. The combinations 宮保 *gōng bǎo* and 醬爆 *jiàng bào*
are also worth remembering.

The next section, *zhū ròu lèi* "pork," lists the following
dishes:

huí guō ròu twice-cooked pork (lit., "return pan
meat": boiled pork, sliced, stir-fried with
vegetables in spicy bean sauce)
jiā cháng ròu piàn home-style pork slices
zhà cài ròu sī pork shreds with pickled kohlrabi
yú xiāng ròu sī fish flavor pork shreds (in spicy garlic
sauce)
jiā cháng yāo huā home-style fancy-cut pork kidney

mù xu ròu moo shu pork (shredded pork and vegetables, stir-fried with scrambled egg, wrapped in pancakes and eaten like tacos)

Characters you should remember: 鍋 *guō* "pan, wok"; 腰 *yāo* "kidney"; 花 *huā* "flower" (used here with reference to the fancy cutting of the kidney)

The following dishes are listed in the section *hǎi xiān lèi* "seafood":

hóng shāo lǐ yú red-cooked carp (braised in soy sauce)
táng cù quán yú sweet and sour whole fish
gān shāo míng xiā dry-cooked large shrimp (in hot sauce)
qié zhī míng xiā large shrimp in tomato sauce
gōng bǎo xiā rén shelled small shrimp stir-fried with chili peppers and nuts
dòu chǐ xiā rén shelled small shrimp in black bean sauce
hóng shāo hǎi shēn red-cooked sea cucumber
xiā rén guō bā shrimp with crispy rice

In this section you have encountered the following important characters: 海 *hǎi* "sea"; 茄 *qié* "eggplant, tomato"; 汁 *zhī* "juice, sauce"; 蝦 *.xiā* "shrimp"; 紅 *hóng* "red". The Cantonese pronunciation of *hǎi xiān* "seafood" is HÓI SÌN, as in the same of the sweet and salty bean sauce that you may know as hoisin sauce.[3]

The next section, *dòu fu lèi* "bean curd," contains the following dishes:

jiā cháng dòu fu home-style bean curd

3. To make it easier for the reader to keep Cantonese pronunciations separate from Mandarin pronunciations, I use capital letters for Cantonese; Mandarin pronunciations are always in lower-case italics.

má pó dòu fu ma po bean curd (bean curd cubes in spicy ground pork gravy)

hóng shāo dòu fu red-cooked bean curd

dōng gū dòu fu bean curd with black mushrooms (lit., "winter mushrooms")

shā guō dòu fu bean curd casserole (lit., "'sand-pot bean curd")

You should learn the character 冬 *dōng* "winter," which appears in the names of many dishes.

The dishes in the next section, *shū cài lèi* "vegetables," are

huǒ tuǐ cài xīn ham with flowering cabbage

jī yóu cài xīn flowering cabbage with chicken fat

yú xiāng qié zi fish flavor eggplant (spicy garlic sauce)

chǎo shuāng dōng stir-fried two winters (black mushroom and bamboo shoot)

The second character in the name of the last dish means "pair," as in 兩雙筷子 *liǎng shuāng kuài zi* "two pairs of chopsticks." 兩冬 *liǎng dōng* is even more common than 雙冬 *shuāng dōng* as a way of referring to the common combination of black mushroom and bamboo shoot.

The dishes listed in the final section, *miàn lèi* "noodle dishes," are

zhá jiàng miàn noodles with bean paste and ground pork sauce (lit., "fried sauce noodles")

dàn dàn miàn noodles with spicy sesame sauce

ròu sī liáng miàn cold noodles with shredded pork

má jiàng liáng miàn cold noodles with sesame sauce

You should learn the characters 麵 *miàn* "noodle, wheat flour," and 麻 *má*, which basically means "hemp" but is part of the word for sesame, 芝麻 *zhī má*, and appears in the names of many dishes that involve sesame paste or

sesame oil. An especially common combination in which it appears is 麻辣 *má là*, which refers to dishes prepared with chili peppers, sesame oil, and brown pepper.

Exercise 1. The following names involve only characters that you should know by heart. Check whether you can translate them into English without looking any of the characters up. Then check whether you know where to find them in the Glossary just in case you ever do need to look them up.

1. 肉片湯   5. 魚片豆腐湯   9. 茄汁蝦球
2. 紅燒鴨   6. 宮保肉丁   10. 麻醬魚片
3. 魚香腰花   7. 鷄油白菜
4. 鷄絲湯麵   8. 麻辣炸鷄塊

Now let's try a second menu, this one a little more elaborate than the last, but not really large by the standards of good Chinese restaurants.

湯類		冷盤類	
魚翅湯(大12.00,中8.00,小5.00)		什錦冷盤(大16.00;小8.00)	
三鮮湯	4.00	棒棒鷄	4.00
酸辣湯	3.50	白切鷄	3.50
蝦仁鍋巴湯	4.00	五香牛肉	3.50
火腿冬瓜湯	4.00	四川泡菜	2.00
蛋花湯	3.00	辣白菜	2.50
點心類		鷄鴨類	
春捲	1.80	宮保鷄丁	5.00
鍋貼(六個)	2.40	腰果鷄丁	5.00
水餃(六個)	2.40	甜酸鷄塊	4.50
大飽子(兩個)	2.00	紅燒鷄	5.00
葱油餅(兩張)	2.00	炒鷄球	4.50
		北京烤鴨	16.00
		八寶全鴨	14.00
		葱爆鴨片	6.75

猪肉類		魚類	
木須肉	5.50	紅燒全魚	7.50
京醬肉絲	6.25	清蒸魚	7.50
甜酸排骨	5.75	炒魚片	6.25
獅子頭	5.50	醋溜魚	6.50
回鍋肉	5.50	紅燒魚翅	12.50
冬筍炒肉絲	5.75	什錦海參	8.50
蝦類		蔬菜類	
甜酸蝦仁	6.25	炒兩冬	5.75
雪豆蝦仁	6.50	素什錦	5.25
炒蝦球	5.75	麻婆豆腐	4.50
鍋巴蝦仁	6.25	家常豆腐	4.50
龍蝦丁	8.25	蠔油芥蘭	4.00
		麵類	
		肉絲炒麵	4.00
		什錦炒麵	4.75
		炸醬麵	3.25
		肉絲湯麵	3.50

Reading from top to bottom in each column, translation of the above (with pronunciations):

Tāng lèi soups
yú chì tāng shark fin soup (lit., "fish wing soup"): *dà*
large, *zhōng* medium, *xiǎo* small
sān xiān tāng three fresh ingredient soup
suān là tāng hot and sour soup
xiā rén guō ba tāng shrimp and crispy rice soup
huǒ tuǐ dōng guā tāng ham and winter melon soup
dàn huā tāng egg drop (lit., "flower") soup

Learn the characters 大 *dà* "large," 中 *zhōng* "medium," 小 *xiǎo* "small," 瓜 *guā* "melon, squash, cucumber," 蛋 *dàn* "egg."

Diǎn xīn lèi pastries
chūn juǎn spring rolls
guō tiē (liù ge) fried ravioli (six pieces) (lit., "pot sticker")
shuǐ jiǎo (liù ge) boiled ravioli (six pieces) (lit., "water ravioli")
dà bāo zi large steamed filled buns (two)
cōng yóu bǐng (liǎng zhāng) scallion pancakes (two)

Learn the characters 水 *shuǐ* "water," 餃 *jiǎo* "ravioli," 飽 *bāo* "steamed filled bun," 葱 *cōng* "scallion," 餅 *bǐng* "pancake." You have just made your first acquaintance with "classifiers," with which Chinese number words must generally be combined. Pancakes and other flat thin objects are counted 一張, 兩張, 三張 "one spread, two spread, three spread"; many objects are simply counted 一個, 兩個, 三個 "one piece, two piece, three piece." (It probably will not be worth your while to learn the classifiers. You should eventually learn the numerals, and you can generally assume that the character that follows a numeral is a classifier.)

Lěng pán lèi cold plates
shí jǐn lěng pán fancy cold plate (*dà* large; *xiǎo* small)
bàng bàng jī bang bang chicken
bái qiē jī white-cut chicken (sliced cold boiled chicken)
wǔ xiāng niú ròu five-spice beef
sì chuān pào cài Szechuan steeped vegetable (a pickle)
là bái cài hot and sour Chinese cabbage

You should remember the combinations 什錦 *shí jǐn* "fancy," which you have undoubtedly encountered in its Cantonese version "subgum," and 四川 *sì chuān* "Szechuan," (Sichuan is literally "four rivers").

Jī yā lèi chicken and duck

gōng bǎo jī dīng chicken cubes fried with chili peppers and peanuts

yāo guǒ jī dīng chicken cubes with cashew nuts (lit., "hip nuts")

tián suān jī kuài sweet and sour chicken pieces

hóng shāo jī red-cooked chicken

chǎo jī qiú stir-fried chicken curls

běi jīng kǎo yā Peking roast duck

bā bǎo quán yā eight-treasure whole duck

cōng bào yā piàn sliced duck quick-fried with scallions

You should learn the characters 果 *guǒ* "fruit, nut" and 全 *quán* "whole" and the combinations 北京 *běi jīng* "Peking" and 八寶 *bā bǎo* "eight treasure." (Beijing is literally "north capital," and 南京 *nán jīng* "Nanking" is "south capital.")

Zhū ròu lèi pork

mù xu ròu moo shu pork

jīng jiàng ròu sī pork shreds in Peking sauce

tián suān pái gǔ sweet and sour spareribs

shī zi tóu lion's head (large meatballs with Chinese cabbage)

huí guō ròu twice-cooked pork

dōng sǔn chǎo ròu sī pork shreds stir-fried with winter bamboo shoot

You should learn the character 筍 *sǔn* "bamboo shoot." Beijing is often abbreviated to just 京 *jīng* "capital."

Xiā lèi shrimp

tián suān xiā rén sweet and sour shelled shrimp

xuě dòu xiā rén shelled shrimp with snow peas (Chinese peapods)

chǎo xiā qiú stir-fried shrimp curls

guō bā xiā rén shelled shrimp with crispy rice

lóng xiā dīng diced lobster (lit., "dragon shrimp")

22

You should learn the characters 雪 *xuě* "snow" and 龍 *lóng* "dragon."

>*Yú lèi* fish
>*hóng shāo quán yú* red-cooked whole fish
>*qīng zhēng yú* clear-steamed fish
>*chǎo yú piàn* stir-fried fish slices
>*cù liū yú* sweet and sour fish
>*hóng shāo yú chì* red-cooked shark fin
>*shí jǐn hǎi shēn* fancy sea cucumber

There are a variety of names for sweet and sour dishes, and you have just met a new one. 醋 means "vinegar" and 溜 means "stir-fry, then add a thick sauce."

>*Shū cài lèi* vegetables
>*chǎo liǎng dōng* stir-fried two winters (bamboo shoot and black mushrooms)
>*sù shí jǐn* fancy mixed vegetarian ingredients
>*má po dòu fu* Ma Po bean curd (cubes of bean curd with minced pork in spicy gravy)
>*jiā cháng dòu fu* home-style bean curd (fried bean curd slices with meats and vegetables in spicy bean sauce)
>*háo yóu jiè làn* Chinese broccoli in oyster sauce

You should learn the characters 兩 *liǎng* "two, both" and 素 *sù* "plain, vegetarian." The latter character is used especially in names of dishes in which meat or fish is simulated with bean curd or a dough, for example, 素火腿 *sù huǒ tuǐ* "vegetarian ham," made of sheets of dried bean curd skin marinated, tied in a tight roll, and steamed.

>*Miàn lèi* noodles
>*ròu sī chǎo miàn* fried noodles with pork shreds
>*shí jǐn chǎo miàn* fancy fried noodles
>*zhá jiàng miàn* noodles with pork and bean-paste sauce
>*ròu sī tāng miàn* noodles in soup with pork shreds

6

Now You Do the Deciphering

You should now be ready to start tackling real menus in real Chinese restaurants. This chapter will simply present you with reproductions of portions of the menus of some excellent Chinese restaurants, first some bilingual menus and then some all-Chinese ones, accompanied by a small amount of commentary that may help you with certain odd or difficult items, though you will be mainly on your own.

Even when a menu gives English translations of the Chinese names of all the dishes, it will often be to your advantage to be able to read the Chinese characters, since the Chinese is often clearer or more specific than the English, and the English is sometimes riddled with errors that render it hard to interpret. Let us, however, start with a bilingual menu whose English is in fact excellent, namely that of the Home Village Restaurant, a Hakka restaurant in New York Chinatown (menu 1).

Note that what is referred to as "egg rolls" in the English name of dish 98 really involves a wrapper of dried bean curd skin, as the Chinese makes clear. By contrast, the English version of dish 95 is more informative than the Chinese version: you have no way of knowing that what the Chinese calls "two crisp" is in fact pig tripe and dried squid. There is no significance to the difference between the characters used to represent tripe in 99–100 and in 101–2. In 101–2 it is called "100 leaves" (this name actually refers specifically to the cow's third stomach—the four stomachs have separate Chinese names), and in 99–100 an otherwise unused character serves as a fancy

正宗客菜　　EXOTIC HAKKA DISHES

91.	三鮮炆鮑	Abalone with Bone Marrows and Boneless Duck Feet 9.25
92.	魚丸炆海參	Braised Fish Ball with Sea Cucumber 7.25
93.	紅燒蝦子海參	Braised Sea Cucumber 8.25
94.	肉丸炆海參	Braised Pork Meat Balls with Sea Cucumber 7.25
95.	生炒雙脆	Sauteed Pig's Stomach and Dried Squid 5.95
96.	油泡肚尖	Sauteed Pig's Stomach 5.95
97.	豉生肚卷	Sauteed Pig's Stomach with Chilli and Black Bean Sauce 4.50
98.	酥炸鮮皮卷	Deep Fried Fresh Meat Egg Rolls 5.25
99.	豉椒炆牛栢葉	Sauteed Tripe with Chilli and Black Bean Sauce 5.25
100.	咸菜炒百葉	Sauteed Tripe with Preserved Vegetable 5.25
101.	糟汁灼牛百葉	Sauteed Tripe with Wine Sauce 5.75
102.	白灼牛百葉	Boiled Tripe 5.75
103.	脆皮炸大腸	Deep Fried Fresh Pig Intestine 5.75
104.	紅燒爾皮角	Deep Fried Assorted Meat Ball with Brown Sauce 5.25
105.	菜扒牛肉丸	Beef Ball with Vegetable 5.25
106.	酥炸爾皮角	Deep Fried Assorted Meat Ball 5.25
107.	梅菜扣肉	Stewed Pork with Preserved Vegetable 5.25
108.	芋頭扣肉	Stewed Pork with Taro 5.50
109.	鹽焗珍肝	Baked Giblets with Salt 4.50
110.	酥炸珍肝	Fried Chicken Giblets 4.50
111.	時菜扒雙丸	Sauteed Beef Ball and Fish Ball with Vegetable 5.75

Menu 1. Courtesy Home Village Restaurant, 20 Mott Street, New York

substitute for the "hundred" character. It is sometimes also written "cypress leaves," using a character that is like the fancy substitute for "hundred" except that it lacks the upper right horizontal stroke. Multiple ways of writing the same thing are, to repeat, a fact of life that you will have to accustom yourself to.

We next have the poultry offerings of Toronto's Yeh Mei Heung, a restaurant that goes in for game specialities, though those dishes appear not on its printed menu but on a blackboard that gives the day's special offerings (menu 2).

The first two characters in dish 14 mean "authentic" and are commonly applied to Tongkiang (東江) style salt-baked chicken. Dish 19 is literally "splendid phoenix returns to nest"; the "nest" is a deep-fried basket made of shredded potato in which the chicken and vegetables are served.

Next we have an excerpt from the Vegetarian's Paradise in New York (menu 3), one of a regrettably small number of Chinese vegetarian restaurants in North America (there are quite a lot of them in Hong Kong and Taipei, representing two distinct vegetarian traditions: the Buddhist tradition in which dried ingredients are widely used and vegetarian simulations of meat dishes are highly prized, and the medical tradition in which fresh vegetables and fresh mushrooms are the center of attraction).

"Sang kan" in dish 54 is a deep-fried gluten dough that is often used as a vegetarian substitute for meat.

We now turn to the seafood section of the menu of the East River, a Hakka restaurant in Berkeley, California (menu 4).

The characters for "hard head" (a variety of croaker) in dish 67 are literally "sublime fish." Note the simplified

version of the character for "crab" in dishes 68–70. The Chinese but not the English makes clear that dishes 75 and 87 contain two varieties of mushroom. The character for "pair," which appears in the name of that dish, recurs in items 80 and 81, with reference to two kinds of squid, dried and fresh.

Our next selection is from the Hainam Restaurant, a noodle shop in New York Chinatown (menu 5).

The not completely legible character translated as "shin" in the rice dishes may in fact be a character for "rump" whose pronunciation is roughly "shin." The heading "fried dishes" is misleading since (as the Chinese indicates) it covers roasted and stewed dishes. "Mon cheong chicken," the second dish under that heading, is a spicy stew of boneless chicken and chicken liver. What is called "chicken legs" in the next two dishes is actually chicken feet, as the Chinese makes clear.

As our final example of a bilingual menu, let us look at the bilingual part of a lunchtime menu from the Blue Heaven in Hong Kong (menu 6).

Note the reference to Yangzhou in the Chinese versions of "noodle in soup: assorted meat" and "fried rice." For fried rice, one is offered a choice of half order, dish, and (rice)bowl. "Shredded beef vermicelli" is actually minced beef with rice-flour vermicelli. "Noodle in soup: pickled chop suey" is a good instance of the Chinese being clearer than the Engish.

We now turn to some monolingual Chinese menus. Let us start with a complete menu, that of Chicago's King Wah Restaurant, which you may wish to use to practice making up full dinner orders from a menu of the length and diversity that you will want to be able to deal with (menu 7).

Note that this menu has separate sections for fish dishes,

雞 鴨 類　　CHICKEN & DUCK

		Whole	Half
14	正宗（炒盬）焗鶏 BAKED CHICKEN IN FRIED SALT	11.00	5.50
15	脆皮炸子鶏 DEEP FRIED CHICKEN CANTONESE STYLE	11.00	5.25
16	金華玉樹鶏 JADE TREE CHICKEN (Sliced Chicken & Ham with Chinese Green)	12.75	6.75
17	菜胆上湯鶏 STEAMED CHICKEN WITH CHINESE GREEN	11.00	5.25
18	蠔油屈鶏 DEEP FRIED CHICKEN WITH OYSTER SAUCE	10.25	5.20
19.	彩鳳還巢 CHICKEN CUBES WITH VEGETABLES IN PHOENIX NEST (Crispy Potatoes)		5.75
20	啤酒焗鶏煲 CHICKEN COOKED WITH BEER IN ORIENTAL POT		5.75
21	鐵扒鶏脯 CHICKEN BREAST SIZZLING ON IRON PLATE		5.50
22	羅定豆豉鶏 BRAISED CHICKEN WITH BLACK BEAN SAUCE		5.25
23	西片鶏柳 SLICED CHICKEN WITH CELERY		4.50

24	咸魚雞煲	CHICKEN WITH SALTED FISH IN ORIENTAL POT	5.95
25	紫羅雞片	SLICED CHICKEN WITH GINGER AND PINEAPPLE	4.50
26	腰果雞丁	DICED CHICKEN WITH CASHEW NUTS	4.50
27	西檸煎軟雞	PAN FRIED BONELESS CHICKEN WITH LEMON SAUCE	5.00
28	時菜雞球	SLICED CHICKEN WITH CHINESE VEGETABLE	4.50
29	北菇蒸滑雞	STEAMED CHICKEN WITH CHINESE MUSHROOM	4.75
30	八珍扣大鴨	BRAISED DUCK WITH ASSORTED MEATS & SEA FOOD	16.25	8.25
31	家鄉扣大鴨	BRAISED DUCK COUNTRY STYLE	16.25	8.25
32	羅漢扣大鴨	BRAISED DUCK WITH MIXED VEGETABLES	16.25	8.25
33	海參北菇扣大鴨	BRAISED DUCK WITH CHINESE MUSHROOM AND SEA CUCUMBER	16.25	8.25
34	荔芋香酥鴨	DEEP FRIED DUCK WITH MASHED-TARO STUFFING	16.25	8.25
35	菜胆扣鴨掌	BRAISED DUCK WITH CHINESE GREEN	14.25	8.25
36	鮑香鴨掌	BRAISED DUCK'S FEET WITH ABALONE	6.50
37	海參鴨掌	SEA CUCUMBER WITH BRAISED DUCK'S FEET	6.00
38	蠔油鴨掌	BRAISED DUCK'S FEET IN OYSTER SAUCE	4.50

Menu 2. Courtesy Yeh Mei Heung Restaurant, 339 Spadina Avenue, Toronto

素 菜 類　DELICIOUS VEGETARIAN DISHES

No.		Dish	Price
38	羅漢上素	BUDDHA'S "DE LUXE" (MIXED VEGETABLES)	
39	酥炸北菇	FRIED DRIED MUSHROOMS	
40	菜花北菇	Broccoli AND DRIED MUSHROOMS	
41	紅燒北菇	DRIED MUSHROOMS IN BROWN SAUCE	
42	紅燒鮮菇	FRESH MUSHROOMS IN BROWN SAUCE	4.75
43	腰果白菌	CASHEW NUTS AND WHITE MUSHROOMS	4.75
44	白汁露筍	ASPARAGUS WITH MAYONNAISE	4.75
45	珍珠露筍	SWEET CORN AND ASPARAGUS	4.75
46	時菜鮑魚菇	ABALONE MUSHROOMS WITH SEASONAL VEGETABLES	4.75
47	合桃菇丁	DICED MUSHROOMS AND WALNUT MEAT	4.75
48	腰果菇丁	DICED MUSHROOMS AND CASHEW NUTS	4.75
49	竹笙菜花	BAMBOO FUNGUS AND CAULIFLOWERS, BRAISED	3.75
50	珍珠紹菜	SWEET CORNS AND TIENTSIN CABBAGE	
51	菜遠雙冬	FRIED BAMBOO SHOOTS & MUSHROOMS WITH VEGETABLE	
52	波羅榆耳	PINEAPPLE AND YU FUNGUS	7.95
53	菜遠鮮菇	FRESH MUSHROOMS WITH VEGETABLE	4.75
54	咖喱生根	★ CURRY "SANG KAN"	4.75
55	咖喱豆腐	★ CURRY WITH BEAN CURD	3.75
56	咖喱鮮菇	★ CURRY WITH FRRESH MUSHROOMS	4.75
57	咖喱鮑魚菇	★ CURRY WITH ABALONE MUSHROOMS	4.75

No.		Dish	Price
58	咖喱珍珠露笋	★ CURRY SWEET CORN AND ASPARAGUS	4.75
57	茄汁根球	"SANG KAN" BALLS WITH TOMATO SAUCE	4.75
60	红烧豆腐	FRIED BEAN CURD IN BROWN SAUCE	3.75
61	鲜菇豆腐	BEAN CURD WITH DRIED FRESH MUSHROOMS	4.75
62	粟米豆腐	BEAN CURD WITH SWEET CORNS	3.75
63	油炸豆腐	FRIED BEAN CURD	3.75
64	酥炸大会	DEEP FRIED COMBINATION	4.75
65	鱼香茄子	★ EGG PLANT WITH chilli SAUCE	3.75
66	干煸四季豆	★ SAUTEED STRING BEANS	3.75
67	腐乳西菜	WATERCRESS WITH PRESERVED BEAN CAKE PASTE	3.75
68	素什锦	MIXED VEGETABLES	4.25
69	麻婆豆腐	★ SPICY BEAN CURD	3.75
70	孔子素鸡	CONFUCIOUS "CHICKEN"	4.75
71	柠檬素鸡	LEMON "CHICKEN"	4.75
72	酥炸素生蚝	DEEP FRIED "OYSTER"	4.75
73	京都素骨	PEKING "SPARE RIBS"	4.75
74	玉树素牛柳	"IRON STEAK" WITH BROCCOLI	4.75
75	甜酸素肉	SWEET AND PUNGENT "PORK"	4.75
76	豉汁素虾球	"PRAWNS" IN BLACK BEAN SAUCE	4.75

Menu 3. Courtesy Vegetarian's Paradise, 48 Bowery, New York

海鮮類 SEA FOOD

65.	清蒸石班	STEAMED ROCK COD .... Seasonal
66.	五柳石班	SWEET AND SOUR ROCK COD .... Seasonal
67.	清蒸崇魚	STEAMED HARD HEAD .... Seasonal
68.	清蒸肉蚧	STEAMED WHOLE FRESH CRAB .... Seasonal
69.	薑葱焗肉蚧	BAKED WHOLE CRAB WITH GINGER AND GREEN ONION. .... Seasonal
70.	豉椒肉蚧	BAKED WHOLE CRAB WITH BLACK BEAN SAUCE ..... Seasonal
71.	生炒大蜆	SAUTEED FRESH CLAMS 4.25
72.	豉椒炒蜆	FRESH CLAMS WITH BLACK BEAN SAUCE 4.25
73.	酥炸生蠔	DEEP FRIED OYSTERS 4.25
74.	薑葱生蠔	BAKED OYSTERS WITH GINGER AND GREEN ONION ... 4.25
75.	雙菰鮑魚	BRAISED ABALONE WITH MUSHROOMS 7.25
76.	生炒帶子	BRAISED SCALLOPS 5.75
77.	蘭豆帶子	SCALLOPS WITH SNOW PEA 5.50

78.	生炒吊片片	FRESH SQUID WITH MIXED VEGETABLES	4.50
79.	生炒鮮魷	BRAISED DRIED SQUID	4.50
80.	生炒雙魷	BRAISED DRIED AND FRESH SQUIDS	4.50
81.	香蝦雙魷	DRIED AND FRESH SQUID WITH PRAWN SAUCE	4.50
82.	鮑魚海參	BRAISED SEA CUCUMBER WITH ABALONE	7.25
83.	椒鹽酥蝦	SPICY SALT BAKED PRAWNS	5.50
84.	干煎蝦碌	DRIED FRIED PRAWNS	5.50
85.	咖喱蝦球	CURRY PRAWNS	5.00
86.	玻璃蝦球	SPECIAL SAUTEED CRYSTAL PRAWNS	6.00
87.	雙菰蝦球	BRAISED PRAWNS WITH MUSHROOMS	5.50
88.	玉蘭蝦球	SAUTEED PRAWNS WITH MIXED VEGETABLES	5.50
89.	腰豆蝦球	PRAWNS WITH CASHEW NUTS	5.50
90.	茉遠蝦球	PRAWNS WITH TENDER GREEN VEGETABLES	5.50
91.	京醬蝦球	PRAWNS WITH LOBSTER SAUCE	5.50
92.	茉遠魚丸	FISH BALL WITH VEGETABLES	4.25

Menu 4. Courtesy East River Restaurant, 2429 Shattuck, Berkeley

蛋麵食品 NOODLES

招牌湯麵
Hai Nam Speical Noodle ----------

淨雲吞
Wonton ----------

雲吞麵
Wonton with Noodle ----------

牛腩雲吞
Brisket with Wonton ----------

牛腩麵
Brisket with Noodle ----------

牛什雲吞
Tripe with Wonton ----------

牛什麵
Tripe with Noodle ----------

牛腩雲吞麵
Brisket & Wonton with Noodle ----------

牛什雲吞麵
Tripe & Wonton with Noodle ----------

火鴨雲吞麵
Fried Duck & Wonton with Noodle ---

切鷄雲吞麵
Boiled Chicken & Wonton w. Noodle-

油鷄雲吞麵
Soy Sauce Chicken & Wonton with
   Noodle ----------

猪扒麵
Pork Chop with Noodle ----------

揚州窩麵
Young Chow Wor Mein ----------

牛肉炒麵
Beef Chow Mein ----------

羊城牛肉炒麵
Beef Chow Mein (Cantonese style) ----------

廣東肉絲炒麵
Shredded Pork Chow Mein
   (Cantonese style) ----------

廣東鷄絲炒麵
Shreaded Chicken Chow Mein
   (Cantonese style) ----------

廣東蝦仁炒麵
Shrimp Chow Mein (Cantonese style)..

鷄球炒麵
Chicken (Chunk) Chow Mein ----------

蝦球炒麵
Har Kew (Shrimp) Chow Mein ----------

海鮮炒麵
Sea Food Chow Mein ----------

什會炒麵
Combination Chow Mein ----------

豉椒排骨炒麵
Spare Rib Chow Mein w. Black Bean
   and Pepper ----------

羊城牛肉炒河
Beef Chow Fun (Cantonese style) ----

豉椒干炒牛河
Beef Chow Fun w. Black Bean
   and Pepper ----------

干炒牛河
Beef Chow Fun   (Pan fried) ----------

滑牛炒河
Beef Chow Fun w. House Special Sc.-

星州炒米粉
Fried Rice Noodle (Singapore style) ~

廈門炒米粉
Fried Rice Noodle (Har Mon style) ----

叉燒撈麵
Roast Pork Lo Mein ----------

牛肉撈麵
Beef Lo Mein ----------

鷄絲撈麵
Shredded Chicken Lo Mein ----------

蝦仁撈麵
Shrimp Lo Mein ----------

薑葱撈麵
Ginger & Scallion Lo Mein ----------

蠔油撈麵
Oyster Sauce Lo Mein ----------

牛腩撈麵
Brisket Lo Mein ----------

牛什撈麵
Tripe Lo Mein ----------

碟飯 DISHES WITH RICE

正宗文昌鷄牌飯
Mon Cheong Chicken Drum on Rice

正宗文昌鷄飯
Mon Cheong Chicken on Rice ----------

馬來咖喱鷄飯
Curry Chicken on Rice
   (Malaysian style) ----------

白切鷄飯
Boiled Chicken on Rice ----------

Menu 5. Courtesy Hainam Restaurant, 67 Bayard Street, New York

油 鶏 飯
Soy Sauce Chicken on Rice -----------
牛 䐑 飯
Shin on Rice -----------
咖喱牛腩飯
Curry Brisket on Rice -----------
牛 腩 飯
Brisket on Rice -----------
牛 什 飯
Tripe on Rice -----------
猪 扒 飯
Pork Chop on Rice -----------
叉 燒 飯
Roast Pork on Rice -----------
叉燒切鶏飯
Roast Pork & Boiled Chicken on Rice --
叉燒油鶏飯
Roast Pork & Soy Sauce Chicken
on Rice -----------
叉燒火鴨飯
Rnast Pork & Fried Duck on Rice -----
芥蘭牛肉飯
Beef with Broccoli on Rice -----------
菜心牛肉飯
Beef w. Chinese Vegetable on Rice ----
青豆牛肉飯
Beef with Green Pea on Rice -----------
番茄牛肉飯
Beef with Tomato on Rice -----------
豆仔牛肉飯
Beef with String Bean on Rice -----------
豆腐牛肉飯
Beet with Bean Curd on Rice -----------
豉汁排骨飯
Spare Ribs w. Black Bean Sauce
on Rice -----------
滑 牛 飯
Beef on Rice -----------
滑蛋牛肉飯
Beef & Egg on Rice -----------
滑蛋蝦仁飯
Shrimp & Egg on Rice -----------

什 會 飯
Combination Soupy on Rice -----------
火腿蛋飯
Ham & Egg on Rice -----------

揚州炒飯
Young Chow Fried Rice -----------
蝦仁炒飯
Shrimp Fried Rice -----------
火腿炒飯
Ham Fried Rice -----------
三 星 飯
Chicken, Ham & Egg on Rice -----------
蠔油肉絲飯
Pork in Oyster Sauce on Rice -----------
蠔油鶏絲飯
Chicken in Oyster Sauce on Rice -----------
豉汁鶏碌飯
Chicken (Chunk) in Black Bean
Sauce on Rice -----------
葱油鶏飯
Chicken in Scallion on Rice -----------
凉瓜牛肉飯
Beef with Bitter Melon on Rice ------
咖喱牛肉飯
Curry Beef on Rice -----------
叉 燒 炒飯
Roast Pork Fried Rice -----------
牛 肉 炒飯
Beef Fried Rice -----------

燒烤鹵味小碟 FRIED DISHES

明爐火鴨
Stove-Fried Duck -----------
正宗文昌鶏
Mon Cheong Chicken -----------
豉椒鳳爪
Chicken Legs w. Pepper & Black Sc. ---
蠔油鳳爪
Chicken Legs with Oyster Sauce -----------
豉 油 鶏
Soy Sauce Chicken -----------
咖 喱 鶏
Curry Chicken -----------
咖喱牛腩
Curry Brisket -----------
五香牛腩
Spicy Brisket -----------
五香牛什
Spicy Mixed Inerior Meat (Beef) -----------
鹵水牛䐑
Shin in Special Sauce -----------

					noodle in soup (tureen)		
蟹	黃	伊	窩	麵	crab cream	$17.50
班	球	窩		麵	garoupa balls	15.50
雞	球	窩		麵	chicken balls	12.00
蝦	球	窩		麵	prawn balls	12.00
鴻	圖	窩		麵	crab meat	10.00
楊	州	窩		麵	assorted meat	9.00
免治牛肉窩米					shredded beef vermicelli	9.00

伊　　麵 e-fu noodle in soup (dish)

蟹	黃	會	伊	麵	crab cream	$14.50
雞	絲	伊		麵	shredded chicken	9.00
蟹	肉	耖	子	麵	crab meat & shrimp seed ..	9.00
會	伊	府		麵	shredded pork	9.00
干	燒	伊		麵	braised noodle	8.00

辦　　麵 braised noodle (dish)

蟹	肉	辦	麵	crab meat	$ 9.00
北	菇	辦	麵	mushroom	7.00
羅	漢	辦	麵	vegetable a la "lor hon"	7.00
义	燒	辦	麵	barbecued pork	7.00
羌	葱	撈	麵	shredded ginger & green onion ..	5.00

炒　　麵 fried noodle (dish)

班	球	炒	麵	garoupa balls	$13.50
雞	球	炒	麵	chicken balls & vegetable ..	11.00
蝦	球	炒	麵	prawn balls	11.00
蝦	仁	炒	麵	shrimp	9.50
蟹	肉	炒	麵	crab meat	8.50
雞	絲	炒	麵	shredded chicken	8.50
珍	肝	炒	麵	chicken giblet	6.80
义	燒	炒	麵	barbecued pork	6.80
排	骨	炒	麵	spice ribs of pork	6.80
八	珍	炒	麵	assorted meat	6.80
肉	絲	炒	麵	shredded pork & bean sprout ..	6.60
牛	肉	炒	麵	sliced beef & vegetable	6.60
星	州	炒	米	fried vermicelli "singapore style" ..	6.20
干	炒	牛	河	rice-noodle with beef & soy sauce ..	5.80

湯　　麵 noodle in soup (bowl)

蟹	黃	生	麵	crab cream	$ 7.00
班	球	生	麵	garoupa balls	6.50
雞	球	生	麵	chicken balls	5.80
蝦	球	生	麵	prawn balls	5.80
燒	雞	生	麵	roasted chicken	5.40
雞	絲	湯	麵	shredded chicken	4.80

Menu 6. Courtesy Blue Heaven Restaurant, 38 Queen's Road, Central, Hong Kong. Prices are in HK$ not US$.

鴨腿生麵	braised duck	$ 4.50
蟹肉會伊麵	crab meat e-fu noodle	4.50
肉絲會伊麵	stewed e-fu noodle	4.50
上湯生麵	noodle in superior soup	4.20
珍肝生麵	chicken giblet	3.60
叉燒生麵	barbecued pork	3.60
肉片生麵	sliced pork	3.60
滑牛生麵	sliced beef	3.60
北菇生麵	mushroom	3.60
牛腩湯麵	beef brisket	3.40
甫魚湯生麵	e-fu noodle in soup	3.40
炸醬淨生麵	pickled chop suey	3.40
火腿雞絲麵	shredded ham & chicken	3.20

飯 類 每 碟

rice (dish)

菜蓮斑球飯	garoupa balls & vegetable	$12.00
菜蓮雞球飯	chicken balls & vegetable ..	8.20
雞絲炒飯	shredded chicken fried rice ..	8.20
菜蓮蝦球飯	prawn balls & vegetable ..	8.20
火腿波蛋飯	sliced ham & eggs	8.20
滑蛋蝦仁飯	shrimps with scrambled egg ..	7.80
蠔油生雞絲飯	shredded chicken with oyster sauce	7.20
粟米雞粒飯	diced chicken with sweet corn ..	7.20
北菇滑雞飯	chicken & mushroom	7.20
菜蓮珍肝飯	chicken giblet & vegetable ..	6.00
粟米肉粒飯	diced pork with sweet corn	5.50
蠔油排骨飯	spice ribs of pork with oyster sauce	5.20
免治肉飯	minced beef	5.20
菜蓮牛腩飯	braised beef brisket & vegetable ..	4.80
楊州炒飯	fried rice .. .. .. 半賣	8.20
	" " .. .. 每碟	5.60
	" " .. .. 每碗	4.00
蟹肉上湯會飯	crab meat in soup .. .. 半賣	9.50
	" " .. 每碗	4.60
鴛鴦雞絲飯	chicken fillet & shrimps .. .. 半賣	15.50
	" " .. .. 每碟	9.00

飯 類 每 碗

rice in bowl

化桶乳豬飯	roasted suckling pig	$ 4.50
皮子油雞飯	soyed chicken	4.20
汁雞肝飯	roasted chicken liver	4.20
蜜明爐燒鵝飯	roasted goose	4.20
蜜汁叉燒飯	barbecued pork	3.60
鹵水珍肝飯	soyed chicken giblets	3.60
鹵味三星飯	mixed soyed meat	3.60
絲苗白飯	plain rice	.90

牛 肉 類

蠔油节的……6.25
香港节的……8.95
中式焗牛柳……7.50
咸菜牛肉……3.25
芥菜牛肉……3.25
搾菜牛肉……3.60
蠔油豆腐牛……2.75
菜遠牛……3.60
番茄牛……3.75
辣椒牛……3.75
芥蘭牛……3.60
升瓜牛……3.60
苦瓜牛……3.60

雞 類

豉汁鶏碌……3.75
喙煙鶏碌……3.75
苦瓜鶏球……3.95
滑鶏球……4.50
杏仁鶏丁……4.50
冬菇燕鶏……4.25
金菜燕鶏……4.25
大鶏三味……11.75
燕窩全鶏……13.95
東江鹽焗鶏 半隻……4.75 全隻……9.25
玉蘭鶏 半隻……4.75 全隻……9.25
冬菇鬱鶏 半隻……4.95 全隻……9.50
针菜鬱鶏 半隻……4.95 全隻……9.50
手撕鶏 半隻……6.20 全隻……12.00

湯 類

紫菜湯 小1.95 中…2.95 大…3.95
豆腐湯 小1.75 中…2.75 大…3.75
芥菜湯 小1.75 中…2.75 大…3.75
冬瓜湯 小1.75 中…2.75 大…3.75
什會湯 小2.75 中…3.75 大…4.75
西洋菜湯 小1.95 中…2.95 大…3.95
搾菜豆腐湯 小1.95 中…2.95 大…3.95
酸菜豆腐湯 小1.95 中…2.95 大…3.95
鶏茸粟米湯 小3.20 中…4.20 大…5.20
生菜魚圓湯 小2.80 中…3.80 大…4.80
芥菜魚圓湯 小2.80 中…3.80 大…4.80

湯類

西洋菜魚圓湯 小3.00 中…4.00 大…5.00
海參魚圓湯 小4.30 中…5.30 大…6.30
魚肚 湯 小3.20 中…4.20 大…5.20
燕窩 湯 小4.00 中…5.00 大…6.00
魚翅 湯 小6.25 中…7.25 大…8.25

雞類

京華脆皮炸雞 半隻…4.75 全隻…9.25
白切雞 …2.15
豉油雞 …2.40
燕鹹雞 …2.50
火腿雞 …3.95
脆皮雞捲 …5.75

鴨類

火鴨 …2.85
無骨火鴨 …5.95
西湖全鴨 半隻…6.00 全隻…11.75
八珍扒鴨 半隻…7.75 全隻…15.25
窩燒全鴨 半隻…6.00 全隻…11.75
琵琶鴨 每隻(預訂) 13.75

鴿類

炸子乳鴿 每隻…2.50
蠔油焗乳鴿 每隻…2.60
冬菇鬱乳鴿 每隻…2.95
針菜鬱乳鴿 每隻…2.95
炸白鴿王 每隻…4.75

牛肉類

墨魚牛 …4.50
蠔油牛 …4.50
子薑牛 …4.50
咖喱牛 …4.25
梅菜炆牛肉 …3.50
冬菇炆牛肉 …4.25

猪肉類

甜酸肉 …3.75
叉燒 …2.75
紅燒豆腐 …3.25
苦瓜肉片 …3.60
搾菜肉片 …3.60
芽菜肉絲 …2.75

Menu 7. Courtesy King Wah Restaurant, 2225 South Wentworth Avenue, Chicago

蛋類

火燒炒蛋……3.50
雞絲蛋……3.75
火腿蛋……3.50
生蝦蛋……3.75

瓜菜類

蠔油净生菜……1.95
油鹽芥菜……1.85
炒芥雪豆……2.95
炒芥菜心……1.85
蠔油净芥蘭……2.10
炒什菜……2.95

飯類

炒飯……2.85

蝦類

炒鮮龍蝦……時價
釀鮮龍蝦……時價
清蒸龍蝦……時價
豉汁蝦球……4.50
雪豆蝦……4.75
苦瓜蝦……4.75
紅燒蝦球……4.60
甜酸蝦球……6.95
炒龍蝦尾……4.50
茄汁蝦碌……4.50
干煎蝦碌……6.75
玻璃蝦球……4.95
喼煙蝦……6.75
四川蝦球……6.75
菜遠蝦球……4.50
生豆蝦粉絲……3.85
生蝦龍蝦糊……4.95

菜遠叉燒……3.60
芥蘭叉燒……3.60
雪豆叉燒……4.50
豆腐叉燒……2.75
八珍豆腐……4.50
紅燒肉……3.75
咸蛋肉餅……3.25
梅菜炆猪肉……3.50
火腿猪肉餅……3.50
豉汁排骨……3.60
甜酸排骨……3.75

魚類

炊白魚……3.50
炆白魚……3.75

牛肉炒飯......2.95
雞炒飯......2.95
蝦炒飯......2.95
火腿炒飯......2.95
揚州炒飯......3.50
牛肉飯......2.85
瓜菜牛肉飯......3.00
雞球飯......3.00
喱喱牛肉飯......3.25
番茄牛肉飯......2.95
蝦球飯......3.00
鮑魚雞球飯......3.50
喱喱蝦球飯......3.25
魚片芥蘭飯......3.00
节的球飯......4.20
白飯......25

螺　類

响螺炒時菜......3.95
蒜瓜油浸炒時螺......5.95
喱喱浸响螺......5.95
炒浸响螺球......5.75

海　味　類

鮑片炒時菜......3.95
蠔油浸鮑片......6.25
炒浸鮑魚角......6.50
炒桂花翅......8.95
乾　粉　絲......3.60
蒸　粉　絲......4.25
蒸魚炒時菜......3.95
炒浸帶菜......5.75
紅燒帶子......4.25
海鮮大什會......6.95
炒大什會......5.75
酥炸生蠔......4.00

白水派魚......時價
紅燒派魚......時價
甜酸派魚......時價
紅燒魚球......4.50
甜酸魚球......4.60
脆皮魚捲......4.25
豆腐魚餅......3.75
芥蘭魚餅......3.75
柬速魚餅......3.75
炒浸魚餅......5.75
魚片炒時菜......3.95
炒浸魚片......5.75
芥蘭魚片......3.75
草菇魚圓......4.75

Menu 7 *(cont.)*

shrimp (and lobster) dishes, conch (sea snail) dishes, and (other) seafood dishes. The fish in the third through fifth fish dishes is pike, and the character with which it is written is not generally used in that meaning (it normally means branch of a river, or faction of a group; it is used for pike in American Chinese because of its phonetic similarity to the English word). The seventh and eighth dishes in the seafood section contain squid, here called by one of the less common of its many Chinese names, literally "wheat fish." In the first two beef dishes, the characters 市的 SÌH TÌK are used to spell out the sound of the English word "steak," without regard to the meaning (namely, "city's") that those characters would normally have.

Next we have half of the Chinese side of the lunchtime menu of the Blue Heaven in Hong Kong (menu 8), of which you saw the bilingual side earlier in this chapter. The remaining page of this menu, which lists dimsam only in Chinese, will appear in chapter 7, which is devoted to dimsam.

The characters here are arranged in really traditional fashion: not only are they mainly arranged into columns, but where they are written in rows they are to be read right-to-left, not left-to-right; thus, the price of the first set lunch is $38 (Hong Kong money), not $83. The column enclosed between dotted lines to the right of the two set lunches lists two specialities. Note the strange characters with which the price of the chicken shreds with shark fin ($11 per bowl) is written. These characters are variant forms that originally served to prevent fraud (note how a deft stroke of the writing brush could change one—into two 二 or ten 十, or ten into one thousand 千). These versions of the numerals are found only in contracts and in checks (where they do in fact prevent fraud) and

▲ 家常小菜 ▼

生炒牛肉絲　八元
栗米魚肚羹　八元
豆腐炆班頭　九元

笋尖煎釀甫　八元
錦綉炒鷄丁　九元
豆腐釀凉瓜甫　九元

珍燒红腐乳　八元
油泡鱆片扎　九元
甫魚鮮菇甫　八元

蠔油腿片扒　九元
檸檬煎鴨甫　八元
油泡鱆木穗　九元

西芹炒腎片　八元
梅子蒸肉排　七元
蘿蔔炆牛腩　八元

金銀炒滑丁　九元
大良葱焗野鷄猪肝　八元
咸香酥炸牛丸　七元

名貴熱葷　三十八元

腰子脆丸戈渣
上素羅漢齋
鮮露筍牛肉
鮮菇滑牛肉
鮮茄滑蝦仁

白雲猪手（每碟）五元
鷄絲炆仔翅（每碗）拾壹元

精選四和菜　二十八元

煎釀凉瓜甫
西芹炒滑肝
金銀炒滑丁
鮮茄牛片湯
（或）即日鮮

例湯：
赤小豆粉葛煲猪膶
啤酒湯（每窩）六元

Menu 8. Courtesy Blue Heaven Restaurant, 38 Queen's Road, Central, Hong Kong

on menus, where they simply add a fancy touch—no cases have been reported of customers adding strokes to numerals on a menu so as to fraudulently raise the prices of their dinners.

For reference purposes, I present here a list of the alternate forms of Chinese numerals: the standard forms, the "popular" forms that often turn up on handwritten menus and in grocery stores, and the fraud-proof forms.

	Standard	Popular	Fraud-proof
yī one	一	| or 一	壹
èr two	二	|| or 二	貳
(*liǎng* two	兩)		
(*shuāng* pair	雙 or 双)		
sān three	三	||| or 三	參
sì four	四	✕	
wǔ five	五	ᡐ	
liù six	六	ㅗ	
qī seven	七	ㅗ	
bā eight	八	ㅗ	
jiǔ nine	九	夂	
shí ten	十		拾
èr shi twenty	二十	廿	
bǎi hundred	百		
qiān thousand	千		
wàn ten thousand	萬		

The popular forms of "one," "two," and "three" are written vertically if the writing is in columns, horizontal if the writing is in rows. An important peculiarity about the use of numbers in Chinese that you should know is that prices are given not in dollars and cents but in dollars, dimes, and cents, for example, $3.25 is 三元二毛五分 *sān yuán èr máo wǔ fen*, literally, "three dollars, two dimes, five cents." When a single numeral follows the character for "dollar," it refers to dimes and not to cents; thus,

一元五 *yì yuán wǔ* means $1.50, not (as you might mistakenly think, by reading it as "one dollar five") $1.05. The following are the alternative ways in which "dollar" and "dime" are written:

dollar 元圓园
dime 毛毫角

Next we turn to a monolingual supplement to the bilingual menu of Hong Kong's Manhattan Restaurant (menu 9). Its Chinese name means "ten thousand happiness" and in Cantonese sounds something like the first two syllables of "Manhattan."

In the upper half ("refined beautiful small dishes"), surprisingly many of the dishes have numbers in their names: the first dish from the right is "three fresh ingredient omlet"; the seventh is "quick-deep-fried two crisp ingredients," the tenth is "three forms quick-fried with scallions" (probably three parts of a pig, e.g., meat, liver, and kidney); the twelfth is "crab meat braised with two kinds of mushrooms"; the thirteenth is "walnuts with two minced ingredients"; and the leftmost is "four treasures in clear soup." On the subject of numbers, note the abbreviation of 二十 *èr shí* "twenty" to 廿 in the prices, one of the rare instances in which a single Chinese character has a pronunciation more than one syllable long. In the lower half, "iron-plate" dishes (precooked ingredients and sauce, poured over sizzling iron griddle) are at the right; the house specialty, Yunnanese chicken (cooked in a peculiar earthenware pot that both steams the chicken and simmers it in the condensed steam), is in the center; and at the left are extravagant specialties such as bear's paw and shark's fin. One probably isn't supposed to understand what "golden dragon spits bright pearls" (the leftmost item) is.

＜精美小菜＞

萬京樓
Manhattan Restaurant Ltd.

芙蓉生炸蝦	廿四元
宮爆明蝦	十六元
糟溜蝦妃	十二元
葱爆蝦仁	八元
鷄絲爆蝦	元
三鮮海參	十四元
芝蔴雙脆	十二元
蟹肉扒豆腐	十元
千炒牛肉	十二元
松燒鳳	十二元
二蟹蒜桃	十八元
瑤柱四寶	十二元
上湯龍鳳	元

鐵板菜式

鐵板牛肉	鐵板蝦球	鐵板魚柳	鐵板豉椒雞	鐵板鮒魚
十八元	廿五元	廿元	廿元	（時價）

特別介紹

原盅田七汽鍋雞

時價 —— 小計 中 大

名菜簡介

全龍吐明珠	正宗金華火方	北京填鴨	砂鍋雞鮑翅	國寶扒翅	長白山熊掌

時價

We conclude this section with the noodle and rice sections of the Chinese-language menu of Lee's Canton Cafe in Chicago (menu 10).

Note that simplified forms appear in place of a couple of characters that by now you know in their traditional forms: 旦 for 蛋 *dàn* "egg", and 云 for 餛, the "won" of wonton. The Chinese name of Lee's Canton Cafe is 廣州樓, and that name appears in the next-to-last dish in the rice section, which could be translated as "house special fried rice." The parenthesized characters in the last two sections inform the customer that in those dishes he has the option of either wheat-flour noodles or rice-flour noodles.

7

Dimsam Menus

In the late morning, the Cantonese like to drink tea and eat pastries, not so much sweet pastries as meat-filled steamed buns, steamed ravioli, and the like, as well as small dishes of such things as meatballs or stuffed duck's feet. The Chinese word for pastry, 点心 DÍMSĀM/ *diǎnxīn*,[4] literally "dot heart," is also used to refer to this kind of brunch, which has by now become beloved by many Occidental residents of North American cities that

---

4. Since dimsam is the one area where a knowledge of Cantonese pronunciations of names of Chinese dishes will be of some use to readers of this book, I will deviate from my usual practice of giving only Mandarin pronunciations and instead also give Cantonese pronunciations. As usual, capital letters will be used to indicate that the pronunciation is Cantonese.

云吞粉麵類
（湯）

云　　　　吞	1.65
加 料 云 吞	1.95
白 切 雞 云 吞	2.95
火 鴨 云 吞	2.95
叉 燒 河 粉(麵)	1.75
加 料 河 粉(麵)	1.95
火 鴨 河 粉(麵)	2.95
白 切 雞 河 粉(麵)	2.95
牛 腩 河 粉(麵)	1.95
牛 肉 河 粉(麵)	1.95
菜 心 牛 肉 河(麵)	2.55
楊 州 窩 麵	5.95
甜 酸 云 吞	3.65

炒粉麵類
（麵粉同價）　（唐庄）

肉 絲 炒 麵(粉)	3.15
叉 燒 炒 麵(粉)	3.75
牛 肉 炒 麵(粉)	3.75
雞 絲 炒 麵(粉)	3.75
菜 心 牛 肉 炒 麵(粉)	3.95
芥 蘭 牛 肉 炒 麵(粉)	4.25
芥 蘭 雞 絲 炒 麵(粉)	4.25
楊 州 炒 麵(粉)	4.75
菜 心 魚 片 炒 麵(粉)	5.75
芥 蘭 魚 片 炒 麵(粉)	5.95
市 的 球 炒 麵(粉)	7.55
番 茄 牛 肉 炒 麵(粉)	3.95
生 蝦 炒 麵(粉)	4.50
叉 燒 撈 麵	3.75
干 炒 牛 河	4.15
豉 椒 牛 河	4.15
牛 肉 麵	2.50
番 茄 牛 肉 麵	2.75
咖 喱 牛 肉 麵	2.60
咖 喱 番 茄 牛 肉 麵	2.85

飯　　類

牛 肉 飯	2.85
白 菜 牛 肉 飯	2.95
番 茄 牛 肉 飯	2.95
咖 喱 牛 肉 飯	3.05
瓜 菜 牛 肉 飯	3.25
雞 球 飯	3.95
雞 球 鮑 魚 飯	4.50
蝦 球 飯	4.35
菜 心 叉 燒 飯	2.95
市 的 球 飯	6.50
叉 燒 且 飯	2.75
火 腿 且 飯	2.75
火 鴨 飯	2.95
叉 燒 炒 飯	2.75
牛 肉 炒 飯	2.95
雞 炒 飯	2.85
生 蝦 炒 飯	2.95
火 腿 炒 飯	2.85
廣 州 樓 炒 飯	3.25
白 飯	.20

粥　　類

牛 肉 粥	1.75
雞 粥	1.75
魚 生 粥	2.65
瘦 肉 粥	1.95
艇 仔 粥	2.25

Menu 10. Courtesy Lee's Canton Cafe, 2300 South Wentworth Avenue, Chicago

have major Chinatowns. Indeed, all the Chinatowns with which I am familiar (including those of London and Amsterdam) have restaurants that serve dimsam, though the English-language menus[5] of these restaurants often provide no hint that they do, and its availability may be advertised only in handwritten posters in Chinese.

In the big dimsam restaurants in Hong Kong, and now also in some in North America, either there is no written menu or the written menu is merely an adjunct to the customer's principal source of food: the waiters and waitresses who walk around the restaurant pushing carts or carrying boxes with large stacks of three or four items, whose names they call out in Cantonese. Customers can inspect the dishes that each waiter is distributing and take whichever ones they want. At the end of the meal, a waiter generally computes the bill by counting the plates on the table (if the dishes are not all the same price, different sizes of plate may be used to correspond to the different prices, or a dish may be served on two stacked plates, indicating that it is twice the price of a "normal" dish). In smaller restaurants (or in bigger ones on their less busy days), customers are instead given a printed order form listing the dishes available, sometimes only in Chinese, sometimes in both Chinese and unintelligible English, sometimes a mimeograph of undecipherable Chinese handwriting. One marks on this form the number of orders wanted of each dish.

Tea is a very important constituent of the dimsam meal, so much so that Cantonese often speak of going to drink tea when they are going to a dimsam brunch. It is a

5. Or French or Dutch language menus in the case of the China-towns of Montreal and Amsterdam, though in fact the best Chinese restaurants in the Netherlands seem to be those whose menus are in English and Chinese but not in Dutch.

good idea, as soon as one is seated at a table, to tell the waiter what kind of tea one wants, since one not only can thereby get more interesting tea than one might otherwise get but can also thereby provide the often not very helpful waiter with evidence that one is really a fellow member of the human race. Often the menu will list the teas that are available. The following are some of the more common ones:

烏龍茶 WÙ LÙHNG CHÀH/*wū lóng chá* oolong tea

香片 HÈUNG PIN/*xiāng piàn* jasmine tea

普洱茶 PU YÍ CHÀH/*pǔ ěr chá* poo nei tea

六安茶 LUHK ON CHÀH/*liú ān chá* lok on tea

鐵觀音茶 TIT GÙN YÀM CHÀH/*tiě guān yīn chá* iron avalokitesvara tea

荔枝茶 LAIH JÌ CHÀH/*lì zhi chá* lichee tea

水仙茶 SÉUI SÌN CHÀH/*shuǐ xiān chá* daffodil tea

菊花茶 GŪK FÀ CHÀH/*jú huā chá* chrysanthemum tea

龍井茶 LÙHNG JÍNG CHÀH/*lóng jǐng chá* dragon well green tea

珠茶 JYŪ CHÀH/*zhū chá* gunpowder green tea

A dimsam menu will generally include several kinds of *bāo* (包 or 飽), that is, stuffed buns made of a wheat flour and yeast dough (generally steamed; if they are baked, the menu will indicate that specially with a character such as 烤 *kǎo*/HĀAU), such as the following:

叉燒飽 CHĀ SÌU BÀAU/*chá shāo bāo* roast pork bao

大飽 DAIH BÀAU/*dà bāo* large bao (with assorted filling)

鷄飽 GÀI BÀAU/*jī bāo* chicken bao

腊腸飽 LAAHP CHÉUNG BÀAU/*là cháng bāo* sausage bao

豆沙飽 DAUH SÀ BÀAU/*dòu sā bāo* sweet bean-
  paste bao
蓮蓉飽 LÌHN YÙHNG BÀAU/*lián rúng bāo* lotus
  seed-paste bao

The last two have sweet fillings and can serve as "dessert"
at the end of your brunch.

Here are some popular pastries of other types:

蝦餃 HĀ GÁAU/*xiā jiǎo* ha gow (ravioli with
  shrimp filling)
粉菓 FÁN GWÓ/*fěn guō* ravioli with rice-four
  wrapper
燒賣 SÌU MAAIH/*shāo mài* shu mai (open-ended
  ravioli with minced meat filling)
芋角 WUH GOK/*yù jiǎo* taro croquette
咸水角 HÀAHM SÉUI GOK/*xiān shuǐ jiǎo* deep-
  fried sticky-rice flour turnover with diced meats
  and vegetables.
蘿蔔糕 LÒH BAAHK GŌU/*luó bo gāo* turnip
  pudding (first steamed, then cut into squares and
  pan-fried)
馬蹄糕 MÁH TÀIH GŌU/*mǎ tí gāo* sweet water-
  chestnut pudding
煎堆 JÌN DÈUI/*jiān duī* deep-fried sticky-rice flour
  puff, with sweet filling and sesame seed coating
蒸粽 JÌNG JUNG/*zhēng jiòng* "Chinese tamale"
  (sticky rice with diced meats and vegetables,
  wrapped in lotus leaf and steamed)

The term SÌU MAAI also covers small meat dishes that
contain no pastry, for example, steamed spareribs. Thus,
there may be more of a difference between 燒賣 and
牛肉燒賣 than just that the former involves pork and
the latter beef: the former will probably be small pork
meat balls in pasta wrappers and the latter somewhat
larger unwrapped beef meatballs.

九龍點心
KOWLOON DIM SUM RESTAURANT

187 DUNDAS STREET W. TORONTO ONT.

電話：977-3773

From 9 a.m. To 5 p.m.　　營業時間：上午九時至下午五時

數量	名稱		數量	名稱	
	蝦　餃 Har Gow	1.00		皮蛋瘦肉粥 Salted Meat & Preserved Egg	1.10
	燒　賣 Siu Mi	1.00		馬　拉　糕 Ma Lai Go	.45
	灌　湯　餃 Goun Ton Gow	1.00		千　層　糕 Chin Jung Go	.45
	牛　肉 Ngau Yuk	1.00		什菓凍豆腐 Doun Dua Foo	.60
	排　骨 Pie Good	1.00		椰　汁　糕 Yer Gup Go	.90
	牛　什 Ngau Gup	1.00		蓮　蓉　飽 Lotus Paste Bun	1.00
	豉椒鳳爪 Fung Jaw	1.00		增設下午茶座及供應粥粉麵食	
	釀　豆　腐 Yuan Dua Foo	1.00		由下午三時至五時	
	煎　粉　菓 Fun Gok	1.00		臘腸雞飯　每盅	1.60
	香煎鮮竹卷 Sin Chut Kuen	1.00		排　骨　飯　每盅	1.60
	煎　鍋　貼 Wor Tip	1.00		煎蛋牛肉飯　每盅	1.60
	酥炸蝦花 Jar Har Fat	1.00		雲　吞　麵	1.35
	芋　角 Woo Gok	1.00		牛　什　麵	1.35
	雞　包　仔 Guy Bow	1.00		水　餃　麵	1.35
	叉　燒　飽 Sha Siu Bow	.45		淨　雲　吞	1.60
	春　卷 Spring Roll	.45		牛肉丸粥	1.30
	蘿　蔔　糕 Law Bak Go	.45		皮蛋瘦肉粥	1.30
	糯　米　雞 Nor My Guy	1.10		淨　水　餃	1.60
	叉燒腸粉 Cha Siu Cheung Fun	1.10		汽水	
	牛肉腸粉 Mgau Yuk Cheung Fun	1.10			
	鮮蝦腸粉 Har Cheung Fun	1.10			

№ 1144

TOTAL	
TAX	

Thank You　PLEASE PAY THIS AMOUNT

Menu 11. Courtesy Kowloon Dim Sum Restaurant, 187 Dundas Street West, Toronto

雅香・茶室（天々茶樓）

雅香

素馨　　普洱　安井
水仙　　龍井　仙　每壺 二毫
觀音　　壽眉
荔枝
菊花　　每位
　　　　普井 三毫
菊

茶室

白糖糕
椰酥汁
蓮蓉飽

◆ 鹹 點 心 ◆

蝦餃　　　　每碟　六毫
粉果　　　　每碟　六毫
燒賣　　　　每碟　六毫
豬肉燒賣　　每碟　六毫
豉汁排骨　　每碟　六毫
牛肉　　　　每碟　六毫
酥炸芋角　　每碟　六毫
三絲春捲粉　每碟　六毫
煎蘿蔔糕　　每碟　六毫
牛肉球　　　每碟　六毫
炸蝦多士　　每碟　六毫
金錢雞　　　每碟　七毫
叉燒球大飽　每碟　五毫

◆ 甜 點 心 ◆

蓮蓉飽　　　每碟　六毫
蛋撻　　　　每碟　六毫
椰汁糕　　　每碟　六毫
白糖糕　　　每碟　六毫
酥皮蛋撻　　每碟　六毫
蓮蓉飽　　　每碟　六毫

歡迎外賣

電話：二八九・六八六五

◆馳名國味◆

國鴨腳	每碟 七毫五仙
國牛筋	每碟 七毫五仙
牛粉腸	每碟 七毫五仙
國牛腩	每碟 七毫五仙

◆粉麵・飯・雲吞◆

五柱香牛筋飯	每碟 一元伍毫伍
蠔油牛腩飯	每碟 一元伍毫伍
冬菇雞絲飯	每碟 一元伍毫伍
牛腩湯麵或粉	每碗 一元三毫伍
牛肉湯麵或粉	每碗 一元三毫伍
叉燒湯麵或粉	每碗 一元一毫伍
生雞絲炒麵或粉	每碟 一元七毫伍
蝦球炒麵或粉	每碟 一元七毫伍
番茄牛肉炒麵或粉	每碟 一元六毫伍
牛肉炒麵或粉	每碟 一元六毫伍
嫁油叉燒炒麵或粉	每碗 一元二毫伍

Menu 12. Courtesy Hang Ah Tea Room, 1 Hang Ah Street, San Francisco

叉燒湯麵

爽滑魚蛋麵

什會湯麵

滑牛湯麵

雞絲湯麵

蟹肉會伊麵

窩麵類

招牌窩麵

鴻圖窩麵

雞球窩麵

會伊窩麵

揚州窩麵

鮮菇雞絲腸

豉椒牛肉河

廈門炒米粉

星洲炒米粉

腸粉類

鮮蝦腸粉

滑牛腸粉

叉燒腸粉

煎蛋火腿飯

中式牛柳飯

揚州炒飯

揚州雞絲飯

時菜牛腩飯

切雞飯

油雞飯

火鴨飯

叉燒飯

酥炸牛肉丸

百花釀荳腐

羊城煎粉果

滑雞鯪魚夾

生菜鯪魚球

珍珠鳳凰球

豬潤鴛鴦夾

椒絲牛栢葉

雞絲春捲

雞粒香芋角

鮮蝦鹹水角

百花釀蟹拑

桂花炸蝦丸

臘味雜白糕

飽　點

蠔油叉燒飽

北菇雞飽仔

五香糯米捲

吉士奶黃飽

蛋黃蓮蓉飽

焗叉燒飽

焗雞尾飽

午市特點

五香牛什
蠔油鴨脚
鮮蝦銀針粉
八珍糯米鷄
猪扒焗意粉
北菇蒸鷄飯
煎蛋牛肉飯
豉汁排骨飯

湯麵類

京都炸醬麵
火鴨湯麵

炒粉麵類

海鮮炒麵
蝦仁炒麵
鷄球炒麵
鷄絲炒麵
招牌炒麵
魚片炒麵
排骨炒麵
牛肉炒麵
肉絲炒麵
蟹肉干燒伊麵
蠔油北菇麵
干炒牛河

飯類

招牌飯
時菜鷄球飯
滑蛋蝦仁飯
滑鷄絲飯
滑蛋牛飯
時菜牛飯
免治牛飯
鮮茄牛飯
酸菜牛飯
時菜班片飯
肉絲飯
豉汁排骨飯

鹹點

薄皮鮮蝦餃
酥皮鷄蛋撻
蟹黃燒賣
腿茸魚翅餃
西菜牛肉
豉汁蒸排骨
鮮蝦蒸粉果
四寶滑鷄札
鮮蝦鳳眼餃
百花釀魚肚
滑鷄絲粉捲
蠔油鮮竹捲

甜點

蓮子紅荳沙
酥皮鷄蛋撻
冰花鳳凰球
合桃蛋馬仔
桂林馬蹄糕
珠糯蓮茸粽
杭仁馬拉糕
冰黃千層夾
蓮茸水晶餅
梳扶哩布甸
真料皮蛋酥

香港灣仔洛克道四十一號
電話：二八一一一二八（五）

輝煌酒樓夜總會

重量質重 十兩足斤

如有價目更改，恕不另行通知

特別介紹

五彩炒（中）	十二元
羅游龍柚添香（中）	十五元
龍鳳四球十二元	
紅梅戲鳳（中）	
鐵板瑪珠四珠	十五元
醬爆雞三片	三十元
雪蛤膏	廿五元
香蕉琵琶蝦	

▲ 精美小菜 ▲

碧綠雙鮮	十五元
桂花炒肝	
椒鹽鳳肝	
椒鹽西肺	
百花炸肝	
北菇鳳爪	
家鄉肉	
碧綠煎鑲豆腐	
鐵板煎鑲豆腐	
蒸釀豆腐	
蒸滑雞	
吊燒雞	
牛柏葉	
蘭度牛肉	
碧綠蒸雙球	
滑蛋蝦仁	
雲耳雞片	
豉汁蒸魚	
豆腐花	
柳花	

▲ 著名煲仔菜 ▲

支竹羊腩煲	
紅炆羊腩煲	
乾炒牛河	
香芋火腩煲	
枝竹火腩煲	
八珍豆腐煲	
生炒糯米飯	
山斑汆湯	
一品窩	
什菜腸煲	
臘腸瑤柱飯	
鴨腎煲	
滑雞煲	
鮮魚腐煲	

底部分類

白灼鮮魷	
北菇燜西油	
生菜鮮肉	
牛腩排	
柳橙滑	

社國安會 謹識
鵲局消遣
海鮮
晚飯

電話：(五)二八一一二八　香港灣仔洛克道四十一號

煇煌酒樓酧夜絕會

金碧煇煌
精質良品

新春鹹點

年樂歡波同慶新春到
年利迎裁賀成恭賀新
盈金滿堂金發埠多花財
大滿四錢時龍壽寄就
利害寶運市暢前貴手

　　　　　　　每　十
　　　　　　　焦　一
　　合時焦行飯每　元

新春甜點

堂華滿客喜賀富閣花
結滿盡滿仕子貴心好
鳳滿金桃賀年壯帛月
鳳皆銀花暢年丹歡團
抹滿庭花放水糕酥笑圓

　毫四元三‥‥歲每

燒烤國味

燒味拼盤　　　　每碟 十二元
烤味拼燒　　　　每碟 十三元
國味燒臘拼　　　每碟 十四元
燒肥叉鳳爪　　　每碟 十八元

明油切汁燒皮水鴨　　廿一元
蠔油燒鵝　　　　　　廿二元
燒鴨　　　　　　　　廿二元
白切雞　　　　　　　廿八元
南乳豬　　　　　　　三十元

鮮羊腩　　　　　　　十二元
明城豬腩　　　　　　十八元
臘腸　　　　　　　　廿一元
潤腸　　　　　　　　廿二元
臘肉　　　　　　　　廿四元

小點

四寶滑雞扎
牛肉燒賣
鮮蝦餃
蝦肉粉果
　　　　　每款三元

點心

棉花雞
花絲潤腸蒸
清蒸燒賣
　　　　　每款四元
鮮蝦腸粉　每件八元

星期美點

	小	中	大	特	頂
點	三元	四元	五元	八元	八元

特價（午市）

上湯三絲雞
翡翠炒上素
上湯水餃
翡翠上湯麵
　　　　　每碗 十二元

牌金價招
鵲局菜 一百四十八元
鵲局菜 一百六十八元

星洲炒米
菜遠炒鮮魷
乾炒牛河
揚州炒飯
　　　　　每碟 十八元
　　　　　　　　廿二元
　　　　　　　　廿九元

You should try to read the Chinese on the samples given here of the order forms that you are likely to encounter in dimsam restaurants. When you are given such a form, you are supposed to write in the appropriate square the number of orders that you want of each dish. If you wish any additional things besides what is listed on the dimsam form, write them in the blank spaces that are usually provided. Keep in mind that noodle dishes (which you might well want to include in a dimsam brunch) come in large portions but dimsam dishes such as those listed above come in small portions: a moderately hungry person can easily eat four or five such portions. Note that ostensibly bilingual menus (or trilingual ones, in the case of the Montreal menu that appears below) often omit translations for some of the items. This is especially common in the case of dishes that Chinese think Occidentals won't like, such as beef tripe and chicken feet; order them—not only will you probably enjoy them, but it will help you convince the waiter that you really mean business. It is also very common for a "translation" on a bilingual menu to be simply a rendering of the Cantonese pronunciation in a spelling system invented by the proprietor. A prize example of that phenomenon is the order form from Kowloon Dim Sum in Toronto (menu 11), in which the "English" consists of little else but idiosyncratic transcriptions of Cantonese pronunciations and is full of typographical errors to boot. Fortunately, by now you probably know enough Chinese that you can ignore such enigmas as "Pie Good" and "Wor Tip" and read the nice clear Chinese that tells you that they are spareribs and fried ravioli respectively.

The menus (12–14) from the Hang Ah, the Cam Fung, and the Glorious are not order forms but supplementary menus listing items that can be ordered in

陸羽茶室　星期三美點

83/12 600f

鹹　品

食小麵飯

上湯鮮蝦絲片兒
鮮雞脯魚燒牛肺腩肉荷針飯粉角
西施烚蒸燒粉菓賣餃
叉家鄉蝦賣蒸燒蝦餃
滑油叉雞飽燒蝦飽
白蠔菌滑餃

紅燒叉絲水辦麵翅
上湯焗肥雞骨飯
米景翅世國蕾焗焗排粒飯班骨飯

甜品

蓮子黃蓉蔴拉蓉糕糕飽粽
置杏仁馬蹄香
紅荳沙晶餃
鮮奶糕

（服務一加牙）

韭五柳五鮮釀杏連王蝦柳燕雲湯蝦薄脆餅菓角椒

菓湘蓮
杏仔合子黑桃露
香杏露堆酥酥角糕露

鮮釀牛桂臘雲腿水侯腸焗腰肉燒蒸粉酥排卷賣賣肉燒排

眉波奶蓮子
山楂油蘿蔴蓉燒
酥雞雲置露酥餃批露夾餅

Menu 15. Courtesy Luk Yu Tea House, 24–26 Stanley Street, Central, Hong Kong

2228 S. WENTWORTH AVE
CHICAGO ILL. 60616

PHONE: (312) 842-7573

Daily Pastry from
9:00 A.M. to 2:00 P.M.

歡 樂 樓

HAPPY GARDEN RESTAURANT

美 點 DUM SUM DUMPLING	件數	價目 PRICE	碟數 QTY	美 點 DIM SUM DUMPLING	件數	價目 PRICE	碟數 QTY
鮮明蝦餃 SHRIMP DUMPLING	3	1.00		叉 燒 飽 B. B. Q. PORK BUN	2	1.00	
鮮明粉果 SHRIMP & meat dumpling	3	1.00		雞 飽 仔 CHICKEN BUN	3	1.00	
乾蒸燒賣 PORK DUMPLING	4	1.00		燕 窩 餃 BIRD-NEST BUN	3	1.00	
北菇燒賣 STUFFED BLACK MUSHROOMS	2	1.00		蓮蓉飽 LOTUS SEED BUN	2	1.00	
牛肉燒賣 BEEF MEAT BALL	2	1.00		豆 沙 飽 BEAN PASTE BUN	2	1.00	
豉汁排骨 SPARERIBS		1.00		鮮蝦腸粉 SHRIMP FUNN ROLL		1.20	
鴨掌燒賣 STUFFED DUCK WEB	2	1.00		滑牛腸粉 BEEF FUNN ROLL		1.20	
雞 札 CHICKEN ROLL	2	1.00		叉燒腸粉 B.B.Q. FUNN ROLL		1.20	

芋 角 TOVO FRIED CAKE	2	1.00	大什會炒麵 SEAFOOD W/noodle	6.25
鹹 水 角 FRIED CAKE(SALTY)	2	1.00	蝦球炒粉或麵 Fresh Shr./Rice Noodle.	6.25
鴨 腳 扎 DUCK FEET	2	1.00	鼓椒牛肉炒粉或麵 Green Pepper Beef/Noodle.	4.75
蘿 白 糕 TURNIP CAKE	2	1.00	星洲炒米粉 FRIED RICE NOODLE	6.25
鼓椒牛百葉 HOT BEEF SLICE *TRIPE*	2	1.00	厦門炒米粉 HA-MOON RICE NOODLE	6.25
糯 米 雞 MOCHI RICE	2	1.80	芥蘭牛肉炒粉粉或麵	5.25
蛋 捷 EGG PUFF	2	1.00		
馬 蹄 糕 Waterchestnut Cake	2	1.00		
煎 堆 FRIED CAKE/Bean Paste	2	1.00	TAX	
水 晶 糕 CRYSTAL CAKE W/Bean Paste	2	1.20	TOTAL	

名茶 菊花 · 60 　普 耳 、水 仙 、
龍井、壽眉、烏龍、香片 · 35

Menu 16. Courtesy Happy Garden Restaurant, 2228 South Wentworth Avenue, Chicago

TABLE NO.

紅 寶 石 酒 家

NO.	點 心 單	ORDER
1	蠔油叉燒包 Char Shiu Bow (2)	
2	蓮 蓉 飽 Lotus Seed Sweet Bow (2)	
3	豆 沙 飽 Dau Sar Sweet Bow (2)	
4	水 餃 Steamed Pork Dumpling (3)	
5	干 蒸 燒 賣 Pork Shiu Mai (3)	
6	雪白鮮蝦餃 Har Gow (Shrimps dumpling) (4)	
7	鴨 脚 札 Opp Cheng (2)	
8	牛 肉 燒 賣 Beef Shiu-Mai (3)	
9	排 骨 燒 賣 Spare Ribs Shiu-Mai	
10	花 菇 燒 賣 Chinese Mushroom Shiu-Mai (2)	
11	白 糖 糕 Sweet Rice Cake (2)	
12	鹹 水 角 Deep Fried Dumpling (2)	
13	芋 角 Fried Taro Ball (2)	
14.	釀 青 椒 Shrimp Stuffed Peppers (2)	
15.	蘿 蔔 糕 Turnips Cake (2)	

CHINESE TEA 中國名茶每位 25¢ ONE PERSON

Menu 17. Courtesy Ruby Restaurant, 609 H Street N.W., Washington, D. C.

特別介紹

五香牛什	Flank Skin w. Spiced Flavor	
廣東肉炒麵	Pork C. Mein. C. Style	
廣東肉炒粉	Pork C. Foon. C. Style	
干炒牛河	Beef C. Foon C. Style	
大集會炒麵	All Mixed Meat C. Mein C. Style	
大集會炒粉	All Mixed Meat C. Foon C. Style	
海鮮炒麵	Sea Food C. Mein	
豉椒牛肉炒米粉	Beef & Pepper. Rice Noodle	
豉椒炒蟹	Fried Crab w. Black Bean Sauce	
羌蔥焗蟹	Fried Crab w. Ginger	
炒石螺	Fried Snails w. Black Bean Sauce	
蠔油鴨掌	Duck Legs in Oyster Sauce	

明　展

Restaurant
Ming Yeng INC.
1051 ST-LAURENT
MONTREAL, QUEBEC, CANADA H2Z 1J6
TEL: (514)861-7413-4

Time Serve
De l'heure 11.00 A.M.
À/to 3.00 P.M.

茶市
由上午十一時至
下午三時

QUANT 數量	茶點	DIM SUM	PRIX 價目	Sub-Total 小計
	透明鮮蝦餃	(4) HAR GAU crevettes/shrimps	1.40	
	頂呱呱鮮粉果	(3) PAN GOR poulet/chicken	1.20	
	鮮美手燒賣	(4) SUI MAI pork dumplings	1.20	
	時拿牛肉賣	(2) SUI MAI boeuf/beef balls	1.20	
	豉汁排骨賣	SPARERIBS (Black Bean Sauce)	1.20	
	三星滑鷄凡	(2) POULET/CHICKEN	.90	
	鮮蝦滑腸粉	SHRIMP CHEUNG - FUN	1.40	
	牛肉滑腸粉	BEEP CHEUNG - FUN	1.20	
	义燒滑腸粉	B.B.Q. PORK CHEUNG - FUN	1.20	
	燒臺义燒飽	(2) CHAR SIU BOW (BBQ Pork Bow)	1.00	
	潮式豆沙飽	(2) PAIN SUCRE/RED BEAN BOW	1.00	
	明風靚大飽	(2) PAIN CHINOIS MAISON	1.30	

牛市特價炒粉麵

平炒牛河 4.90
SAUTÉ DE BOEUF
NOUILLES DE RIZ FRY
SLICED BEEF
WITH RICE NOODLE
QUANT 數量　S

乾炒牛河 4.90
BOEUF TRANCHÉ AU POIVRO
EN SAUCE GREEN NOUILLES
BEEF WITH GREEN PEPPER
AND RICE NOODLE
QUANT 數量　15

什錦大炒麵 4.90
CHOW MEIN CANTONNAIS
CANTONESE CHOW MEIN
QUANT 數量　3

星期日日日至星期六
美日園國遊迎阖府
點市會意惠茶陞外賣理

	Item	Price		
家鄉鳳爪大包	(2) HUM SHUI KOK porc/pork	.90	星洲炒米粉 SAUTÉ DE PORC AUX VERMICELLES CHINO VERMICELLI SINGAPORE STYLE	4.90
五香茄子角	(2) WO KOK (Deep Fried Taro)	1.20	QUANT 數量	3
腊味蘿白糕	(2) LOR PAK GO (Turnip Cake)	.90		
荷葉糯米飯	LOR MAI GUY riz/rice	1.50		
豉汁牛肉菜	BLACK BEAN SAUCE. TRIPE	1.20		
蠔豉鴨掌	OYSTER SAUCE DUCK WEB	1.20		
豉汁鳳爪	FUNG CHAO (Chicken Claw)	1.20		
血食馬拉糕	(2) MA LAI GO gateau/cake	.90		
香煎馬蹄糕	(2) WATER CHESTNUT JELLO CAKE	.90	SUB TOTAL	
啊吹蛋撻腥	EGG CUSTARD TART	.90		
豆沙糕仔	CHIT CHAI Red Bean/sucre	.90	SOUS TOTAL SUB TOTAL	
脆口春卷	CRISPY SPRING ROLL/ROULEAU	1.00	TAX/TAXE	
茶每位	THE PAR PERSONNE/TEA PER PERSON	.25	TOTAL 總額	
		SOUS TOTAL SUB TOTAL		

Menu 18. Courtesy Restaurant Ming Yeng, 1051 boulevard Saint-Laurent, Montreal

三喜大酒樓

THREE HAPPINESS

THREE HAPPINESS REST.
2130 S. Wentworth Ave.
Chicago, Ill. 60616
Tel. 791-1228

THREE HAPPINESS REST.
209 W. Cermak Rd.
Chicago, Ill. 60616
Tel. 842-1964

TABLE NO:

DATE:

QUAN. 碟數	DIM SUM		QUAN. 碟數	DIM SUM	
	叉燒火焙飽 Char Siu Bow	1.20		榛蚵煎堆 Gin Duey (Sesame Seed Puff)	1.20
	梘雞燒飽 Chicken Bow	1.20		荷葉糯米雞 Naw Mi Guy (Sweet Rice & Meat Wrapped)	2.25
	叉燒腸粉 Char Siu Chong Fun	1.20		椰汁糕 Coconut Milk Gelatin Square	1.20
	鮮蝦腸粉 Fresh Shrimp Chong Fun	1.25		蓮蓉飽 Leen Yung Bow (Lotus Seed Steamed Bun)	1.20
	牛肉腸粉 Beef Chong Fun	1.20		鵪油馬拉糕 Malayan Cake (Brown Sugar Cake)	1.20
	鮮尖蝦餃 Fresh Shrimp Har Gau	1.20		糯米糍 Coconut Mochi	1.20
	西荞牛肉燒賣 Beef Meat Ball	1.20			
	干蒸燒賣 Pork Siu Mai	1.20			
	三喜燒賣 Three Happiness Siu Mai	1.20			

		CHOW MEIN Or RICE NOCDLE	
蟹黃燒賣 Crab Roe Siu Mai	1.20	滑肉條炒粉或麵 Pork W/ Thin or Rice Noodle	5.25
豉汁排骨 Spare Ribs W/ Black Beans Sauce	1.20	肩牛炒粉或麵 Beef W/ Thin or Rice Noodle	5.25
鳳冠餃 Fung Kun Gau	1.20	又燒炒粉或麵 Char Siu W/ Thin or Rice Noodle	5.25
魚翅餃 Ye Chi Gau	1.20	蝦球炒粉或麵 Fresh Shrimp W/ Thin or Rice Noodle	7.25
豉汁鳳爪 Chicken Feet W/ Garlic Sauce	1.20	魚片炒粉或麵 Fresh Fish W/ Thin or Rice Noodle	7.25
雞潭麻鴨掌 Stuffed Duck Feet	1.20	雞球炒粉或麵 Chicken W/ Thin or Rice Noodle	5.25
牛肚 Beef Tripes	1.20	火鴨炒粉或麵 Roast Duck W/ Thin or Rice Noodle	6.75
牛百葉 Beef Tripe	1.20	什會炒粉或麵 Mixed Seafood W/ Thin or Rice Noodle	7.25
肉絲粉角 Shredded Pork Fun Guen	1.20	豉椒牛肉炒粉麵 Green Pepper Beef W/ Thin or Rice Noodle	5.75
蚝油雞扎 Chicken & Char Siu Stuffed	1.20	星洲炒米粉 Singapore Fried Rice Noodle	5.75
羅白糕 Pan Fried White Turnip Cake	1.20	干炒牛河 Dry Pan Fried Rice Noodle W/ Beef	5.25
蝦多士 Shrimp Toast	1.20	芥蘭牛肉炒粉或麵 Beef Broccoli with Thin or Rice Noodle	6.25
香脆春卷 Spring Roll	1.20		
炸蒸芋角 Fried Taro Root	1.20		
家鄉鹹水角 Ham Sui Kok (Meat Filled)	1.20		

Menu 19. Courtesy Three Happiness Restaurant, 2130 South Wentworth Avenue, Chicago

addition to the items that are brought around on carts. The Luk Yu, Hong Kong's oldest and most respected dimsam restaurant, has different specialities every week (at the top it says—printed right to left—"Luk Yu Tearoom, the Week's Dimsam, solar calender March 26 to April 1"), and their order form has the fanciest names for the dishes that I have seen on any such form (menu 15). Do not be dismayed to find much of it very hard to interpret. You will at least be able to identify major components of most of the items (e.g, the fifth item from the right is some kind of beef-filled ravioli). You'll also find it easier to get your bearings if you pay attention to the headings: the upper half of the menu is "salty items," the lower right corner contains "rice and noodle dishes," and the rest of the lower half is "sweet items."

Certain Mandarin restaurants serve a Northern version of a dimsam brunch, including such items as 油條 *yóu tiáo* "Chinese crullers," 小籠包 *xiǎo lóng bāo* "ravioli served in steamer basket," 葱油餅 *cōng yóu bǐng* "scallion pancake," 燒餅 *shāo bǐng* "grilled bun," and such cold dishes as 辣白菜 *là bái cài* "hot and sour Chinese cabbage," and 薰魚 *xūn yú* "smoked fish," as well as various noodle dishes.

8
Restaurant Names

If you have gotten this far in the book, you will be in a position to make a stab at reading the names of Chinese restaurants. You will in fact find it of some use to pay

attention to the Chinese names of Chinese restaurants, since they may give you information about the restaurant that is not contained in the English name, and since they often appear on the menu as part of the names of specialties of the house. Besides, it's fun to show off your knowledge when (as is often the case) there is no connection between the English and Chinese names of the restaurant.

The name of a Chinese restaurant often is something that would be meaningful to a Chinese but would mean nothing to most Westerners. For example, a restaurant that once was one of Chicago's finest (to my deep regret, it has gone out of business) called itself "Mandarin House" in English but 峨嵋大飯店 *é méi dà fàn diàn* in Chinese. The Chinese name, which incorporates the name of a mountain range in Sichuan and is identical to the name of Beijing's most famous Sichuanese restaurant, told one that the restaurant not only served Sichuanese food but aspired to very high standards in that cuisine, which one could not guess from the English name. In other cases, the Chinese characters on the front of a restaurant may provide you with warning that you should stay away, as in the case of the Sydney, Australia, restaurant whose sign bears the English name "E—— Chinese Restaurant" and the Chinese characters 洋菜 *yáng cài* "occidental food."

The Chinese name of a restaurant often contains or is accompanied by characters that indicate what cuisine it serves, for example:

京菜 *jīng cài* Peking cuisine
川菜 *chuān cài* Szechuan cuisine
粤菜 *yuè cài* Cantonese cuisine
滬菜 *hù cài* Shanghai cuisine
淮揚菜 *huái yáng cài* North Yangtze cuisine
江浙菜 *jiāng zhè cài* Jiangsu-Zhejiang cuisine

客菜 *kè cài* Hakka cuisine
潮州菜 *cháo zhōu cài* Teochiu (eastern Canton) cuisine
素菜 *sù cài* vegetarian cuisine
教門菜 *jiào mén cài* Moslem cuisine

There are also innumerable completely transparent terms for cuisines, consisting simply of the name of a province or region and 菜, for example, 福建菜 *fú jiàn cài* "Fukien cuisine."

The name of a Chinese restaurant frequently ends in one of the following combinations:

飯店	*fàn diàn* rice shop	園	*yuán* garden
飯館	*fàn guǎn* rice hall	亭	*tíng* pavilion
樓	*lóu* inn	居	*jū* residence
酒樓	*jiǔ lóu* tavern	堂	*táng* hall
酒家	*jiǔ jiā* wine house	餐廳	*cān tīng* dining room
菜館	*cài guǎn* food hall		

These expressions often appear in expanded forms such as 大飯店 *dà fàn diàn* "big rice shop."

Many restaurants are named after Chinese places, for example, 北京飯店 *běi jīng fàn diàn* "Peking Restaurant." The following are some place names that you may encounter in names of restaurants:

	Cities	Provinces
Northern China	北京 *běi jīng* Peking	
	天津 *tiān jìn* Tientsin	
		山東 *shān dōng* Shantung
		河北 *hé běi* Hopei
		蒙古 *méng gǔ* Mongolia

Central China	上海	shàng hǎi		
		Shanghai		
	蘇州	sū zhōu	江蘇	jiāng sū
		Soochow		Kiangsu
	南京	nán jīng		
		Nanking		
	楊州	yáng zhōu		
		Yangchow		
	杭州	háng zhōu	浙江	zhè jiāng
		Hangchow		Chekiang
	寧波	níng po		
		Ningpo		
	溫州	wēn zhōu		
		Wenchow		
	漢口	hàn kǒu	湖北	hú běi
		Hankow		Hupei
	武漢	wǔ hàn		
		Wuhan		
Western China	重慶	chóng qìng	四川	sì chuān
		Chungking		Szechuan
	成都	chéng du		
		Chengtu		
	長沙	cháng shā	湖南	hú nán
		Changsha		Hunan
			雲南	yún nán
				Yunnan
Southern China	廣州	guǎng zhōu	廣東	guǎng dōng
		Canton		Canton
	汕頭	shàn tóu		
		Swatow		
	福州	fú zhōu	福建	fú jiàn
		Foochow		Fukien
	廈門	xià mén		
		Amoy		
	桂林	guì lín	廣西	guǎng xī
		Kweilin		Kwanghsi
			江西	jiāng xī
				Kianghsi

Places outside the People's Republic of China:

香港 *xiāng gǎng* Hong Kong
九龍 *jiǔ lóng* Kowloon
澳門 *ào mén* Macau
台灣 *tái wān* Taiwan
台北 *tái běi* Taipei
馬來亞 *mǎ lái yà* Malaya
星州 *xīng zhōu* Singapore

Rivers and other geographic features:

長城 *cháng chéng* Great Wall
長江 *cháng jiāng* Yangtze River
楊子江 *yáng zi jiāng* Yangtze River
廣江 *huáng jiāng* Yellow River
珠江 *zhū jiāng* Pearl River
東江 *dōng jiāng* East River (tributary of Pearl River)

The following are some of the famous restaurants in Beijing that are described in Kenneth K. C. Lo's *Peking Cooking*; their names are occasionally adopted by restaurants elsewhere, especially those that purvey the cuisine in which their Beijing namesakes specialize.

Moslem-influenced Northern cuisine:

烤肉宛 *kǎo ròu wǎn* Wan Barbecued Meat
回民食堂 *huí mín shí táng* Moslem Dining Hall
東來順 *dōng lái shùn* (famous for lamb hot pot)
全聚德 *quán jù dé* (famous for Peking duck)
便意坊 *biàn yì fāng* (famous for Peking duck)

Imperial palace cuisine:

坊膳 *fǎng shàn*
沙鍋居 *shā guō jū* (famous for simmered pork)

Shandong cuisine:

豐澤園 *fēng zé yuán*
同和居 *tóng hé jū*
春元樓 *chūn yuán lóu*

Shanghai and other Eastern Chinese cuisines:

森隆飯居 *sēn lóng fàn jū*
玉華食堂 *yù huá shí táng*

Fujian, Jiangxi, Yunnan, and other Southern cuisines:

康東南菜館 *kāng dōng nán cài guǎn* Kang's Southeastern Dining Room

Sichuan cuisine:

峨嵋酒家 *é méi jiǔ jiā* Omei Tavern

9

Familiar Characters in Unfamiliar Forms

Variant Forms of Characters

If you have gone through the examples given so far and looked up the characters, you have found in a number of cases that an unfamiliar character was merely an alternative way of writing a Chinese word for which you already knew "the" character. Much as you may curse the perversity of people for whom several thousand words each written with a different character is not enough of a burden on the memory, the existence of variant forms of characters is a fact of life that you will simply have to contend with.

I will proceed to list the principal ways in which variant

forms have come about, partly in order to help you make intelligent guesses as to whether an unfamiliar character is a variant form of one you know (and there will be many occasions when you will have to guess: while I have listed many variant forms in the Glossary, it is impossible to list them all, since new ones get created all the time), and partly to reassure you that the perversity of the Chinese is not total.

1. In many cases, variant forms of a character involve fairly natural simplifications of some part of the character. For example, while the "standard" form of the "vegetable" radical consists of two crosses ⁺⁺, it is more often written with the horizontal parts of the two crosses joined 艹. Similarly, a row of dots may be replaced by a line, as in 鱼 instead of 魚.

2. A variant of a character may involve the same elements just placed differently; for example, the "tick" at the top of such characters as the one for "white" 白 may fall anywhere from the middle to the far left. Similarly, the character for "dot" may be written either 點 or 点.

3. "New" characters are often formed by adding an appropriate radical to an old character. For example, by adding the "vegetable" radical to 豆 *dòu* "bean," a new form 荳 of the same character was created. Other examples of this are the addition of the "eating" radical to 包 *bāo* "wrap, steamed bun" to yield 飽 "steamed bun," and the addition of the "fire" radical to *xūn* 薰 "smoked" (which actually contains that radical to begin with, in the form of the row of dots at the bottom) to yield 燻.

4. The phonetic is sometimes replaced by a simpler one that has the same pronunciation as the given character, except perhaps for tone. For example, 蝦 *xiā* "shrimp" is popularly simplified to 虾 by substitution of the character 下 *xià* "down" for the original phonetic (叚 *jiǎ* "false")

of the character. This sort of variant character not only involves less writing but also gives more information about the pronunciation: in the classical system of characters, the phonetic need only rhyme with the word represented by the whole character, but in these new variant characters, the phonetic generally not only rhymes but begins with the same consonant as does the word that the whole character represents.

5. In some variant forms, parts of the character are left out. For example, another variant of 點 *diǎn* "dot" is 点.

6. There are also many miscellaneous substitutions. For example, the character for *ji* "chicken" has the forms 鷄, 雞, 鸡, and 难.

Simplified Characters

The People's Republic of China has officially adopted a system of characters in which many of the traditional characters have been eliminated altogether (other characters are used in their place) and many characters have been given new shapes that involve considerably less writing. For example, the popular form 虾 for "shrimp" is now the official one, and 東 *dōng* "east" is now written 东; characters whose left half is the "speech" radical 言 now have 讠 instead. To a large extent, this system of simplified characters consists in the adoption of already existing variant characters in place of the traditional chatacters from which they have arisen. For example, the simplified form of the "speech" radical has existed for centuries in handwriting and has now been adopted into the system of printed characters. I have not attempted to include official simplified characters in the Glossary except where they coincide with popular simplified forms that are in common use among North American Chinese.

Handwritten Characters

The ability to read printed Chinese does not carry with it the ability to read handwritten Chinese. The relationship between the printed forms of Chinese characters and the forms that they assume when written rapidly by a native Chinese is quite complicated, and no system has been devised for determining from a handwritten character what its printed form is, or for looking up characters on the basis of their handwritten rather than their printed forms. Moreover, it is often difficult to tell where one handwritten Chinese character ends and the next one begins.

I thus admit defeat. I am unable to teach the readers of this book how to decipher handwritten menus, and indeed I can not really claim to be able to read them proficiently myself—I can still only identify bits and pieces of handwritten menus, unless the handwriting sticks very close to the printed forms, and I feel proud of myself when I manage to puzzle out more than a little of a menu that is handwritten. After you have become proficient in the reading of printed Chinese menus, you will know enough characters and know enough names of Chinese dishes that you will be in a position to make good guesses as to what some of the unintelligible characters ought to be. Your guessing will be helped considerably if you keep in mind that all of the nonstandard ways of simplifying characters that were taken up earlier in this chapter are very common in handwritten Chinese.

Beyond that quite fragmentary advice, all that I can offer the reader in the way of help with Chinese handwriting are a few samples of handwritten Chinese, side-by-side with their printed equivalents, to give some idea of what can happen in Chinese handwriting. We have, in order, the week's special dishes from Chicago's Won

Kow and Toronto's Tung Kong, and special set dinners from Berkeley's East River and New York's Home Village Restaurant (menus 20–23). (Handwritten menu supplements advertising set dinners are especially common.)

10

Writing Out Your Order

In Chinese restaurants in North America, Chinese customers often write out their orders on a slip of paper and hand their written order to the waiter. If you can write out your order legibly in Chinese characters, you will increase the likelihood that your waiter will treat you as a real customer and not as an interloper.

To get to where you can write out an order in Chinese, you should start by copying Chinese characters for practice. Here are some pointers that will help you produce writing that your waiter will be able to read.

1. In writing a Chinese character, you go from left to right and from top to bottom. For example, in writing 油 *yóu* "oil," you go through the following steps:

1 丶	5 氵冂
2 丶	6 氵冃
3 氵	7 油
4 氵丿	8 油

Drawing the strokes in the traditional order helps considerably to make your characters look authentic, since the order of the strokes controls the way that the pen moves and thus the kinds of connections between strokes

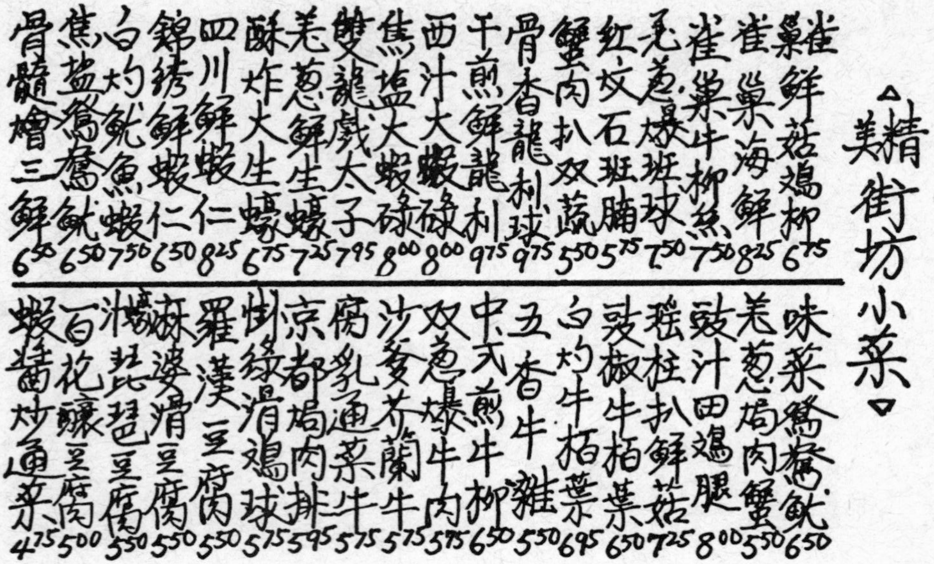

Menu 20. Courtesy Won Kow Restaurant, 2237 South Wentworth Avenue, Chicago

精美街坊小菜

雀巢鮮菇鷄柳	6^{75}
雀巢海鮮	8^{25}
雀巢牛柳絲	7^{50}
羗葱爆班球	7^{50}
紅炆石班腩	5^{75}
蟹肉扒雙蔬	5^{50}
骨香龍利球	9^{75}
干煎鮮龍利	9^{75}
西汁大蝦碌	8^{00}
焦鹽大蝦碌	8^{00}
雙龍戲太子	7^{95}
羗葱鮮生蠔	7^{25}
酥炸大生蠔	6^{75}
四川鮮蝦仁	8^{25}
錦綉鮮蝦仁	6^{50}
白灼魷魚蝦	7^{50}
焦鹽鴛鴦魷	6^{50}
骨髓燴三鮮	6^{50}

味菜鴛鴦魷	6^{50}
羗葱焗肉蟹	5^{50}
豉汁田鷄腿	8^{00}
瑤柱扒鮮菇	7^{25}
豉椒牛栢葉	6^{50}
白灼牛栢葉	6^{95}
五香牛雜	5^{50}
中式煎牛柳	6^{50}
雙葱爆牛肉	5^{75}
沙爹芥蘭牛	5^{75}
腐乳通菜牛	5^{75}
京都焗肉排	5^{95}
掛綠滑鷄球	5^{75}
羅漢豆腐	5^{50}
蔴婆滑豆腐	5^{50}
蠔汁琵琶豆腐	5^{50}
百花釀豆腐	5^{00}
蝦醬炒通菜	4^{75}

Menu 20. Courtesy Won Kow Restaurant, 2237 South Wentworth Avenue, Chicago

東江鹽焗雞　半隻 7⁰⁰　全隻 13⁵⁰
百花釀蟹拑　2⁰⁰

煲仔菜

八珍豆腐煲 5⁴⁵
東江豆腐煲 5²⁵
紅炆斑腩煲 5⁷⁵
崧陸生腩煲 5⁷⁵

鐵板名菜

鐵板龍利球 9⁷⁵
鐵板海鮮 7⁵⁰
鐵板牛柳 6⁹⁵
鐵板滑雞(肉) 6⁵⁰
鐵板沙爹牛(肉) 6⁵⁰
鐵板豆腐 5⁴⁵

湯羹美類

蟹肉燴羹
西湖牛肉羹 5⁹⁵
花膠燴鴨絲 5³⁵
錦繡豆腐羹 5⁵⁰
八寶辣湯 6²⁵
酸辣湯 5⁵⁰ 7⁹⁵

Menu 20 (cont.)

┌─────────────────────────┐
│ 特別介紹 │
│ │
│ 鹽焗雞　每半隻 7⁰⁰　每隻 13⁵⁰ │
│ 江蟹拼 │
│ 東花釀 │
│ 百花釀蟹　每只 2⁰⁰ │
└─────────────────────────┘

○名馳煲仔菜○

東江豆腐煲　5²⁵
八珍豆腐煲　5⁹⁵

紅炆班腩煲　5⁷⁵
柱候牛腩煲　5⁷⁵

○鐵板名菜○

鐵板豆腐　5⁹⁵
鐵板沙爹牛　6⁵⁰
鐵板豆豉雞　6⁹⁵
鐵板龍利海鮮　7⁵⁰
鐵板牛柳球　9⁷⁵

○湯羹類○

酸辣湯　5⁵⁰
八寶辣醬柱湯　7⁹⁵
西洋菜魚丸湯　6²⁵
錦綉魚丸湯
花膠豆腐羹　5⁵⁰
西湖牛肉羹　5⁹⁵
湖牛燴鴨羹　5²⁵
牛肉冬菇絲　5⁵⁰
冬茸

Menu 20. (*cont.*)

Menu 21. Courtesy Tung Kong Restaurant, 393 Dundas Street West, Toronto

鐵板沙爹牛肉 6⁰⁰　　白家白灼鮮中蝦 7⁵⁰　　涼瓜鄉炒牛肉 6⁰⁰　　涼鄉鮮釀中蝦 5⁵⁰　　脆瓜瓜釀雙寶 6⁵⁰　　五柳皮炒牛腩 5⁰⁰　　椒鹽焗石斑 7⁵⁰　　干煎板大鮮魷 5⁰⁰　　酥炸石斑塊 7⁰⁰　　羌膠釀生蠔 8⁵⁰　　魚柱煀海大蝦 9⁵⁰　　瑤柱釀生蠔 9⁵⁰　　大扒茄瓜 5⁵⁰　　扒釀瓜 5⁰⁰　　甫魚奶瓜 7⁰⁰　　例湯 3⁵⁰

羌葱牛柏葉 6⁵⁰　　龍鬚菜 4⁵⁰　　柱侯蘿白牛腩 5⁰⁰　　蘿白牛腩 5⁵⁰　　溫公扣牛 5⁰⁰　　牛腩齋煲 6⁵⁰　　菜膽根煲 6⁵⁰　　白通菜根鮮魷 6⁵⁰　　醬爆通菜牛 7⁵⁰　　蝦醬通菜乳根 5⁰⁰　　椒絲腐乳鮮魷 6⁵⁰　　鐵板中牛肉 6⁵⁰　　韭菜豆焗腐 4⁵⁰　　琵琶豆腐 5⁵⁰　　茸菜豆豉中牛 6⁵⁰　　百花釀蟹紅鷄 7⁵⁰　　時鮮鮑腐子 6⁵⁰　　脆奶鮮掌片仁蝦 7⁰⁰

Menu 21. Courtesy Tung Kong Restaurant, 393 Dundas Street West, Toronto

時菜 清蒸 燦烤 和菜

48: 鮮果凍乳

甲

龍利

龍利

和菜

乙

薑葱焗龍蝦球

骨香碧古利龍球　燒焗

時菜碧古利　焗

乳鴿春　清蒸

和菜甲

清蒸時鮮

香波海上鮮

椒鹽焗咕嚕肉

時菜炒鮮魷

東江霸王牛肉塊

錦繡豆腐羹

足八位　$48⁰⁰

每只　2⁰⁰　11⁰⁰

全只　14⁰⁰　8⁰⁰

半條　22⁰⁰

全條　12⁰⁰

半條　16⁰⁰

和菜乙

珍珠蝦醬

時菜炒石班

金牌鹽焗鮮魷

例湯

金牌炒牛肉塊

足五位　$24⁰⁰

Menu 21. (*cont.*)

大菜（可口）

海鮮煲

清蒸石班
豉汁蒸蟹
蒜蓉蒸蝦
砂窩海鮮
玉枝瑤柱甫
鮑魚焗肉蟹
鮮菇扒時菜

Menu 22. Courtesy East River Restaurant, 2420 Shattuck, Berkeley

海鮮餐　45.00（六人）

珊瑚鮮菇湯

酥炸生蠔

雀巢鮮帶子蟹

薑蔥焗大蜆

豉椒蒸海斑

清蒸斑球

Menu 22. Courtesy East River Restaurant, 2429 Shattuck, Berkeley

湘　雞　燒　腿　湯

東　江　釀　全　雞

東　江　豆　至　鴨

梅　江　酥　肉　鴨

菜　菜　香　扣　丸

紫　蓉　炒　双　丸

（四至五人）

清　東
鶏　江
鹽　釀
焗　豆
豆　腐
腐　鶏

東
江
酥
肉
排
丸

江
瑤
膠
鶏
羹
湯

東
江
鹽
焗
鶏

梅
菜
香
扣
肉
丸

菜
遠
炒
雙
丸

Menu 22. (cont.)

Menu 23. Courtesy Home Village Restaurant, 20 Mott Street, New York

豐盛和菜　105.⁰⁰

鮮菇扒玉掌
花雕焗鮮雞
柱甫玉樹蝦的
鹽煎鱈魚龍鱈
四寶蔘焗土鱿
瑤柱鵠巢雪耳
弍熱葷
紅燒

奉送西
楊香合米焗
芝沙律
脆皮芝士
家鄉土皮
鄉合時焗
煎伊生布
鹽炒府甸
龍府
鱈麵飯
蝦飯菓布甸
的菓匈

Menu 23. Courtesy Home Village Restaurant, 20 Mott Street, New York

or deformations of strokes that occur naturally in rapid writing.

2. Two lines forming an "upper right corner" ㄱ are written as a single stroke, as in step 5 above. Thus, the character for *huí* "return" (as in 回鍋肉 "twice-cooked pork") is written with six strokes, and is counted as having six strokes in traditional dictionaries (though in our Glossary it counts as having eight strokes):

1 丨		4 冋	
2 冂		5 回	
3 冂		6 回	

3. Don't overlook minute hooks and twiddles. For example, some vertical strokes have a hook at the bottom and others don't: 手 *shǒu* "hand," 干 *gān* "dry." If you wrote "hand" without the hook, or "dry" with one, slight though that difference is, the character would be harder for a Chinese to recognize.

4. Try to recognize the pieces of which a complicated character is built. If you recognize that the left half of 鷄 consists of ⺈ above 幺 above 大, you will find it easier to reproduce the character intelligibly than if you just regard it as a mass of strokes. Similarly, the top of 醬 *jiàng* "sauce" consists of 爿 plus 夅 (which is in turn 夂 over 寸) and the bottom is 酉. This will also help you to come closer to the standard order of writing the strokes, since the strokes of a "piece" are consecutive except (as with 回, discussed above) where one "piece" completely surrounds another.

Exercise 1

Using the menus reproduced in chapter 6, choose a dinner consisting of a pork dish, a seafood dish, a poultry dish, a vegetable dish, and a soup, and write out the characters.

Exercise 2

Make up your own exercises: imagine a visit to a Chinese restaurant with a group of your friends (decide how many of them there will be!), and using the menus in chapter 6 or any other Chinese menu that you can get hold of, choose an appropriate quantity and variety of dishes for that group and write out your order. Be sure to achieve variety both in the flavors of the dishes and in the ingredients that go into them. Don't forget to order rice (白飯) and tea (茶).

11

The Pronunciation of Chinese

Mandarin

This book is concerned with how to read printed Chinese, not with how to speak Chinese or how to understand spoken Chinese. However, it would be foolish to overlook pronunciation entirely, since a knowledge of the pronunciation of words can be a great help in remembering them. I have accordingly given the pronunciations of all Chinese words discussed above and have indicated in the Glossary the pronunciations of all the words listed there. However, it will take a bit of explanation before you are able to read off the pronunciations of the characters, since Chinese has several sounds and combinations of sounds that do not occur in English or the better-known European languages and since there are some unfamiliar things about the use of letters in the system of transcription used here (the PINYIN system) that require an explanation.

The pinyin system of transcription, which is the official system of the People's Republic of China and is now widely used in the English-speaking world in transcribing Chinese names, is not the only system of representing Chinese sounds in the Roman alphabet. Many pre-1970s publications and the catalogs of many libraries use the older Wade-Giles system of transcription, which involves spellings such as "Ch'ingtao, Kueichou" for what are written "Qingdao, Guizhou" in pinyin. There is also the Yale system of transcription, used in some important pedagogical works on Chinese, though otherwise not widely employed, in which those names are rendered "Chingdau, Gweijou," as well as popular spellings such as "Tsingtao, Kweichow," which in many cases represent no systematic scheme of transcription but have been created ad hoc by foreign journalists and travelers.

The explanation of the use of the various letters and combinations of letters in pinyin are given in alphabetic order, so as to make life easier for the reader who has to refer back to this section when he can't remember how some combination is pronounced.

a (see also *ai, ao, ian*). Pronounced as in Italian or Spanish, or as in English "father."

ai. The *a* sound followed by a *y* sound. Thus *mai* sounds like the English word "my."

ao. The *a* sound followed by a *w* sound; thus *bao* sounds like the first syllable of English "bow-wow."

b. Pronounced as in English;[6] thus *bao* sounds like the first syllable of English "bow-wow."

c (see also *ch*). Pronounced like the "ts" of "bets."

6. More accurately, Mandarin *b* is a VOICELESS UNASPIRATED STOP and is in fact closer to the "p" of "spin" than to the "b" of "bin." However, English "b" is so close to the desired sound that English speakers can simply pronounce a "b" and get a quite satisfactory result. If your native language is not English, it may help if you identify the *b* of Mandarin with the "p" of French or Spanish.

ch. This is one of two Mandarin sounds that both resemble English "ch" but are actually distinct (the other sound is the one written *q*); *ch* represents a "ch" sound pronounced with the tip of the tongue moved back and raised so that it touches the middle of the hard palate, that is, it is a RETROFLEX "ch" sound. (The tongue position just described is roughly the one with which many American and Welsh speakers pronounce "r"). The same tongue position is used in Mandarin *r*, *sh*, and *zh*. Thus, *chao* is pronounced like the English word "chow," except that the tongue must have the retroflex position just described.[7]

d. Pronounced like "d" in English "dog."[8]

e (see also *ei*, *er*, *ie*, *ue*). Pronounced like the "a" of English "sofa" or "gorilla" (a lax central vowel). In Mandarin this is a full-fledged vowel, not just an unstressed variant of other vowels, the way it is in English. You wouldn't be too far off if you gave it the "short u" sound of words like "fun" or "mud"; thus, *ben* sounds something like English "bun," except that the vowel of "bun" is a little bit off.

ei. Pronounced like the "ay" of "may"; thus *mei* sounds like "may."

er. In this combination, the vowel of often sounds more like *a* than like *e*. Thus *zher* often sounds very like English "jar."

f. Pronounced like English "f." Thus, *fou* is pronounced like English "foe."

g. Pronounced like "g" in English "god" (see footnote 8); thus *gei* sounds like English "gay."

---

7. The sound of Mandarin *ch* is ASPIRATED, that is, it ends with an h-like puff of air. Since English "ch" is normally pronounced aspirated, English speakers should have no trouble getting this detail of the pronunciation of Mandarin *ch* right, though speakers of languages such as French and Spanish will have to do some work to master it.

8. This sound is voiceless unaspirated; see footnote 6.

h. A very noisy "h," sounding as much like the "ch" of German "Bach" as like English "h."

i (see also *ai*, *ei*, *ia*, *ie*, *iu*). Pronounced like the "ee" of "seed" (thus, *ti* sounds like English "tea"), except in two sorts of combinations in which it has rather peculiar sounds that do not normally occur in European languages. In the combinations *ci*, *si*, and *zi*, the *i* has the sound of a "z" used as a vowel; thus to pronounce *sì* "four" correctly, one must keep the tongue in the position it has for the *s* and vocalize, thereby producing the buzzing sound of a "z." In the combinations *chi*, *ri*, *shi*, and *zhi*, the *i* has the sound of a Chinese *r* used as a vowel; as in the case of *ci*, *si*, and *zi*, one pronounces the *i* by keeping one's tongue in the position it has for the consonant and vocalizing. In the Yale system of transcription, *z* an *r* are in fact used to represent these sounds, for example, where the pinyin system writes *ci* and *chi*, the Yale system has *tsz* and *chr*.

ia. *ian* is pronounced "yen," as in *mian*. Otherwise *ia* occurs only in the combinations *jia*, *qia*, and *xia*, in which the *a* is pronounced the way that *a* normally is and the *i* serves mainly as a reminder of the PALATAL pronunciation of the *j*, *q*, or *x*.

ie. Pronounced like the "ye" of "yet."

iu. Pronounced like the "yoe" of "yoeman," that is, as a "y" followed by an "o." In the combinations *jiu*, *qiu*, and *xiu*, the "y" sound may not be heard as something separate but is simply absorbed into the palatal sound of the *j*, *q*, or *x*.

j. This is one of two sounds in Mandarin that both resemble English "j" but are actually distinct (the other sound is written *zh*). *j* is a palatal sound (as are *q* and *x*), while *zh* is a retroflex sound (like *ch*, *r*, and *sh*). To pronounce *j*, try to pronounce English "j" and "y" together: you make the sound not with the tip of the tongue but with the part of the body of the tongue that is an inch or so behind the tip; as

the tongue releases its contact with the roof of the mouth, it should be in the position it would have for a "y" sound. (see footnote 8).

k. Pronounced like the "k" of English 'kill" or the "c" of "cool".[9]

l. Like the "l" of English "look." In combinations like *lia*, *lie*, and *lüan*, the "l" takes on a "y" color like what is written "gl" in Italian.

m. Pronounced like English "m."

n (see also *ng*). Like English "n." Note, however, that it does not take on an "ng" sound when the following syllable begins with *k* or *g*. Thus, the first syllable of *hàn kŏu* is pronounced "han," not "hang."

ng. Pronounced like English "ng."

o (see also *ao*, *ou*, *uo*). Pronounced like the "aw" in "law"; thus *mo* is pronounced like English "maw." In the combination *ong*, the *o* is pronounced like the "oo" of English "foot."

ou. Pronounced like the "o" of English "go."

p. Pronounced like the "p" of English "pin" (see footnote 9).

q. This is the palatal counterpart of *ch*. It sounds something like English "ch" but has the palatal articulation that is described above for *j*.

r. Pronounced like an American or Welsh "r" except that the lips are not rounded. The tip of the tongue is pulled back and raised to near the middle of the hard palate. This sound is pronounced with enough friction that it often sounds as much like a French "j" as like an American "r."

s (see also *sh*). Pronounced like English "s" as in "sin." It never has the "z" sound found in words like "reason".

sh. This is one of two sounds that resemble English "sh" the other one is written *x*). *Sh* is a retroflex sound (see the description of *ch*) and *x* a palatal

9. This sound is aspirated; see footnote 7.

sound (see the description of *j*).

t. Pronounced like the "t" of English "ten" (see footnote 9).

u (see also *iu*, *ou*, *ua*, *ue*, *ui*, *uo*). This is the sound of "oo" in "food," except in the combinations *ju*, *qu*, *xu*, *yu* (i.e., those in which it follows a palatal consonant or *y*), when it has the sound of German *ü*, a high front rounded vowel. When *u* is written between a consonant and a vowel, as in *ruan* or *zhuang*, it is pronounced like a "w," except that when the consonant is *j*, *q*, *x*, or *y* it represents the sound that is to German *ü* as "w" is to "u," that is, the sound written *u* in French *lui*.

ü. This represents the sound of German *ü*. That sound is usually written *u* (which generally works out all right, since the preceding consonant generally enables you to tell which of its two sounds *u* should have), but in the combinations *lü* and *lüan* it is necessary to have a special symbol for the *ü* sound, so as to avoid confusion with *lu* and *luan*.

ue. This represents the *ü*-like "w" sound followed by the "e" of "yet," as in *jue* or *lue*.

ui. Pronounced like English "way." Thus *sui* sounds like English "sway."

uo. This represents "w" followed by the "aw" sound of "law."

w. Pronounced like the "w" of English "wall."

x. This is one of two sounds that resemble English "sh" (the other one is written *sh*); *x* is a palatal sound and *sh* a retroflex sound (see the description of *j*).

y. Pronounced like "y" in English "yet."

z (see also *zh*). Pronounced like the "ds" of English "roads" (see footnote 8).

zh. This is one of two sounds that both resemble English "j" (the other sound is written *j*); *zh* is a retroflex sound (see the description of *ch*) and *j* a palatal sound.

Chinese is a tone language, that is, its words can differ not only with regard to what consonants and vowels they contain but also with regard to the pitch on which they are pronounced. For example, the following four words have exactly the same consonant and vowel but are pronounced with different tones:

mā mother; *má* numb; *mǎ* horse; *mà* scold

The diacritics that appear on the vowels in these examples represent the four tones of Mandarin Chinese. The first tone, written with ¯, is a level high tone. The second tone, written with ´, is a rising tone that goes up from a mid to a high pitch. The third tone, written with ˇ, is a low tone, except that when it is at the end of a phrase it is pronounced with a sharp rise at the end, and when it is followed by another third tone it is pronounced like a second tone. The fourth tone, written `, is a falling tone that starts on a high pitch and ends on a mid or low pitch (low at the end of a phrase, mid otherwise). The tones can be represented graphically in the following diagrams:

Vowels on which no tone mark appears are unstressed: they have no distinctive tone of their own and are simply fitted into the melody to go along with the tones on the surrounding syllables.

Cantonese
Where Cantonese pronunciations have been given in this book, the Yale system of transcription has been used, printed in capital letters to keep it clearly distinct from the

pinyin transcriptions of Mandarin pronunciation. There is also an older system of transcription of Cantonese known as the Meyer-Wampe romanization, as well as the informal use of English spelling conventions that provides the most common spellings of Hong Kong place names and of names of Cantonese foods. To illustrate the differences, Kowloon (an informal spelling) is transcribed GÁULÙHNG in the Yale system and KAULUNG (or KAU²LUNG⁴, including the numbers that indicate tones) in the Meyer-Wampe system.

In the Yale transcription of Cantonese, as in pinyin, B, D, G, and J represent voiceless unaspirated sounds (see footnote 6 above) and P, T, K, and CH represent aspirated sound footnote 7 above). However, Cantonese does not make any distinction between retroflex and palatal sounds the way that Mandarin does, and CH and J have roughly their English values (though often sounding something like "ts" and "dz" respectively).

Cantonese has words beginning with NG. These are pronounced exactly as written, i.e., NGÁAP "duck" begins with the same sound that you pronounce at the end of the word "song." It even has a couple of words that begin with that sound and have no vowel at all, such as NGH "five" (the H here indicates low tone, in accordance with the system of representing tones that is explained below). When P, T, or K is at the end of a word, it is to be pronounced UNRELEASED, that is, instead of using the "clear" pronunciation of the final consonant that speech teachers encourage you to use in words like "mop, rot, rock," in which you make an "explosion" on the final consonant, you should do precisely what speech teachers tell you not to do. The proper Cantonese pronunciation of, for example, NGÁAP ends with your simply closing your lips for the P and not releasing that closure to make the "bang" or "pop."

The pronunciation of the vowel letters is as in pinyin except for the following points. A and AA represent two different vowel sounds: A is like the vowel of English "but" or "mother," AA like the vowel of English "spa" or "father," except that at the end of a syllable the latter sound is written A rather than AA, for example, GĀ "house" is pronounced as if it were written GĀA. E is pronounced as in English "let" except in the combinations EI and EU. As in pinyin, EI is pronounced like the vowel of English "late." EU represents a vowel that does not exist in Mandarin or in English, namely the vowel that is written ö in German or eu in French, as in schön or il pleut. For this vowel, the tongue is in the position for the vowel of "late" or "let" but the lips are rounded.

Cantonese distinguishes more different tones than Mandarin. Like Mandarin, it has level, rising, and falling tones, but these are on a high pitch for some words and on a low pitch for others. The letter H is written after a vowel to indicate low pitch, and level, rising, and falling tones are marked by ‾, ´, and `, as in Mandarin. Thus, GĀ is a high, level pitch, GÁ is high rising, GÀ is high falling, GÁH is low rising, and GÀH is low falling. A low, level pitch ought then to be written by combining the level sign with an H, that is, GĀH; however, the level sign is omitted and GAH is written instead, since there is nothing else that would be written with an H and no tone mark. In addition, there is a mid level tone, which is written with no H and no tone mark, for example, GA is mid level.

This description of Cantonese tones applies to literary Cantonese. In the ordinary spoken Cantonese of Hong Kong, the two falling tones have been turned into level tones: GĀ and GÀ are both pronounced as high, level tones, and GÀH is pronounced as an extra-low, level tone, lower than the tone on GAH.

12

Answers to Exercises

Chapter 2

Exercise 1
1. Shrimp slices
2. Chicken shreds
3. Stir-fried beef slices
4. Deep-fried fish slices
5. Pan-fried chicken curls
6. Stir-fried three shredded ingredients
7. Stir-fried chicken cubes
8. Steamed fish slices
9. Cold shrimp "salad"
10. Steamed beef chunks

Chapter 3

Exercise 1
1. Stir-fried Chinese cabbage
2. Stir-fried beef slices
3. Deep-fried carp
4. Stir-fried squid
5. Celery salad
6. Stir-fried abalone slices
7. Steamed carp
8. Pan-fried beef slices

Exercise 2
1. Chinese cabbage stir-fried with sliced abalone
2. Pickled kohlrabi stir-fried with shredded pork
3. Fish slice fried rice
4. Sliced beef chow mein (fried noodles)
5. Shredded chicken and "red-in-snow" chow mein
6. Celery stir-fried with sliced pork

Chapter 4

Exercise 1
1. L5a.3b
2. L3b.9c
3. L3c.9a
4. L6a.10
5. Ulla
6. E4a.4
7. T1a.7
8. T4a.13b
9. T8*7
10. L3a.6a
11. L3*2
12. L6b.16
13. U6c
14. L6*13
15. T4b.7a
16. L3a.12a
17. E3a.8
18. L9*4a
19. L8a.9a
20. L6c.4
21. L10*8
22. L10.11a
23. T4a.20
24. L10*13
25. E4a.12

Chapter 5

Exercise 1
1. Sliced pork soup
2. Red-cooked duck
3. Fish flavor fancy-cut pork kidneys
4. Shredded chicken and noodles in soup
5. Sliced fish and bean curd soup
6. Gong bao diced chicken
7. Chinese cabbage with chicken fat
8. Deep-fried chicken chunks in chili and sesame sauce
9. Shrimp curls in tomato sauce
10. Sliced abalone in sesame sauce

13

Directions for Finding Characters in the Glossary

1. Decide whether the character that you are looking up divides up into a left and a right half, into a top and a bottom, or into an enclosure and an enclosed, or does not divide up in one of those ways. In carrying out this step, note the following:

a. If there are two ways in which a character might divide into left and a right half or into a top and a bottom (as in the case of 湖, where it is not obvious whether the middle part should be assigned to left half or to right half, or 富, where it is not obvious whether the middle part should be assigned to top or to bottom), divide it so that as little as possible is assigned to the left half or to the top. Thus, 湖 is treated as having a three-stroke left half, not a nine-stroke left half, and 富 is treated as having a four-stroke top, not a five-stroke or nine-stroke top.

b. A character is treated as dividing into two parts only if it is normal to leave some space between the two parts. Thus, 古 is treated as a six-stroke indivisible character, not as having a two-stroke top and a four-stroke remainder.

2. Count the strokes in the top, the left half, the enclosure, or (if the character is "indivisible") the whole character. In carrying out this step, note the following (contrary to traditional practices in counting strokes):

a. Each "corner" is taken as the beginning of a new stroke; thus 口 counts as four strokes and 糸 counts as seven strokes.

b. "Hooks" at the ends of strokes do not count as separate strokes; thus, 丁 counts as two strokes, not three, and 虫 counts as six strokes, not seven.

3. Look for the left half, the top, the enclosure, or the whole character in the indexes given below of left halves, tops, enclosures, and indivisible characters. These are arranged according to number of strokes. If you find the element that you are looking for, go on to step 4. If you do not find it, try the following possibilities:

a. Perhaps you counted the strokes wrong, or perhaps you aren't counting strokes exactly the same way that I am. Try raising or lowering the stroke count by one (or by two, if the stroke count is fairly high) and see if you find the element under a different stroke number.

b. Perhaps what you have identified as dividing into two parts is treated here as indivisible, or vice versa. If the opposite of the decision you arrived at is remotely conceivable, try that as an alternative.

c. Perhaps the character involves one of the simplifications that were described in chapter 9; review that chapter, then search for things of which the element that you are looking for might be a simplified form.

4. The index in which you found the left half, top, enclosure, or whole character gives a page number below that element. Turn to that page of the Glossary. If what you are looking up is an indivisible character, you will find it on that page. Otherwise, the page to which you have turned is where listings of characters with the given left half, top, or enclosure begin. The characters with that element are arranged according to the number of strokes in the remainder. Count the strokes in the remainder, then look in the appropriate place in the listing for the given left half, top, or enclosure. If you do not find it, you may have the stroke count wrong and should try again, raising or lowering the stroke count.

5. It will often be quicker to bypass the indexes of character parts and simply search the pages where the parts of a given number of strokes are listed. To facilitate this, the margins are provided with a display of the elements listed in that section of the Glossary, with brackets marking which elements are listed on a given page and the one facing it.[10] You can locate an element of a given number of strokes by opening the Glossary to any page of the appropriate section, noting where the element that you seek is in the list in the margin, and then flipping the pages until that element is between the brackets. For

10. Where a section takes up only a couple of pages, elements from consecutive sections are displayed together, as on pages 114–29, where the one-stroke and two-stroke left halves appear together in the marginal guides (the one-stroke left halves take up barely more than a page of the Glossary). In cases like that of pages 156–57, where a pair of facing pages takes in the end of one section and the beginning of another, the characters from the first section are displayed in the margin of the left page and those from the second section in the margin of the right page, and only one bracket appears in each margin. Thus, the bracket in the margin of page 156 indicates that that page begins with characters having the left half 扌, and the bracket in the margin of page 157 indicates that that page ends with characters having the left half 身.

example, to find a character with the five-stroke left half 阝 , open the Glossary to any page whose margin has the heading L5, find 阝 in the list in the margin, and then, if the brackets are above or below it, flip the pages back or forward until you reach a page where 阝 is between the brackets. You will ultimately reach pages 144–45, which list the following elements in the margin, indicating that that pair of facing pages begins with characters having the left half 阝 and ends with characters having the left half 禾 and thus should include the character with the left half 阝 that you are looking for.

L5
⌐
月
日
礻
示
禾
⌐
段
將
矮
旗

6. Cross-references are given in terms of a system of naming characters, in which L, T, E, and U indicate whether the character has a left half, a top, or an enclosure, or is indivisible. This letter is combined with numbers for stroke counts, and small letters are used to distinguish elements that have the same stroke count. For example, the character 清 is given the name L3b.9c, indicating that it has a three-stroke left half (the "b" indicates that it involves the second of the three-stroke left halves listed below) and a nine-stroke remainder (the "c" indicates that it is the third of the characters listed

below that have the left half L3b combined with a nine-stroke remainder). Characters involving a left half, a top, or an enclosure that does not occur in any other character listed here are grouped together at the end of the appropriate categories of the given number of strokes, under headings such as "Miscellaneous Five-stroke Left Halves." They are arranged in increasing order of the number of strokes in the remainder. For examples, T5*4b (the name for the character 冊) indicates the second character listed in which a miscellaneous five-stroke top is combined with a four-stroke remainder.

7. Inevitably, some characters that you look up simply will not be listed here. I apologize in advance for all instances in which inadvertence or ignorance on my part has caused you to go on a fruitless search through the Glossary or to miss out on interesting dishes whose Chinese names are not listed here. I will be most grateful to any readers who are kind enough to call to my attention any omissions or errors in the Glossary, or any faults in its organization, which is aimed at making it easy to find characters but which may fall short of that goal. Please send corrections and additions to James D. McCawley, Department of Linguistics, University of Chicago, 1010 East 59th St., Chicago, Illinois 60637, USA.

Index to Left Halves

L1	丿⊗ 114	丿⊗ 115	丨⊗ 115	**L2**	亻⊗ 115	冫⊗ 117	頂 117	**L3**	扌⊗ 117
氵⊗ 120	犭⊗ 126	土⊗ 127	彳⊗ 128	又⊗ 129	北 129	竹 129	加 129	怪 130	順 130
鳩 130	**L4**	木⊗ 130	火⊗ 134	口⊗ 136	王⊗ 138	女⊗ 139	牛⊗ 140	阝⊗ 140	孔 141
划 141	幼 141	峨 141	預 141	**L5**	月⊗ 141	日⊗ 144	衤⊗ 145	示⊗ 145	禾 145
段 146	將 146	矮 146	旗 146	**L6**	米⊗ 146	虫⊗ 148	石⊗ 150	弓⊗ 151	礻⊗ 152
郊 152	胡 152	瓶 152	翔 152	鴨 152	**L7**	糹⊗ 153	辛⊗ 155	缶⊗ 155	東⊗ 155
刨 156	甜 156	雜 156	艇 156	貓 156	豬 156	鴿 156	鵝 156	**L8**	酉⊗ 156
金⊗ 158	豆⊗ 159	足⊗ 160	車⊗ 160	臣⊗ 160	乳 161	釆⊗ 161	野 161	教 161	瓠 161
賜 162	鵓 162	護 162	**L9**	肯⊗ 162	乾 163	新 163	就 163	群 163	靚 163
類 163	鵉 163	鶴 163	**L10**	倉⊗ 163	革⊗ 164	剝 164	都 165	殼 165	雜 165
龍 165	鶉 165	**L11**	奚⊗ 166	馬⊗ 166	麥⊗ 166	鷸 166	**L12**	隹⊗ 167	瓢 167
鹹 167	歸 167	**L13**	魚⊗ 167	骨⊗ 170	鄂 170	點 171	麒 171	翻 171	
L14	影 171	**L15**	歐 171						

Read indexes from left to right. ⊗ indicates relation of element to rest of character.

Index of Tops

T1 一 171	**T2** 亠 173	亼 174	⺈ 175	台 175	公 176	余 176	肴 176	
T3 吉 176	士 176	丷 177	艹 177	尖 177	奇 177	盲 177	冠 177	貢 178
T4 艹 178	宀 186	圭 188	木 189	屮 189	口 190	夕 190	冬 190	孚 191
吞 191	灸 191	孟 191	雀 191	熊 191	**T5** 旦 191	辛 192	禾 192	疋 193
炙 193	岳 193	春 193	背 194	益 194	蛊 194	柴 194	**T6** 竹 194	罒 195
此 196	羊 196	穴 196	常 197	癸 197	点 197	脊 197	帶 197	貴 197	巢 198
發 198	**T7** 覀 198	唇 198	梨 198	臭 198	热 199	番 199	盘 199	蜇 199
袈 199	棗 199	蒙 199	鯊 199	鴛 199	**T8** 隹 200	羽 200	真 200	無 200
骨 201	琵 201	普 201	腐 201	翡 201	**T9** 雪 201	魚 202	黑 203	煮 203
塩 203	黎 203	餐 203	**T10** 髟 204	保 204	碧 204	蠶 204	**T11** 喋 204
腎 205	**T12** 敝 205	熱 205	**T13** 將 205	魚 205	燙 205	盤 206	驚 206
鷹 206	**T14** 22	點 206	擘 206	鱟 206	鬱 206	雙 206	蟹 207	響 207	甕 207
鹽 207								

Index of Enclosures

Index of Indivisible Characters

U1	一 215	丨 215	**U2**	十 216	丁 216	人 216	七 216	亠 216	**U3**
大 216	干 217	上 217	下 217	千 217	九 217	刀 218	士 218	土 218	丫 218
才 218	**U4**	木 218	山 218	火 219	毛 219	牛 219	手 220	口 220	心 220
丸 220	子 220	文 221	天 221	王 221	井 221	斗 221	爪 221	夫 222	戈 222
尤 222	升 222	午 222	太 222	厶 222	六 222	廿 222	**U5**	水 222	五 223
生 223	玉 224	瓜 224	中 224	片 224	方 225	甘 225	月 225	平 225	末 225
巴 225	本 225	禾 226	丘 226	日 226	去 226	屯 226	正 226	**U6**	白 226
四 227	皮 227	石 227	米 228	羊 228	耳 228	田 228	古 228	瓦 229	衣 229
目 229	虫 229	甲 229	申 229	占 229	及 229	只 229	老 230	氷 230	朱 230
冬 230	**U7**	西 230	百 230	肉 231	夾 231	舌 231	出 231	血 232	母 232
成 232	赤 232	糸 232	**U8**	金 232	長 233	貝 233	武 233	里 234	色 234
車 234	克 234	幸 234	甫 234	两 234	**U9**	東 234	虎 235	果 235	兩 235
角 235	串 235	兒 236	呂 236	美 236	**U10**	南 236	咸 236	重 236	面 237
兔 237	姜 237	羌 237	**U11**	馬 237	麥 238	爽 238	兔 238	鬼 238	**U12**
烏 238	鹵 238	**U13**	黃 239	島 239	鳥 239	**U14**	粵 239	象 239	

Glossary

L1 One-Stroke Left Halves

L1a ノ⊗

L1a.1a 八 *bā* eight

八寶菜 *bā bǎo cài* eight treasures (eight fancy ingredients; sometimes vegetarian, sometimes mixed seafoods and meats)

八寶飯 *bā bǎo fàn* eight-treasure rice pudding

八寶鍋珍 *bā bǎo guō zhēn* preserved fruits, coated with rice flour and fried in oil (Sichuan)

八美和睦 *bā měi hè mù* eight peaceful beauties (tray of cold appetizers; Taiwan)

炸八塊 *zhá bā kuài* deep-fried chicken pieces (Beijing)

八角 *bā jiǎo* anise (lit., "eight corners")

八爪魚 *bā zhǎo yú* octopus (lit., "eight-claw fish")

八帶魚 *bā dài yú* octopus (lit., "eight-belt fish")

L1a.1b 儿 *-r* diminutive suffix, as in 鍋貼儿 *guō tiēr* fried ravioli (abbreviation of U9g 兒)

L1a.2 小 *xiǎo* small

小炒 *xiǎo chǎo* stir-fried meat shreds and mixed vegetables (Guangdong)

小菜 *xiǎo cài* small dishes of appetizers, esp. pickled vegetables

烤小猪 *kǎo xiǎo zhū* roast whole piglet

L1b)⊗

L1b.2 川 *chuān* river; Szechuan (Sichuan)
四川 *sì chuān* Szechuan
川菜 *chuān cài* Szechuan cuisine
川炸文武肉 *chuān zhá wén wǔ ròu* vegetables with two
   kinds of pork (Fujian)

L1c |⊗

L1c.1 ‖ *èr* two (popular form of T1a.1; used only when
   the characters are arranged vertically)

L1c.2 ‖‖ *sān* three (popular form of T1a.2; used only when
   the characters are arranged vertically)

L2 Two-Stroke Left Halves

L2a ⌠⊗

L2a.2a 仁 *rén* kernel
蝦仁 *xiā rén* shelled shrimp
杏仁 *xìng ren* almond
五仁月餅 *wǔ rén yuè bǐng* moon cake with five-nut filling
L2a.2b 什 *shí* diverse; ten
什錦 *shí jǐn* fancy (the Cantonese pronunciation of these
   characters, SAHP GÁM, is often spelled "subgum")
什景 *shí jǐng* fancy
什錦菜 *shí jǐn cài* shredded vegetables boiled in syrup
牛什 *niú shí* beef diaphragm, tripe, etc.
L2a.2c 化 *huà* transform
化皮全乳猪 *huà pí quán rǔ zhū* spit-roasted whole suckling pig
叫化鷄 *jiào hua jī* beggar's chicken (marinated chicken
   encased in clay and cooked in charcoal pit)

L2a.3a 他 *tā* he, other
他似蜜 *tā sì mì* candied sweet and sour lamb slices (lit.,
   "it's like honey"; folklore has it that the dowager
   empress exclaimed that on first tasting this dish;
   Beijing)

ノ
ノ ｜
｜
亻
冫
頂

L2a.3b 付　*fù* abbreviation for E3a.12a 腐

L2a.4a 仙　*xiān* fairy; cent; fresh (pun on L13.6a 鮮)
百花仙島　*bǎi huā xiān dǎo* hundred-flower fairy island
(uncured bacon deep-fried with shrimp paste and
served with crab sauce; Guangdong)
炒八仙　*chǎo bā xiān* stir-fried eight fairies (a Cantonese
mixed seafood dish)
仙掌　*xiān zhǎng* boneless duck feet

L2a.4b 件　*jiàn* classifier used for counting miscellaneous
things
每碟三件　*měi dié sān jiàn* three pieces per dish

L2a.5a 伊　*yī* he, she
伊麵　*yī miàn* or 伊府麵 *yī fu miàn* deep-fried noodles
L2a.5b 伍　*wǔ* five (fraud-proof form of U5b 五)
L2a.5c 位　*wèi* person
名茶每位二毫五仙　*míng chá měi wèi èr háo wǔ xiān*
famous teas 25¢ per person
L2a.5d 体　*tǐ* body (simplified form of L13b.15)

L2a.6 何　*hé* what; a Chinese family name
何禿麵　*hé tū miàn* a kind of egg noodle (named after
"Bald He")

L2a.7 佛　*fó* Buddha
蒸佛手白菜　*zhēng fó shǒu bái cài* steamed Buddha's
hand cabbage (stuffed Chinese cabbage)
佛跳墻　*fó tiào qiáng* Buddha jumps wall (a stew of
chicken, duck, pig's feet, and numerous dried seafoods in wine soup stock, prepared in a huge wine jar;
Fujian)
佛手瓜　*fó shǒu guā* chayote (lit., "Buddha's hand
melon")

L2a.9a 條　*tiáo* strip (classifier used for counting long
thin things)
油條　*yóu tiáo* Chinese cruller
L2a.9b 倭　*wō* Japan (ancient name)
倭瓜　*wō guā* cushaw (a type of pumpkin)

L2a.10 個　*gè* classifier used for counting miscellaneous
things

一個麵　*yì ge miàn* (YĀT GO MIHN) one portion of noodles (sometimes given on menus as "yatcamen," after the Cantonese pronunciation)

每個三毫　*měi gè sān háu* 30¢ a piece

L2a.12 假　*jiǎ* false

假燒鵝　*jiǎ shāo é* mock roast goose (made of roasted chitterlings or of bean curd skin stuffed with shredded vegetables)

假梅子　*jiǎ méi zi* mock plums (bean curd skin stuffed with minced shrimp and deep-fried)

L2b 冫⊗　the "cold" radical (do not confuse with L3b 氵⊗)

L2b.5a 冷　*lěng* cold

冷菜　*lěng cài* cold meats, etc., as appetizers

L2b.5b 冰　*bīng* ice

冰糖　*bīng táng* rock sugar

冰淇淋　*bīng jī lín* ice cream

L2b.5c 冲　*chōng* to rinse

冲菜　*chōng cài* (CHŪNG CHÒI) a kind of pickled turnip (Guangdong)

L2b.9 凍　*dòng* jelly

凍鷄　*dòng jī* jellied chicken

凍頂茶　*dòng dǐng chá* a variety of Oolong tea (named after a region in central Taiwan)

L2* Miscellaneous Two-Stroke Left Halves

L2*10 頂　*dǐng* peak, best

頂湯　*dǐng tāng* best quality soup stock

L3 Three-Stroke Left Halves

L3a 扌⊗　the "hand" radical

L3a.1 扎　*zhā* to stab; stylus

扎猪蹄　*zhā zhū tí* pig's feet simmered in salty stock
扎裹肉　*zhā lǐ ròu* fried stewed pork rib (Fujian)
扎燒猪排　*zhā shāo zhū pái* spareribs, each with slices of
　　chicken and ham tied to it with a strip of seaweed,
　　deep-fried and then simmered (Sichuan)

L3a.2a 扒　*pá* to braise, *bā* to stir
扒海羊　*pá hǎi yáng* braised shark fin with lamb kidney
L3a.2b 打　*dǎ* to hit; dozen
打邊爐　*dǎ byān lú* a type of fondue or hot pot

L3a.3 托　*tuō* to support (used for the English word
　　"toast")
蝦托　*xiā tuō* shrimp toast

L3a.4a 扣　*kòu* to reduce
扣肉　*kòu ròu* thrice-cooked pork (uncured bacon, first
　　boiled, then deep-fried, then steamed with seasonings)
扣四寶湯　*kòu sì bǎo tāng* four-treasure steamed soup
　　(Shanghai)
L3a.4b 抓　*zhuā* to scratch, grasp
抓鈴儿　*zhuā língr* crisp deep-fried stuffed bean curd skin
抓搶牛肉片　*zhuā qiàng niú ròu piàn* beef slices stir-fried
　　rapidly (lit., "grabbed from the pot"; Guangdong)
抓鷄虎　*zhuā jī hǔ* a kind of badger
L3a.4c 抄　*chāo* to fold (one's arms or hands)
抄手　*chāo shǒu* wonton (Sichuan dialect word, lit.,
　　"folded hands")

L3a.5a 拌　*bàn* mix
涼拌茄子　*liáng bàn qié zi* "salad" of cold steamed
　　eggplant
L3a.5b 拉　*lā* pull
拉皮　*lā pí* pasta in sheet form
棗泥拉糕　*zǎo ní lā gāo* steamed cake with date filling
L3a.5c 把　*bà* handle
把子肉　*bà zi ròu* stewed pork rib meat (Shandong)
L3a.5d 拖　*tuō* to drag, dredge
苔菜拖黄魚　*tái cài tuō huáng yú* yellow fish in batter
　　coated with seaweed and deep-fried (Shanghai)
L3a.5e 拑　*qián* claw (of crab, etc.)
L3a.5f 拆　*chāi* to take apart

鮑魚拆掌　*bào yú chāi jǎng* abalone with boned goose feet

L3a.5g 批　*pī* (PĀAI) pie

L3a.6a 拼　*pīn* to piece together (= L3a.8b)

L3a.6b 担担麵　*dàn dan miàn* cold noodles with spicy seasame sauce (Sichuan)

L3a.6c 抽　*chōu* to pull; soy sauce (Cantonese)
老抽　*lǎu chōu* thick soy sauce
生抽　*shēng chōu* thin soy sauce

L3a.6d 拔　*bá* to pull
拔絲蘋果　*bá sī píng guo* candied apples

L3a.7a 拾　*shí* ten (fraud-proof variant of U2a 十)

L3a.7b 招　*zhāo* to beckon
招牌　*zhāo pái* shop signboard; house special

L3a.7c 指　*zhǐ* finger
炸班指　*zhá bān zhǐ* deep-fried chitterling segments (Sichuan)

L3a.8a 排　*pái* raft; to arrange in a row
排骨　*pái gǔ* spareribs, pork chop
排翅　*pái chì* whole shark fin
西炸小蝦排　*xī zhá xiǎo xiā pái* batter-fried shrimp "slabs" (small shrimps skewered together)

L3a.8b 拼　*pīn* to piece together
拼盤　*pīn pán* plate of assorted cold appetizers

L3a.8c 掛　*guā* to hang
掛爐鴨　*guā lù yā* Peking roast duck (lit., "hang-roasted duck")
掛爐乳豬　*guā lù rǔ zhū* roast suckling pig

L3a.8d 捆　*kǔn* to tie
捆燒排骨　*kǔn shāo pái gǔ* pork and shredded ingredients tied into rolls, with sweet and sour sauce (Fujian)

L3a.10a 捲　*juǎn* roll
春捲　*chūn juǎn* spring roll
捲心菜　*juǎn xīn cài* round cabbage

L3a.10b 提　*tí* grape

L3a.12a 撻　*dá* (DAAHT) tart
撻沙魚　*dá shā yú* flounder

L3a.12b 搶　*qiǎng* to rob

扌
辶
犭
亻
又
北
竹
加
怪
順
鳩

搶白菜 *qiǎng bái cài* quick-fried Chinese cabbage with chili peppers and brown pepper

L3a.14 撈 *lāo* to drag for, fish up; to mix (Cantonese)
撈麵 *lāo miàn* lo mein (seasoned mixed noodles)

L3a.15 擂 *lèi* ring (arena for martial contests)
擂沙圓 *lèi shā yuán* sticky-rice flour dumplings in sweet bean paste (Shanghai)

L3a.16 擢 *zhuó* to extract
擢淨 *zhuó jìng* preserved ginger

L3a.22 攢 *cuán* to assemble
攢絲襍燴湯 *cuán sī zá huì tāng* mixed fancy ingredients in soup (Sichuan)

L3b ⺡⊗ the "water" radical (do not confuse with L2b ⼎⊗)

L3b.2 汁 *zhī* juice
薑汁魷花 *jiāng zhī yóu huā* fancy-cut squid with ginger sauce
茄汁明蝦 *qié zhī míng xiā* prawns in tomato sauce

L3b.3 池 *chí* pond
池菇 *chí gū* arrowhead

L3b.4a 沙 *sā* or *shā* sand
豆沙 *dòu sā* sweet bean paste
沙爹 *sā tiē* satay (grilled meat with spicy sauce; the name is a Malay word)
沙茶 *sā chá* satay
沙茶牛腩 *sā chá niú nán* beef tenderloin slices in chili and tea-leaf sauce (Hunan)
沙其馬 *sā qí mǎ* fried dough strips with sesame, sugar, and raisins
沙丁魚 *shā dīng yú* sardine
沙魚 *shā yú* shark
沙河粉 *shā hé fěn* a kind of flat rice-flour noodle
白糖沙翁 *bái táng shā wēng* sugared raised donuts
沙拉 *sā lā* salad
沙果儿 *shā guǒr* crabapple

沙田柚　*shā dián yòu* Guangxi pomelo
沙葛　*shā gé* yam bean (yam-like root of a legume)
L3b.4b 汕　*shàn* basket for catching fish
汕頭　*shàn tóu* Swatow (city in eastern Guangdong
　　Province)

L3b.5a 汽　*qì* steam, vapor
汽鍋蒸鷄　*qì guō jēng jī* chicken steamed in special
　　earthenware pot (Yunnan)
L3b.5b 注　*zhù* to pour
注油鰻魚　*zhù yóu mán yú* deep-fried marinated sliced eel
　　(Fujian)
L3b.5c 汾水　*fén shuǐ* a tributary of the Yellow River
汾酒　*fén* jiǔ sorghum wine from the Fenshui region

L3b.6a 油　*yóu* oil
雞油　*jī yóu* chicken fat
油條　*yóu tiáo* Chinese cruller
油豆腐　*yóu dòu fu* fried bean curd
油浸魚　*yóu jìn yú* oil-soaked fish
油皮　*yóu pí* fresh bean curd skin
油菜　*yóu cài* rape; stir-fried bok choi (Guangdong)
油魚　*yóu yú* squid (variant of 魷魚 *yóu yú*)
油燜筍　*yóu mèn sǔn* braised bamboo shoots
L3b.6b 洋　*yáng* ocean; occident
洋葱　*yáng cōng* onion (lit., "occidental scallion")
洋山芋　*yáng shān yù* potato
洋菜　*yáng cài* agar-agar (gelatin made from seaweed)
洋魚　*yáng yú* stingray
洋桃　*yáng táo* kiwi fruit, Chinese gooseberry
洋燒排參　*yáng shāo pái shēn* spareribs and sea cucumber
　　simmered with potatoes (Fujian)
洋焗什錦　*yáng jū shí jǐn* mixed sliced cooked meats in
　　thick gravy (Fujian)
L3b.6c 河　*hé* river
河粉　*hé fén* flat rice-noodles (Guangdong)
河間爆肉　*hé jiān bào ròu* rapid-fried sliced beef fillet
泡椒河鰻　*pào jiāo hé mán* river eel braised with pickled
　　hot peppers (Sichuan)
L3b.6d 泥　*ní* mud; mash
茄泥　*qié ní* mashed cooked eggplant refried

扌
氵
犭
土
彳
又
北
竹
加
怪
順
鳩

棗泥鍋餅　*zǎo ní guō bǐng* pancakes filled with date paste

泥鰍　*ní qiú* a kind of small eel; smelt

L3b.6e 洗　*xǐ* to wash

洗沙蕎包　*xǐ shā qiáo bāo* steamed buckwheat buns with
　　sweet bean-paste filling (Yunnan)

L3b.6f 派　*pài* faction; pie

派魚　*pài yú* pike

L3b.6g 洪　*hóng* great flood

洪都雞　*hóng dū jī* deep-fried chicken pieces stewed with
　　chili peppers (Jiangxi)

L3b.6h 波　*pō* wave (also nonstandard simplified form of
　　T4a.9a 菠 spinach)

L3b.7a 津　*jīn* short for 天津 *tiān jīn* Tientsin

津白　*jīn bái* Tientsin cabbage

L3b.7b 泡　*pào* to steep, marinate

泡菜　*pào cài* vegetables pickled in spicy brine (Sichuan)

泡椒　*pào jiāo* pickled chili peppers (Sichuan)

上湯泡魚生　*shàng tāng pào yú shēng* hot soup poured
　　over raw fish slices (Hunan, Guangdong)

L3b.7c 活　*huó* live

活蝦　*huó xiā* live shrimp

L3b.7d 浙　*zhè* Chekiang

浙江　*zhè jiāng* Chekiang

江浙菜　*jiāng zhè cài* cuisine of the Kiangsu-Chekiang
　　region

浙醋　*zhè cù* Chekiang sweet rice-vinegar

L3b.7e 流　*liú* to flow

流浪雞　*liú làng jī* boiled whole chicken with hot sauce
　　(Jiangxi)

L3b.8a 酒　*jiǔ* wine, liquor

酒蒸鴨　*jiǔ zhēng yā* duck steamed in wine

酒釀　*jiǔ niàng* fermented rice

啤酒　*pí jiǔ* beer

L3b.8b 淮　*huái* the Huai River; name of several counties

淮河　*huái hé* Huai River (in Henan, Anhui, and Jiangsu)

淮楊菜　*huái yáng cài* Yangchow area cuisine

淮山　*huái shān* a long thin tuber (Jap. *yamaimo*)

淮杞　*huái qǐ* boxthorn

淮杞羊頭蹄　*huái qǐ yáng tóu tí* lamb head and feet
　　stewed with yam and boxthorn (Guangdong)

L3b.8c 淋　*lín* drip

油淋雞　*yóu lín jī* oil-dripped chicken (Northern version of Cantonese deep-fried chicken)

L3b.8d 淡　*dàn* light (color); bland taste

淡水蝦仔　*dàn shuǐ xiā zi* freshwater shrimp

淡菜　*dàn cài* dried sea mussel

L3b.8e 洞　*dòng* cave

洞庭　*dòng tíng* a lake in northern Hunan Province

洞庭蝦片　*dòng tíng xiā piàn* sliced prawns and vegetables in white sauce (Hunan)

L3b.9a 海　*hǎi* sea

上海　*shàng hǎi* Shanghai

海南　*hǎi nán* Hainan

海南鷄飯　*hǎi nán jī fàn* chicken cooked with rice in coconut milk (Hainan)

海鮮　*hǎi xiān* seafood

海鮮醬　*hǎi xiān jiàng* (HÓI SÌN JEUNG) hoisin sauce

海參　*hǎi shēn* sea cucumber

海胡瓜　*hǎi hú guā* sea cucumber

海鼠　*hǎi shǔ* sea cucumber

海蜇皮　*hǎi zhé pí* jellyfish skin

海膽　or 海胆　*hǎi dàn* sea urchin

海帶　*hǎi dài* a tough, salty type of seaweed (Jap. *konbu*)

酥海帶　*sū hǎi dài* pork wrapped in konbu and simmered in vinegar (Shandong)

海鰻　*hǎi mán* conger eel

海扇　*hǎi shàn* scallop

海瓜子　*hǎi guā zi* a small bivalve

海鞘　*hǎi qiào* sea squirt

海米　*hǎi mǐ* dried shrimp

海底松　*hǎi dǐ sōng* jellyfish

海腸子　*hǎi cháng zi* a type of edible sea worm

海紅魚唇　*hǎi hóng yú chún* fish lips with crab roe and red oil

海棠　*hǎi táng* crabapple

海棠百花菇　*hǎi táng bǎi huā gū* black mushrooms steamed with shrimp stuffing

L3b.9b 涼　*liáng* cold

涼拌　*liáng bàn* "salad" of cold ingredients with dressing

涼拌茄子　*liáng bàn qié zi* steamed eggplant served cold with dressing

涼瓜　*liáng guā* bitter melon

涼麵　*liáng miàn* cold noodles

涼捲　*liáng juǎn* cold glutinous rice pudding with sesame (Hangzhou)

L3b.9c 清　*qīng* clear

清蒸魚　*qīng zhēng yú* steamed fish

清湯白菜　*qīng tāng bái cài* Chinese cabbage in clear soup

清眞菜　*qīng zhēn cài* Moslem cooking

清燉蹄膀　*qīng dùn tí bǎng* pork shoulder stewed in clear broth

L3b.9d 清　alternate form of L3b.9c

L3b.9e 淖　*nào* mud

雞淖脊髓　*jī nào jǐ suǐ* stir-fried minced chicken and pig's spinal cord (Sichuan)

L3b.9f 淹　*yān* to drown, soak

淹肉　*yān ròu* salted pressed pork (Zhenjiang)

L3b.10a 湯　*tāng* soup

酸辣湯　*suān là tāng* hot and sour soup

上湯　*shàng tāng* clear soup stock

湯卷　*tāng juǎn* fish head, fat, and intestine in earthenware pot (Shanghai)

鷄絲湯麵　*jī sī tāng miàn* noodles with shredded chicken in soup

L3b.10b 湘　*xiāng* ancient name of Hunan

湘江　*xiāng jiāng* river in Hunan

湘菜　*xiāng cài* Hunanese cuisine

湘綺蝦片　*xiāng qǐ xiā piàn* shrimp slices with ham and vegetables in white sauce (Hunan)

L3b.10c 涮　*shuàn* to rinse

涮羊肉　*shuàn yáng ròu* Mongolian lamb fondue

L3b.10d 混沌　*hún tún* wonton (usually written 餛飩)

L3b.10e 渝　*yú* Chungking (Chongqing)

L3b.10f 浸　*jìn* dip, soak

浸魚　*jìn yú* poached fish

L3b.10g 渣　*zhā* dregs, lees

豆腐渣　*dòu fu zhā* dregs from making bean milk

L3b.11a 湖　*hú* lake

湖南　*hú nán* Hunan

湖北　*hú běi* Hupei

西湖　*xī hú* West Lake (Hangzhou)

西湖豆腐　*xī hú dòu fu* bean curd in fancy sweet and sour sauce

西湖醋魚　*xī hú cù yú* West Lake fish (poached whole fish in sweet vinegar sauce; Hangzhou)

西湖全鴨　*xī hú quán yā* West Lake whole duck (duck cut down middle and flattened out, stewed with mixed meats and vegetables)

L3b.11b 滋　*zī* to nourish

滋補牛尾　*zī bǔ niú wèi* nourishing oxtail potroast

L3b.11c 温　*wēn* lukewarm

溫景山笋　*wēn jǐng shān sǔn* boiled bamboo shoot in sweet and sour sauce (Anhui)

溫州　*wēn zhou* Wenchow (a port city in Zhejiang Province)

L3b.11d 滇　*tián* Yunnan

滇式牛肉　*tián shì niú ròu* Yunnan-style beef (beef cubes and mushrooms in spicy gravy)

L3b.12a 滷　*lǔ* gravy

滷雞肫肝兒　*lǔ jī zhūn gār* chicken giblets simmered in gravy

明滷雞腳　*míng lǔ jī jiǎo* chicken legs in clear gravy

大滷麵　*dà lǔ miàn* noodles in thick soup with meats, vegetables, and egg

L3b.12b 滿　*mǎn* abundant; Manchuria

滿州　*mǎn zhōu* Manchuria

滿蒙菜　*mǎn měng cài* Manchu-Mongol cuisine

L3b.12c 滾　*gǔn* to roll

滾筒排骨　*gǔn tóng pái gǔ* vegetables wrapped in thin pork slice, deep-fried

驢打滾兒　*lǘ dǎ gǔr* rolling donkeys (boiled sticky-rice flour dumplings rolled in bean-flour and nut coating)

L3b.12d 渝　*yú* ancient name for Chongqing (alternate form of L3b.10e)

L3b.12e 溫　alternate form of L3b.11c

L3b.13a 溜　*liū* stir-fry, then add thick sauce

L3

扌
氵
犭
±
彳
又
北
竹
加
怪
順
鳩

溜黃菜　*liū huáng cài* scrambled egg with meat and vegetables in thick sauce

醋溜魚片　*cù liū yú piàn* fish slices in sweet and sour
sauce

L3b.13b 滑　*huá* slip (used for glossy thick sauces)

魚滑湯　*yú huá tāng* fish chowder

滑蛋牛肉　*huá dàn niú ròu* beef in scrambled egg

L3b.14a 滬　*hù* Shanghai area

滬杭菜　*hù háng cài* Shanghai-Hangchow cuisine

L3b.14b 濟　*jǐ* varied, elegant

濟南　*jǐ nán* Tsinan (capital of Shandong Province)

L3b.14c 潮　*cháo* tide

潮州　*cháo zhōu* Teochow (area in eastern Guangdong
Province whose principal city is Swatow)

L3b.14d 潤　*rùn* moist and soft; liver

燒豬潤　*shāo zhū rùn* barbecued pork liver

L3b.15a 澄　*chéng* clear

澄湖秋月　*chéng hú qiū yuè* clear like autumn moon (an
appetizer plate containing crab)

L3b.15b 漲　*chàng* to swell

漲蛋　*chàng dàn* omlet

L3b.15c 澳　*ào* deep water

澳門　*ào mén* Macau

澳門方脷　*ào mén fāng lì* Macau sole

L3b.16a 鴻　*hóng* great

鴻圖窩麵　*hóng tū wō miàn* noodles in crab sauce

L3b.16b 潺　*chán* sound of flowing water; slippery

潺菜　*chán cài* a mucilaginous leafy green vegetable, used
in soups

L3b.19 瀨　*lài* name of a river

瀨粉　*lài fěn* thin rice-flour noodles, served in soup with
roast pork, duck, or goose (Guangdong)

L3b.20 灌　*guàn* to pour

灌腸　*guàn cháng* a kind of sausage with chitterling casing

L3c 犭⊗ the "beast" radical (also occurs in the
form 犭⊗)

L3c.7 狗　*gǒu* dog

上豉燜狗肉　*shàng chǐ mén gǒu ròu* dog meat simmered with black beans (Guangdong)

狗棍魚　*gǒu gùn yú* lizard fish

狗不里包子　*gǒu bù lǐ bāo zi* pork-filled steamed buns (Tianjin)

L3c.8 狸　*lí* wildcat

L3c.9a 猪　*zhū* pig

猪肝　*zhū gān* pork liver

猪閏　*zhū rùn* pork liver

猪排　*zhū pái* pork chop

猪爪　*zhū zhǎo* pig's trotter

乳猪　*rǔ zhū* suckling pig

猪及第粥　*zhū jí dì zhòu* rice porridge with pork, pig liver, and pork kidney (Guangdong)

猪𨤲栄　*zhū la cài* a type of cabbage

L3c.9b 猫　*māo* cat

猫耳朵　*māo ěr dou* cat's ears (a Zhejiang noodle dish)

生燴老猫公　*shēng huì lǎo māo gōng* stewed cat meat (Guangdong)

L3c.10 猴　*hóu* monkey

猴魚　*hóu yú* porpoise

猴頭　*hóu tou* a kind of mushroom

雞燋猴頭　*jī kào hóu tou* steamed mushroom-stuffed chicken (Shandong)

L3c.14 獅子　*shī zi* lion

獅子頭　*shī zi tóu* lion head (large meatballs stewed with cabbage leaves)

獅子滾繡球　*shī zi gǔn xiù qiú* stewed pigeon eggs and fried jellyfish (Beijing)

L3d 土 the "earth" radical

L3d.3 地　*dì* earth

地栗　*dì lì* water chestnut

地瓜　*dì guā* sweet potato

L3d.6 坨　*tóu* heap

127

扌
彳
犭
壬
彳
北
竹
加
怪
順
鳩

坨子肉　*tóu zi ròu* boiled pork, steamed with chili peppers (Sichuan)

L3d.8 堆　*duī* pile
脆皮煎堆　*cuì pí jiān duī* (CHEUI PEÌH JÌN DÈUI) deep-fried ball of glutinous rice-flour dough with sweet filling

L3d.11a 塔　*tǎ* (TAAP) pagoda; tart
鍋貼魚塔　*guō tiē yú tǎ* sandwiches of bread, fish, and ham, batter-fried
蛋塔　*dàn tǎ* egg-custard tart
L3d.11b 塊　*kuài* chunk
炸八塊　*zhá bā kuài* deep-fried chicken pieces (Beijing)

L3d.12a 填　*tián* to fill in
北京填鴨　*běi jīng tián yā* Peking duck
L3d.12b 塘　*táng* embankment
塘蒿　*táng hāo* chrysanthemum vegetable (Jap. *shungiku*)

L3d.13a 塌　*tā* collapse
鍋塌豆腐　*guō tā dòu fu* bean curd pan-fried in egg batter (Beijing)
L3d.13b 墩　*dūn* mound
四鮮白菜墩　*sì xiān bái cài dūn* Chinese cabbage pieces covered with four ingredients and steamed in serving bowl (Shanghai)

L3d.18 壜　*tán* earthenware pot

L3e 辶⊗ the "walking" radical

L3e.8 後　*hòu* rear, after
後腿　*hòu tuǐ* hind leg

L3e.15 衡　see L3e.16a 衡

L3e.16a 衡　*héng* to weigh; horizontal beam
衡山　*héng shān* a mountain in Hunan
衡陽　*héng yáng* Hengyang (city in Hunan Province)
衡陽牛柳　*héng yáng niú liǔ* beef tenderloin slices in hot sauce, served on bed of watercress (Hunan) (see also T5*4b)

L3e.16b 徽 *huī* honorable

徽州 *huī zhōu* Hweichow

安徽 *ān huī* Anhwei

L3f 又⊗ the "again" radical

L3f.3 双 abbreviated form of T16*3 雙 *shuāng* pair

L3f.13 鸡 popular form of L11a.8 雞 *jī* chicken
   (= L11a.13)

L3* Miscellaneous Three-Stroke Left Halves

L3*2 北 *běi* north

北京 *běi jīng* Peking

北平 *běi píng* Peiping (name for Beijing current among
   Nationalists; avoids the suggestion that Beijing is the
   current capital)

北京烤鴨 *běi jīng kǎo yā* Peking roast duck

河北 *hé běi* Hopei

湖北 *hú běi* Hupei

北瓜 *běi guā* a type of pumpkin

北菇 *běi gū* large round black mushrooms

L3*3 竹 *zhú* bamboo

竹笙 *zhú shēng* bamboo fungus

竹蓀 *zhú sūn* bamboo fungus

竹筍 *zhú sǔn* summer bamboo shoot (small thin bamboo
   shoot)

竹籠肉 *zhú lóng ròu* ground pork, potato, and rice flour,
   steamed in bamboo mugs (Sichuan)

竹節鴿盅 *zhú jié gē zhōng* minced pigeon soup steamed
   in bamboo cups (Hunan)

L3*4 加 *jiā* to add

加料 *jiā liào* garnish

加吉魚 *jiā jí yú* snapper, bream

扌
氵
犭
土
彳
又
北
竹
加
怪
順
鳩

L3*6 怪 *guài* strange

怪味腰花 *guài wèi yáo huā* sliced pork kidney with pungent aromatic sauce (lit., "strange flavor kidney flowers")

L3*10 順 *shùn* favorable

順慶羊肉粉 *shùn qìng yáng ròu fěn* stewed lamb meat and lamb organs with rice-flour noodles (Sichuan)

順德白灼腰肝 *shùn dé bái shāo yāo gāo* poached pork kidney and liver, topped with raw ginger and scallions (Guangdong)

L3*13 鳩 *jiū* pigeon

L4 Four-Stroke Left Halves

L4a 木⊗ the "tree" radical

L4a.1 札 *zhá* stylus
雞札 *jī zhá* chicken feet

L4a.3 杧 *máng* mango
香杧 *xiāng máng* mango

L4a.4a 杞 *qǐ* boxthorn
L4a.4b 杓 *sháo* container; ladle
白杓玻璃蝦 *bái sháo bō li xiā* boiled shrimp with garnish and dipping sauces
L4a.4c 杯 *bēi* cup
一杯茶 *yì bēi chá* a cup of tea

L4a.5a 松 *sōng* pine (also used as a substitute for T10a.8 鬆 hair; floss)
松子全魚 *sōng zi quán yú* whole fried fish with pine nuts
松鼠魚 *sōng shǔ yú* squirrel fish (a version of sweet and sour whole fish)
松花蛋 *sōng huā dàn* thousand-year egg
松花肉 *sōng huā ròu* chopped meat and vegetables mixed with beaten egg and fried (Fujian)
松菌 *sōng jùn* pine mushroom (Jap. *matsutake*)

松鬚菜　*sōng xū cài* coriander leaf (lit., "pine mustache vegetable")

松鷄　*sōng jī* grouse

L4a.5b 板　*bǎn* board

板鴨　*bǎn yā* pressed duck

鐵板牛柳　*tiě bǎn niú liǔ* beef steak on hot griddle

L4a.5c 枇　*pí* (PÈIH) loquat; pie

枇杷　*pí ba* loquat

L4a.5d 杭　*háng* to sail

杭州　*háng zhōu* Hangchow

L4a.5e 枝　*zhī* branch

花枝　*huā zhī* cuttlefish

枝竹　*zhī zhú* a type of dried bean curd skin

L4a.5f 柱　*zhù* pillar

柱侯醬　*zhù hóu jiàng* a type of fermented bean paste

L4a.6a 桂　*guì* cinnamon; Kwangsi Province

桂花　*guì huā* sweet olive

桂林　*guì lín* Kweilin

桂圓　*guì yuán* dried longan

桂皮　*guì pí* cinnamon

桂魚　*guì yú* salmon

L4a.6b 柳　*liǔ* willow; tender cut of meat

牛柳　*niú liǔ* beef tenderloin

柳葉魚　*liǔ yè yú* bread spread with shredded fishmeat and deep-fried (Shandong)

五柳全魚　*wǔ liǔ quán yú* five-willow whole fish (in sweet and sour sauce with shredded vegetables; Hangzhou)

花柳菜　*huā liú cài* broccoli

L4a.6c 桃　*táo* peach; walnut

桃仁　*táo rén* shelled walnut

桃核　*táo hé* peach kernel

桃花泛　*táo huā fàn* deep-fried crispy rice with tomato sauce (Beijing)

櫻桃　*yīn táo* cherry

雙桃銀耳　*shuāng táo yín ěr* white wood ears with peaches and cherries

L4a.6d 柿　*shì* persimmon

西紅柿　*xī hóng shì* tomato

L4a.6e 柚子　*yòu zi* pomelo

柚皮　*yòu pí* pomelo peel

L4

[木 火 口 王 女 牛 阝 孔 划 幼 峨 預]

蠔油扒柚皮　*háo yóu pá yòu pí* stewed pomelo peel with oyster sauce

金山柚　*jīn shān yòu* grapefruit

L4a.6f 相　*xiāng* to meet

相思糕　*xiāng sī gāo* lovesickness pudding (made of red beans, sugar, and agar-agar; Zhejiang)

滷舌相紅鬆　*lǔ shé xiāng hóng sōng* stewed pork tongue and shredded carrot (as two halves of a cold appetizer plate)

L4a.6g 柏　*bǎi* cypress, cedar (used as pun on 百 *bǎi* hundred)

柏葉　*bǎi yè* third stomach of cow

L4a.7a 核　*hé* walnut; sweetbreads

核桃　*hé tao* walnut

核桃雞丁　*hé tao jī dīng* diced chicken with walnuts

L4a.7b 根　*gēn* root

軟根　*ruǎn gēn* thin sliced cooked gluten dough

L4a.7c 枸杞頭　*gǒu qǐ tóu* boxthorn shoots

枸杞子　*gǒu qǐ zi* boxthorn seeds

L4a.7d 桔　*jú* tangerine (see L4a.15a)

桔燒巴　*jú shāo bā* pork chunks marinated in wine lees and batter-fried

L4a.7e 栢　fancy nonstandard variant of U7b

栢葉　*bǎi yè* third stomach of cow

L4a.8a 棒　*bàng* stick, club

棒棒雞　*bàng bàng jī* bang bang chicken (cold shredded chicken with spicy sesame sauce; Sichuan)

L4a.8b 桶　*tǒng* cask, pail

桶鷄　*tǒng jī* a variety of salt-cured chicken, steamed and sliced (Sichuan)

桶子油雞　*tǒng zi yóu jī* soy sauce chicken (Guangdong)

L4a.8c 棋　*qí* Chinese chess

棋盤雞　*qí pán jī* chessboard chicken (chicken, boned, flattened, and deep-fried, with sauce)

L4a.8d 梗　*gěng* stem

青梗菜　*qīng gěng cài* green cabbage

L4a.8e 桐　*tóng* paulownia

桐蒿　*tóng hāo* chrysanthemum vegetable (Jap. *shungiku*)

L4a.8f 梭　*suō* shuttle for weaving

梭魚　*suō yú* barracuda
梭子蟹　*suō zi xiè* blue crab

L4a.9a 梅　*méi* plum
酸梅蒸鴨　*suān méi zhēng yā* duck steamed with sour
pickled plums
梅菜　*méi cài* a kind of mustard green
梅雪爭春　*méi xuě zhēn chūn* baked apple, banana, and
egg (Shandong)
梅開二度　*méi kāi èr dù* plum blooms twice (stir-fried
squid pieces and cauliflower)
酥炸梅肉　*sū zhá méi ròu* minced pork and vegetables
wrapped in bean curd skin and deep-fried

L4a.9b 椒　*jiāo* pepper
花椒　*huā jiāo* brown (Sichuan) pepper
青椒　*qīng jiāo* green pepper
辣椒　*là jiāo* chili pepper
泡椒　*pào jiāo* pickled chili peppers (Sichuan)

L4a.10a 楊州　*yáng zhōu* Yangchow
楊子江　*yáng zi jiāng* Yangtze River
楊梅　*yáng méi* strawberry
L4a.10b 榆　*yú* elm
榆耳　*yú ěr* elm fungus
L4a.10c 椰　*yé* coconut
椰菜　*yé cài* round cabbage; cauliflower
椰汁荔芋鷄煲　*yé zhī lì yù jī bào* casserole of chicken,
taro, and coconut sauce
L4a.10d 榛子　*jiān zi* hazelnut
L4a.10e 椿　*chūn* camelia
香椿頭　*xiāng chūn tóu* salted dried camelia shoots

L4a.11a 榨　*zhà* to squeeze, wring
榨菜　*zhà cài* spicy pickled kohlrabi (Sichuan)
榨菜肉絲湯　*zhà cài ròu sī tāng* shredded pork and
Szechuan pickle soup
L4a.11b 槓丸　*gàng wàn* pork balls (Taiwan)

L4a.12a 樣　*yàng* appearance; kind
醬爆三樣　*jiàng bào sān yàng* three parts of the pig (meat,
liver, kidney) quick-fried with bean paste
L4a.12b 橄　*gǎn* olive
橄欖　*gǎn lǎn* olive; broccoli

樟
灬⊗
口⊗
玉⊗
女⊗
牛⊗
阝⊗
孔
划
幼
峨
預

L4a.12c 樟 *zhāng* camphor

樟茶鴨 *zhāng chá yā* tea-leaf and camphor smoked duck (Sichuan)

L4a.12d 榴 *liú* pomegranate

石榴 *shí liú* pomegranate

榴連 *liú lián* durian

L4a.14 橙 *chén* orange

香橙焗童雞 *xiāng chén jú tóng jī* chicken simmered in orange sauce

L4a.15a 橘 *jú* tangerine

金橘 *jīn jú* (GÀM GWÀT) kumquat

橘餅 *jú bǐng* sugar-preserved kumquats in slab form

L4a.15b 橋 *qiáo* bridge

過橋麵 *guō qiáo miàn* crossing the bridge noodles (noodles with soup and condiments to be mixed by the eater; Yunnan)

馬安橋 *mǎ ān qiáo* eel

L4a.16a 檸 *níng* lemon

檸檬 *níng méng* lemon

檸檬鷄 *níng méng jī* chicken in lemon sauce (Guang-dong)

L4a.16b 櫻桃 *yīng táo* cherry; frog legs

L4a.25 欖 *lǎn* olive; large black bean

欖角炊占補魚 *lǎn jiǎo chuī zhān bǔ yú* whitefish steamed with large black beans or dried olives (Guangdong)

L4b 火⊗ the "fire" radical

L4b.2 灯 *dēng* lamp (popular form of L4b.14c 燈)

L4b.4a 炒 *chǎo* to stir-fry

炒麵 *chǎo miàn* fried noodles

炒菁綠茶 *chǎo jīng lǜ chá* a kind of green tea (lit., "stir-fried leek flower green tea")

L4b.4b 炊 *chuī* to cook, boil, steam

L4b.4c 炆 *wén* to simmer

L4b.4d 灼 *shāo* to roast, scald

L4b.5a 炸 *zhá* to deep-fry

炸醬麵　*zhá jiàng miàn* noodles with fried bean-paste sauce (Beijing)

炸八塊　*zhá bā kuài* deep-fried chicken pieces (Beijing)

L4b.5b 炕　*kàng* to broil

L4b.5c 炖　*dùn* alternate form of L4b.14b

L4b.6a 烘　*hōng* to bake, roast

韮黃烘蛋　*jiǔ huáng hōng dàn* chive omlet

L4b.6b 炻　*pin* alternate form of L4b.11a 煸

L4b.6a 炯　*wén* alternate form of L4b.4c 炆

L4b.7a 烤　*kǎo* to bake, roast

北京烤鴨　*běi jīng kǎo yā* Peking roast duck

烤麵包　*kǎo miàn bāo* toasted bread

L4b.7b 烟　*yān* to smoke (simplified form of L4b.10 煙)

烟香雞　*yān xiāng jī* aromatic smoked chicken

L4b.7c 炮　*bāo* to roast, barbecue

L4b.9a 焗　*jú* to bake

葱薑焗蠔　*cōng jiāng jú háo* oysters baked with scallion and ginger (Guangdong)

L4b.9b 燒　see L4b.12a

L4b.10 煙　*yān* to smoke

禁止吸煙　*jìn jǐ xī yān* smoking prohibited

L4b.11a 煸　*bian* to stir-fry precooked ingredients over a strong fire

乾煸牛肉絲　*gān bian niú ròu sī* dry-cooked shredded beef (Sichuan)

L4b.11b 煨　*wēi* to simmer, bake

L4b.11c 焗　*jū* to stew precooked ingredients in soup (Fujian)

L4b.12a 燒　*shāo* to roast with sauce

叉燒　*chā shāo* (CHĀ SÌU) roast pork tenderloin (roasted on spit)

燒賣　*shāo mài* (SÌU MAAIH) shumai (open-ended ravioli; often used in names of other steamed small dishes involving minced meat but not necessarily pasta, e.g., the next item; Guangdong)

鴨掌燒賣　*yā zhǎng shāo mài* steamed stuffed duck feet

紅燒魚　*hóng shāo yú* red-cooked fish (simmered in soy sauce; originally made with caramelized sugar)

杮
火⊗
叮⊗
王⊗
女⊗
牛⊗
阝
孔
划
幼
峨
預

燒酒　*shāo jiǔ* brandy or other distilled spirits
燒餅　*shāo bǐng* griddle biscuits (served with Mongolian barbecue)
L4b.12b 熗　*qiàng* to quick-poach (used for seafood)

L4b.14a 燜　*mèn* to simmer in covered pot
火腿豆燜飯　*huǒ tuǐ dòu mèn fàn* cooked rice reheated with ham and beans (Yunnan)
L4b.14b 燉　*dùn* to stew; to cook in bain-marie
L4b.14c 燈　*dēng* lamp
燈影牛肉　*dēng yǐng niú ròu* lamp shadow beef (spiced beef, steamed, then deep-fried; Sichuan)
炸燈籠仔鷄　*zhá dēng lóng zǐ jī* chicken steamed, boned, wrapped in net fat and batter-fried, served with sugar-preserved garlic (Sichuan)

L4b.15 燴　*huì* to mix together foods cooked separately
什錦燴飯　*shí jǐn huì fàn* rice mixed with fancy ingredients

L4b.16a 爆　*bào* to explode; to saute rapidly over very high flame
醬爆鷄丁　*jiàng bào jī dīng* quick-fried diced chicken in bean-paste sauce
L4b.16b 煿　*kào* to simmer in earthenware pot
煿排骨　*kào pái gǔ* deep-fried spareribs, simmered in sweet and sour sauce (Shandong)

L4b.18 爐　*lú* stove

L4b.19 爛　*làn* overripe; cooked soft
爛糊　*làn hú* stewed cabbage with duck fat (Suzhou)

L4b.22 熼　*bian* alternate form of L4b.11a

L4c 口⊗ the "mouth" radical

L4c.3a 叫　*jiào* to call
叫化子鷄　*jiào hua zǐ jī* beggar's chicken (chicken encased in clay and cooked in charcoal pit; Sichuan, Yunnan)
L4c.3b 吐　*tǔ* to spit
吐絲 or 吐司 or 吐斯　*tǔ sī* toast
吐那魚　*tǔ na yú* tuna fish

L4c.4a 吃　*chī to eat*

小吃　*xiǎo chī* snacks

黄魚二吃　*huáng yú èr chī* yellow croaker cooked two ways (e.g., the body red-cooked, plus a soup made of the head and tail)

L4c.4b 吤　*gā* nonstandard character used in following compound

吤喱　*gā lǐ* curry (cf. L4c.7a)

L4c.4c 叫　alternate form of L4c.3a

L4c.5 味　*wèi* flavor

四味蝦片　*sì wèi xiā piàn* sliced shrimp in four-flavor sauce (Hunan) or with four different sauces

川味涼麵　*chuān wèi liáng miàn* cold noodles with Szechuan sauce

味精　*wèi jīng* monosodium glutamate

請你別用味精　*qǐng ni bié yòng wèi jīng* please don't use monosodium glutamate

L4c.6a 咕　*gū* fancy alternate form of U6i

咕咾肉　*gū lǎo ròu* sweet and sour pork

咕嚕肉　*gū lǔ ròu* sweet and sour pork

L4c.6b 咬　*yǎo* to bite

魚咬羊　*yú yǎo yáng* fish bites lamb (deep-fried lamb-stuffed fish; Anhui)

L4c.7a 咖　*kā* character used in transcribing foreign words

咖喱　*kā lǐ* curry

咖啡　*kā fēi* coffee, café

L4c.7b 哈　*hā* peal of laughter

哈蜜瓜　*hā mì guā* honeydew melon

L4c.7c 咭　*jí* fancy alternate form of T3a.4a

咭汁　*jí zhī* Worcestershire sauce

L4c.8a 响　*xiǎng* to ring, resound (simplified form of T16*10)

炸响鈴　*zhá xiǎng líng* deep-fried ringing bell (stuffed bean curd skin, deep-fried very crisp)

响螺　*xiǎng luó* conch

L4c.8b 咯　*luò* to cough

咯嗒　*luò tǎ* boiled dough balls

L4c.10a 啤　*pí* beer

木
火
口
王
女
牛
阝
孔
划
幼
峨
预

啤酒　*pí jiǔ* beer

L4c.10b 啫　*zhě* fancy alternate form of 者 *zhě* 'whoever'

啫啫雞　*zhě zhě jī* chicken with scallions in casserole

啫喱　*zhě lí* jelly

L4c.11 唧　*jí* fancy form of 急 *jí* "quick"

唧汁　*jí zhī* Worcestershire sauce

L4d 王⊗　the "jewel" radical

L4d.4 玫　*méi* rose

玫瑰　*méi guì* rose

玫瑰露　*méi guì lù* a kind of rose brandy

玫瑰水　*méi guì shuǐ* sweetbriar juice

玫瑰鍋炸　*méi guì guō zhá* deep-fried egg-dough cakes
　　with fragrant syrup (Shandong)

玫瑰干貝　*méi guì gān běi* scallops in red oil

L4d.5 珍　*zhēn* treasure

珍肝　*zhēn gān* chicken giblets

珍珠肉丸　*zhēn zhū ròu wàn* pearl meatballs (meatballs
　　rolled in glutinous rice and steamed)

珍珠菜　*zhēn zhū cài* corn; pearl greens

珍珠猪排　*zhēn zhū zhū pái* deep-fried bread and pork
　　chop sandwiches (Sichuan)

珍絲　*zhēn sī* bean threads, peastarch noodles

L4d.6a 玻　*bō* glass

玻璃　*bō li* glass (used in names of dishes with glazed
　　appearance)

玻璃肉　*bō li ròu* candied deep-fried pork

玻璃蝦球　*bō lí xiā qiú* transparent (i.e., plain) stir-fried
　　shrimp curls

L4d.6b 斑　*bān* group

斑魚　*bān yú* grouper

斑指　*bān zhǐ* pig's large intestine

L4d.6c 珠　*zhū* pearl

珠聯璧合　*zhū lián bì hé* pearl joins jade (duck stuffed
　　with mushrooms, dried scallops, and lotus seeds,
　　steamed in sauce)

珠油　*zhū yóu* bead molasses

珠茶　*zhū chá* gunpowder tea (green)

L4d.7a 球 *qiú* (KĀU) curl, "ball" (piece of meat or fish
  that curls up as it cooks; sometimes rendered as
  "kow" or "kew" on menus)
L4d.7b 珊 *shān* coral
珊瑚 *shān hú* coral
珊瑚玉樹鷄 *shān hú yù shù jī* coral jade tree chicken
  (chicken and crab meat or ham, served on bed of
  green vegetable)
L4d.7c 琉 *liú* glossy, glazed
琉璃 *liú li* porcelain
琉璃鴿蛋 *liú li gē dàn* quail eggs and straw mushrooms
  in shiny sauce
L4d.8 斑 *bān* mottled, striped (short for 石斑 *shí bān*
  grouper)
斑鳩 *bān jiū* wood dove
斑指 *bān zhǐ* pig's large intestine

L4d.9 琥 *hǔ* amber
琥珀 *hǔ pò* amber

L4d.11 瑤 *yáo* jade
瑤柱 *yáo zhù* scallop, esp. dried

L4e 女⊗ the "woman" radical

L4e.3 好 *hǎo* good
好霉干菜 *hǎo méi gān cài* a type of dried mustard green

L4e.4a 奶 *nǎi* milk
奶湯 *nǎi tāng* thick soup
奶油菜心 *nǎi yóu cài xīn* flowering cabbage in white
  sauce
炒鮮奶 *chǎu xiān nǎi* fried milk (stir-fried egg-white-milk
  mixture, served over deep-fried noodles; Guangdong)
奶酪 *nǎi lào* a pudding made of milk and agar-agar
L4e.4b 如 *rú* as
如意捲 *rú yì juǎn* shrimp and pork rolls fried in egg
  batter (lit., "as you like it rolls")

L4e.6 娃 *wá* baby
娃娃魚 *wá wá yú* lit., "baby fish" (also known as 狗魚
  gǒu yú)

木
火
口
王
女
牛
阝
孔
划
幼
峨
预

L4e.12 嫩 *nèn* tender

L4f 牛⊗ the "cow" radical

L4f.3 牡 *mǔ* male animal
牡丹 *mǔ dan* tree peony
牡丹魚 *mǔ dan yú* turtle
椰茸牡丹酥 *yé róng mǔ dan sū* crisp coconut pastries
牡蠣 *mǔ lì* oyster

L4f.3b 牠似蜜 *tā sȝ mì* empress dowager lamb shreds
(lit., "It's like honey"; candied lamb shreds in sweet
bean sauce)

L4f.6 特 *tè* special
特式 *tè shì* specialties

L4f.17 犢 *dú* calf
犢肉 *dú ròu* veal

L4g 阝⊗ the "yin-yang" radical

L4g.5 附 *fù* to be attached
附油蓮米 *fù yóu lián mǐ* lotus seeds steamed with fatty
pork and rock sugar (Guizhou)

L4g.8 陸 *lù* mainland
陸海空湯 *lù hǎi kūng tāng* land-sea-air soup (contains,
e.g., pork, fish, chicken)

L4g.9a 陳 *chén* stale (common Chinese surname)
陳皮 *chén pí* dried tangerine peel (used widely in Chinese
herbal medicine)
陳皮雞 *chén pí jī* chicken pieces fried with dried tangerine peel and chili peppers (Sichuan)
陳麻婆豆腐 see E3a.8 麻婆豆腐 *má po dòu fu*
L4g.9b 陰 *yīn* female half of the yin-yang contrast
陰陽菠菜鷄蓉湯 *yīn yáng pō cài jī róng tāng* yin-yang
spinach and chicken soup (thick chicken and spinach
soups served in a single bowl in form of yin-yang
symbol; Fujian)

L4g.10 陽 *yáng* sun; male half of the yin-yang contrast
太陽餅 *tài yáng bǐng* sun cake (meat-filled flaky pastry;
Fujian)

L4* Miscellaneous Four-Stroke Left Halves

L4*1 孔 *kǒng* Chinese family name; Confucius

孔夫子 *kǒng fu zǐ* Confucius
孔雀 *kǒng què* peacock
孔明肉 *kǒng míng ròu* pork side cut in spiral shape and
  simmered (Sichuan)

L4*2 划 *huá* to row

划水 *huá shuǐ* fish tail (lit., "row water")

L4*3 幼 *yòu* young, immature

幼麟龍魚 *yòu lín lóng yú* Macau sole

L4*7 峨 *é* lofty

峨嵋 *é méi* Mount Omei, a Buddhist resort in Sichuan,
  after which many Sichuanese restaurants are named

L4*10 預 *yù* beforehand

預定 *yù dìng* to be ordered in advance

L4*10a 帽 *mào* hat
和菜戴帽 *hé cài dài mào* mixed ingredients wearing a hat
  (stir-fried shredded meats and vegetables with omlet
  on top)
帽貝 *mào bēi* limpet

L5 Five-Stroke Left Halves

L5a 月⊗ the "meat" radical

L5a.3a 肚 *dǔ* stomach
魚肚 *yú dǔ* fish stomach (actually, airbag)
肚板 *dǔ bǎn* first stomach of cow or other ruminant; flat
  tripe
肚葫蘆 *dǔ hú lu* second stomach; honeycomb tripe
蜂窩肚 *fēng wō dǔ* second stomach; honeycomb tripe

月日礻示禾段將矮旗

肚散旦　*dǔ sàn dàn* third stomach (a kind of honeycomb tripe)

千層肚　*qiān céng dǔ* third stomach

肚蘑菇　*dǔ mó gū* fourth stomach (flat tripe)

肚膅　*dǔ dāng* fish steak

L5a.3b 肝　*gān* liver

滷肝　*lǔ gān* liver simmered with soy sauce and spices, served cold

L5a.3c 肘　*zhǒu* pork shoulder

L5a.3d 肋　*lè* ribs

肋條　*lè tiáo* ribs

L5a.5a 肥　*féi* fatty

肥腸　*féi cháng* large intestine

肥龍會鴨紅　*féi lóng huì yā hóng* duck intestines simmered with duck blood (Guangdong)

L5a.5b 肫　*zhūn* gizzard

肫肝　*zhūn gān* gizzard and liver

L5a.5c 胗　*zhēn* gizzard

L5a.5d 肺　*fèi* lung

肺藏　*fèi zàng* lung

L5a.6a 肢　*zhī* limb, wing, leg

L5a.6b 胎　*tāi* fetus

鳳胎魚翅　*fēng tāi yú chì* chicken stuffed with shark fin (Fujian)

L5a.7a 朐　*qú* dried flank meat

L5a.7b 豚　*tún* suckling pig

L5a.7c 胹　*lí* tongue; sole (fish)

L5a.8a 脫　*tō* to remove, take off

脫骨雞　*tō gǔ jī* boneless chicken

L5a.8b 脯　*pú* flesh; breast (of poultry); *fǔ* preserved fruit

梅醬炸鴨脯　*měi jiàng zhá yā pú* deep-fried duck meat with plum sauce

L5a.8c 脚　*jiǎo* foot

豬脚凍　*zhū jiǎo dòng* jellied pig's feet

脚魚　*jiǎo yú* turtle (more commonly written with U6n)

L5a.8d 胴　*dòng* large intestine

L5a.8e 脖　*bó* neck (of poultry)

L5a.8f 胰　*yí* soap; second stomach of duck

燴鴨胰　*huì yā yí* duck stomach with thick sauce
　　(Shandong)
L5a.8g 胸　*xiōng* chest
胸腺　*xiōng xiàn* sweetbreads (thymus; lit., "chest glands")

L5a.9a 臘　*là* cured (meat)
生爆臘肉　*shèng bào là ròu* stir-fried preserved meat with
　　vegetables
臘腸　*là cháng* (LAAHP CHÉUNG) Chinese sausage
臘八豆　*là bā dòu* fermented soybeans (Jap. *nattō*)
湖南臘肉　*hú nán là ròu* thin-sliced Hunanese lean bacon
　　stir-fried with leek and chili peppers
L5a.9b 脆　*cuì* crisp
脆皮鴨　*cuì pí yā* crispy skin duck
炸脆　*zhá cuì* sweet deep-fried wonton skins
生炒雙脆　*shēng chǎo shuāng cuì* stir-fried pig tripe and
　　dried squid (Hakka)
L5a.9c 脾　*pí* sweetbreads (pancreas)
L5a.9d 腌川　*āng chuān* dirty river (fish and salt pork soup;
　　Shanghai)

L5a.10a 腸　*cháng* intestine, sausage
香腸　*xiāng cháng* Chinese sausage
腸粉　*cháng fěn* (CHÈUNG FÁN) rice-flour sheets with
　　filling, rolled up and steamed
L5a.10b 腩　*nǎn* meat for stewing (chuck steak, etc.)
L5a.10c 腱　*jiàn* beef or lamb shank
L5a.10d 腫　*zhǒng* swollen
火腫　*huǒ zhǒng* ham
L5a.10e 腌　*yān* to salt; salted (alternate form of L8a.9b)

L5a.11a 腰　*yāo* hip; kidney; cashew nut
腰花　*yāo huā* fancy-cut kidney slices
腰豆　*yāo dòu* cashew nut
蝦仁雙腰　*xiā rén shuāng yāo* shrimp with pork kidney
　　and cashew nuts
腰窩方子　*yāo wō fàng zi* pork rib meat
L5a.11b 腿　*tuǐ* leg
火腿　*huǒ tuǐ* ham
素火腿　*sù huǒ tuǐ* vegetarian ham (made from bean curd
　　skin)
L5a.11c 腳　*jiǎo* leg, foot (alternate form of L5a.8c)

月日衤示禾
段將矮旗

L5a.11d 脛　*jìng* shank

L5a.12a 膗　*chuái* nonstandard character used in following compound

膗肉　*chuái ròu* fatty pork

L5a.12b 膃　*wèn* nonstandard character used in following compound

膃肭劑　*wèn nà jì* dried genitals of male otter (used for promoting fertility)

L5a.12c 膘　*piao* fatty pork

L5a.12d 腱　*jiàn* tendon; gizzard

L5a.13a 腦　*nǎo* brain

蟹粉腦膏　*xiè fěn nǎo gāo* beef brain and crab meat steamed in soup

上腦　*shàng nǎo* beef shoulder roast

L5a.13b 膠　*jiāo* glue

蝦膠　*xiā jiāo* a sticky paste made from seasoned ground shrimp meat

膠荀　*jiāo sǔn* wild rice shoots

L5a.15a 膽　*dǎn* gall bladder; thermos jug

海膽　*hǎi dǎn* sea urchin

蟹肉焗菜膽　*xiè ròu jú cài dǎn* flowering cabbage with crab sauce in casserole

L5a.15b 膾　*kuài* minced meat

L5a.20 膘　*biau* fatty pork

L5a.21 臘　*là* see L5a.9a

L5b 日⊗ the "sun" radical

L5b.5 明　*míng* bright; Ming dynasty

明蝦　*míng xiā* prawn; whole large shrimp

明爐乳豬　*míng lú rǔ zhū* roast suckling pig

L5b.6 時　*shí* time

時菜　*shí cài* vegetable in season

時價　*shí jià* seasonal price

L5b.7 昭　*zhāo* bright

昭通麵　*zhāo tōng miàn* vermicelli in soup (Yunnan)

L5b.9 晾　*liàng* to dry in the air

晾干肉　*liàng gān ròu* dried meat

L5b.16 曝　*pù* to dry in the sun
曝腌魚　*pù yān yú* sun-dried salted fish

L5c 礻⊗　the "divine" radical

L5c.4 祁　*qí* vigorous
祁門　*qí mén* Keemun county (Anhui), after which a
celebrated black tea is named

L5c.6a 神　*shén* god
神仙　*shén xiān* fairy
神仙雞　*shén xiān jī* chicken stewed in earthenware pot
L5c.6b 祝　*zhù* to congratulate
祝壽蟠桃　*zhù shòu pán táo* fancy peach-shaped steamed
buns with sweet filling

L5c.8 裡　*lǐ* nonstandard character used in following
compound
裡肌　*lǐ jī* pork tenderloin

L5c.11 福　*fú* good fortune
福建　*fú jiàn* Fukien
福州　*fú zhōu* Fuchow province
五福魚丸　*wǔ fú yú wàn* fancy fish balls in soup (Sichuan)
全家福　*quán jiā fú* happy family (mixed seafoods and
meats in thick sauce)
福壽全　*fú shòu quán* turtle simmered with mountain and
sea delicacies (Guangdong)
福祿鷄冠餃　*fú lù jī guàn jiǎo* lucky cockscomb steamed
chicken ravioli (Guangdong)

L5d 示⊗　alternate form of L5c

L5e 禾⊗　the "grain" radical

L5e.2 利　*lì* profit
利馬豆　*lì mǎ dòu* lima beans

L5e.4a 和　*hé* peace, harmony
和菜戴帽　*hé cài dài mào* mixed ingredients wearing a hat

月

日

礻示

禾

段

將

矮

旗

(stir-fried shredded meats and vegetables with omlet on top)

L5e.4b 秋 *qiū* autumn

L5e.10 稱 *chēng* to weigh
稱開洋 *chēng kāi yáng* a kind of dried shrimp

L5e.12 穗 *suì* ear of grain

L5* Miscellaneous Five-Stroke Left Halves

L5*6 段 *duàn* section

醋烹蝦段 *cù pēng xiā duàn* sweet and sour shrimp segments
炸段宵 *zhá duàn xiāo* bananas filled with preserved fruit and deep-fried (Beijing)

L5*8 將 *jiàng* general (of army)

將軍 *jiàng jūn* general (of army)
將軍過橋 *jiàng jūn guò qiáo* general crosses bridge (fried fish in soup; Jiangsu)

L5*9 矮 *ǎi* short

矮 *ǎi guā* Chinese eggplant

L5*10 旗 *qí* flag

旗魚 *qí yú* swordfish

Six-Stroke Left Halves

L6a 米⊗ the "rice" radical

L6a.5a 粉 *fěn* flour; powder; rice-flour noodles
米粉 *mǐ fěn* rice-flour noodles
炒粉 *chǎo fěn* stir-fried rice-flour noodles

腸粉 *cháng fěn* rice-flour noodle sheet wrapped around filling

粉果 *fěn guǒ* (FÁN GWÓ) ravioli with skin of rice flour (Guangdong)

粉蒸排骨 *fěn zhēng pái gǔ* spareribs dredged in seasoned rice flour and steamed (Sichuan)

粉東西 *fěn dōng xi* flour things (sliced meats and vegetables dredged in rice flour and steamed in huge steamer; Jiangxi)

粉葛 *fěn gé* kudzu (a root sometimes used in soups)

粉絲 *fěn sī* bean threads; peastarch noodles

粉皮 *fěn pí* peastarch noodle in sheet form

粉條 *fěn tiáo* flat peastarch noodles

粉酒 *fěn jiǔ* Fenyang wine

L6a.5b 粒 *lì* granule

雞粒 *jī lì* minced cooked chicken

L6a.5c 粑 alternate form of U5m 巴

L6a.6 粘 *nián* to glue

粘糖蘋果 *nián táng píng guo* sugar-coated apple fritters

L6a.9a 粽 *jiòng* (JÙHNG) Chinese tamale (glutinous rice and diced meats and vegetables, wrapped in leaf and steamed)

豬油夾沙粽 *zhū yóu jiā shā jiòng* glutinous rice ball filled with sweet bean paste and steamed in bamboo leaf

L6a.9b 糝 porridge

L6a.10 糕 *gāo* cake, pudding

年糕 *nián gāo* New Year's sweet rice-flour cake

羊糕 *yáng gāo* jellied lamb

炸鷄糕 *zhá jī gāo* paste of chicken meat, pork, and egg white, steamed until set, then cut into strips and deep-fried (Sichuan)

蘿白糕 *luó bài gāo* (LO BAAHK GOU) turnip pudding (steamed, then sliced and pan-fried)

L6a.11a 糊 *hú* paste

蝦龍糊 *xiā lóng hū* shrimp in lobster sauce

糊辣肉鷄 *hú là ròu jī* deep-fried chicken with gravy of dried chili peppers (Sichuan)

L6a.11b 糍 *cí* a type of rice-flour pasta

L6

糍巴 *cí bā* a rice-flour pasta, served steamed or fried

L6a.11c 糁 *sǎn* grain of rice, etc.; rice mixed in meat soup and boiled to a porridge

L6a.11d 糭 alternate form of L6a.9a

L6a.12 糖 *táng* sugar; candy
糖醋魚 *táng cù yú* sweet and sour fish
冰糖 *bīng táng* rock sugar

L6a.13 糟 *zāo* wine lees
糟溜田雞腿 *zāo liū tián jī tuǐ* frog legs with wine lees sauce
糟雞 *zāo jī* boiled chicken marinated in wine lees (Fujian)

L6a.16 糯 *nuò* glutinous rice
糯米 *nuò mǐ* glutinous rice
糯米雞 *nuò mǐ jī* Chinese tamale (sticky rice and chicken pieces wrapped in lotus leaf and steamed); chicken with sticky-rice stuffing

L6b 虫⊗ the "bug" radical

L6b.3 虾 *xiā* shrimp (popular form of L6b.12a)

L6b.4a 蚧 *xiè* crab (popular form of T16*6)
L6b.4b 蚌 *bàng* clam
L6b.4c 蚝 *háo* oyster (popular form of L6b.16)

L6b.5 蚋 *ruì* mussel (lit., "gnat")

L6b.6a 蛇 *shé* snake
三蛇湯 *sān shé tāng* soup made with three kinds of snake meat
L6b.6b 蚵 *ké* a type of oyster (Taiwan)
L6b.6c 蛙 *wā* frog

L6b.7 蛤 *gé* clam
蛤蜊 *gé lí* clam
蛤蚧蛇 *gé xiè shé* lizard
蛤蟆雞 *gé má jī* hairy pea and fried chicken casserole (Beijing)
鳥蛤 *niǎo gé* cockle (lit., "bird clam")

L6b.8a 蜂 *fēng* bee
蜂蜜 *fēng mì* honey
蜂窩 *fēng wō* beehive
蜂窩肚 *fēng wō dǔ* honeycomb tripe (second stomach of cow)
蜂窩豆腐 *fēng wō dòu fu* honeycomb bean curd (bean curd boiled so that it puffs up)
L6b.8b 蚬 *xiǎng* conch (variant of L4c.8a)
蚬螺 *xiǎng luó* conch
L6b.8c 蚬 *xian* mussel, clam
L6b.8d 蜘 *chē* fancy form of U8g 車 *chē* vehicle
蜘螯 *chē ao* large crab
蜘螯豆腐湯 *chē ao dòu fu tāng* crab and bean curd soup (Jiangsu)

L6b.10 蝤 *qiú* nonstandard character, used in following compound
蝤蛑 *qiú mou* a type of crab

L6b.11a 螞 *mǎ* ant
螞蟻 *mǎ yǐ* ant
螞蟻上樹 *mǎ yǐ shàng shū* ants climb a tree (spicy ground beef sauce poured over deep-fried bean threads; Sichuan)
螞螂 *mā lang* dragonfly
螞螂雞塊 *mā lang jī kuài* chicken and deep-fried bean curd skin with thick sauce (Beijing)
螞蚱 *mǎ zhà* grasshopper
干炸螞蚱 *gān zhá mǎ zhà* deep-fried grasshoppers (Yunnan)
L6b.11b 蝴 *hú* butterfly
蝴蝶 *hú dié* butterfly
蝴蝶蝦 *hú dié xiā* butterfly shrimps

L6b.12a 蝦 *xiā* shrimp
龍蝦 *lóng xiā* lobster
明蝦 *míng xiā* large shrimp
蝦片 *xiā piàn* sliced shrimp; shrimp chips (Malay *krupuk*)
蝦龍糊 *xiā lóng hú* shrimp in lobster sauce (Guangdong)
蝦餃 *xiā jiǎo* (HĀ GÁU) shrimp ravioli

米[虫石弓衤]
郊
胡
瓶
翔
鴨

蝦仁　*xiā rén* shelled small shrimps
蝦米　*xiā mǐ* dried shrimps
蝦膏　*xiā gāo* shrimp paste
蝦吐司　*xiā tǔ sī* shrimp toast
蝦多司　*xiā duō sī* shrimp toast
L6b.12b 螃　*páng* crab
螃蟹　*páng xie* crab
賽螃蟹　*sài páng xie* imitation crab foo yung (made with thin-sliced fish; Shandong)
L6b.12c 蝸　*guā* snail
蝸牛　*guā niú* snail

L6b.13a 螺　*luó* large snail; conch
螺蛳　*luó shī* large snail; conch
石螺　*shí luó* small land snail
螺絲捲　*luó sī juǎn* fancy steamed rolled buns of snail-like shape
螺旋　*luó xuán* spiral
燒螺旋肉　*shāo luó xuán ròu* pork side cut in spiral shape and simmered (Sichuan)
L6b.13b 蟠　*pán* to curl up
蟠桃　*pán táu* a type of small flat peach

L6b.14a 蟳　*xun* crab
三絲蟳丸　*sān sī xun wàn* soup with crab balls and three shredded ingredients (Fujian)
L6b.14b 蟶　*chēng* razor clam, mussel

L6b.15 蠑　*róng* top shell
蠑螺　*róng luó* top shell

L6b.16 蠔　*háo* oyster
蠔油牛肉　*háo yóu* oyster sauce
蠔士　*háo shì* dried oyster

L6b.17 蠣　*lì* oyster
蠣蟥　*lì huáng* oyster

L6c 石⊗ the "rock" radical

L6c.4 砂　*shā* sand
砂鍋　*shā guō* earthenware pot; casserole (lit., "sand pot")
砂鍋魚頭　*shā guō yú tóu* fish head casserole

L6c.5 砵 *bē* nonstandard character used in transcribing foreign words
砵酒 *bē jiǔ* (BUHT JÁU) port wine

L6c.6 硃 *zhū* cinnabar
硃砂豆腐 *zhū shā dòu fu* stir-fried mashed bean curd (Beijing)

L6c.8 碎 *suì* break, broken
碎米雞 *suì mǐ jī* diced chicken with chopped peanuts in hot sauce (Sichuan)
碎肉大紅腸 *suì ròu dà hóng cháng* sausage of chitterling stuffed with minced pork

L6c.10a 碟 *dié* dish
每碟一元 *měi dié yī yuán* one dollar per plate
L6c.10b 碌 *lù* green jasper; rough
干煎大蝦碌 *gān jiān dà xiā lù* grilled prawns in shell
L6c.10c 礆 *jiǎn* alkaline
礆粉 *jiǎn fěn* baking soda
礆粽 *jiǎn jiòng* sweet Chinese tamale
L6c.10d 碩 *shí* eminent
碩果長青 *shí guǒ cháng qīng* stir-fried garlic shoots, pressed bean curd, and peanuts

L6c.11 碗 *wǎn* bowl, esp. rice bowl
一碗飯 *yì wǎn fàn* one bowl of rice

L6d 弓⊗ the "bow" radical

L6d.6 弦 *xián* string (of bow or musical instrument)
雪白雙弦 *xuě bái shuāng xián* quick-fried shredded beef tripe and bamboo shoot (Beijing)

L6d.9 張 *zhāng* classifier for counting flat objects
六張餅 *liù zhāng bǐng* six pancakes
千張茄子 *qián zhāng qié zi* thousand-layer eggplant (spiced fried eggplant slices)
千張 *qián zhāng* bean curd pressed into thin sheets

L6d.12 粥 *zhōu* (JŪK) rice porridge; congee
魚生粥 *yú shēng zhōu* congee with fish slices
白粥 *bái zhōu* plain congee

米
虫
石
弓
衤
郊
胡
瓶
翔
鴨

L6e 衤⊗ the "clothing" radical (do not confuse with L5c 衤⊗)

L6e.8 襍 *zá* miscellaneous (alternate form of L10*8)

L6e.9 裙 *qún* apron

裙帶菜 *qún dài cài* a kind of seaweed (lit., "apron-string vegetable"; Jap. *wakame*)

L6* Miscellaneous Six-Stroke Left Halves

L6*4 郊 *jiāo* suburbs

郊外菜蘟 *jiāo wài cài yuán* suburban vegetable garden (parboiled mixed greens)

L6*5a 胡 *hú* Northern barbarians of ancient times

胡椒 *hú jiāo* black pepper
胡蘿蔔 *hú ló bo* carrot
胡桃 *hú táo* walnut
胡荽 *hú suī* coriander leaf
胡葱 *hú cōng* scallion
爆胡 *bào hú* beef grilled on metal plate (Beijing)
胡肘 *hú zhǒu* stewed grilled pork leg

L6*5b 瓶 *píng* bottle

瓶保山瑞 *píng bào shān ruì* turtle in sealed casserole or porcelain jar

L6*8 翔 *xiāng* to soar

翔鷹拼盤 *xiāng yīng pīn pán* soaring hawk appetizer plate

L6*13 鴨 *yā* duck

北京烤鴨 *běi jīng kǎo yā* Peking roast duck

火鴨　*huǒ yā* (FÓ NGÁAP) barbecued duck
(Guangdong)
鴨泥麵包　*yā ní miàn bāo* fried bread with minced duck
　　sauce (Beijing)
板鴨　*bǎn yā* pressed duck
子薑鴨片　*zǐ jiāng yā piàn* sliced duck with sweet and
　　sour sprouting ginger

Seven-Stroke Left Halves

L7a 糸⊗　the "silk" radical

L7a.3 紅　*hóng* red
紅燒魚　*hóng shāo yú* red-cooked fish (simmered in soy
　　sauce)
紅油水餃　*hóng yóu shuǐ jiǎo* boiled ravioli with chili oil
小紅頭　*xiǎo hóng tóu* little red heads (small steamed
　　buns, filled with sugar and fatty pork; Anhui)
紅斑　*hóng bān* red grouper
紅菜頭　*hóng cài tóu* beet
紅衫魚　*hóng shān yú* red snapper (lit., "red shirt fish")
紅綠雙凍　*hóng lǜ shuāng dòng* jelly of red and green
　　beans (Zhejiang)
紅綠絲　*hóng lǜ sī* pickled shredded red and green fruit
紅毛丹　*hóng máo dān* rambutan (fruit similar to lychee)
紅紋鵝掌　*hóng wén é zhǎng* red-cooked goose feet
紅糟　*hóng záo* red fermented rice paste
雞紅　*jī hóng* jellied chicken blood (Guangdong, Hakka)

L7a.5a 紙　*zhǐ* paper
紙包雞片　*zhǐ bāo jī piàn* deep-fried paper-wrapped
　　chicken slices
L7a.5b 紐　*niǔ* knot; used in transcribing foreign names
紐約　*niǔ yuē* (NÁU YEÙK) New York

L7a.6a 細　*xì* fine, small
細粉　*xì fěn* bean threads; vermicelli
細饊子　*xì sǎn zi* deep-fried dough strips (Shandong)
L7a.6b 絨　*róng* velvet
雞絨　*jī róng* chicken velvet (minced chicken mixed with
　　egg white)

L7a.7a 絲 *sī* thread, shred
粉絲 *fěn sī* bean threads; peastarch noodles
干絲 *gān sī* shredded pressed bean curd
三絲湯 *sān sī tāng* three shredded ingredient soup
絲苗白飯 *sī miáo bái fàn* plain rice
絲瓜 *sī guā* ridged gourd; zucchini

L7a.7b 紹 *shào* to bring together
紹菜 *shào cài* celery cabbage
紹子魚 *shào zi yú* fish with spicy meat sauce (Sichuan)
紹興 *shào xīng* Shaohsing, a city in Zhejiang, after which
  a famous variety of rice wine is named

L7a.7c 結 *jié* to join, connect
結瓜 *jié guā* hairy melon (also written with T6a.11)

L7a.8 綫 alternate form of L7a.11

L7a.9a 網 *wǎng* net
網油 *wǎng yóu* net fat (pig's abdominal fat, which is in
  thin sheets that can be used for wrapping food that is
  then steamed or batter-fried)
網油鳳肝卷 *wǎng yóu fèng gān juǎn* chicken liver rolls
  wrapped in net fat

L7a.9b 綉 *xiù* embroidery
綉球鷄胗 *xiù qiú jī shēn* chicken gizzard and pork,
  stewed with spices (Beijing)

L7a.10a 綠 *lǜ* green
綠豆 *lǜ dòu* mung bean
綠豆沙 *lǜ dòu sa* sweet porridge of mung beans
綠茶 *lǜ chá* green tea
綠花椰菜 *lǜ huā yé cài* cauliflower

L7a.10b 經 *jīng* to plan, arrange
經濟 *jīng jì* economy
經濟麵 *jīng jì miàn* simple cold noodles (Sichuan)

L7a.11 線 *xiàn* line, wire
線粉 *xiàn fěn* rice vermicelli; bean threads
米線 *mǐ xiàn* rice vermicelli
麵線 *miàn xiàn* wheat-flour vermicelli
赤線 *chì xiàn* red snapper

L7a.12 縐 *zhòu* crepe

縐紗元蹄　*zhòu shā yuán tí* steamed whole pork shoulder (Guangdong)

L7a.17 繡　*xiù* embroidery (alternate form of L7a.9b)

L7b 辛⊗　the "bitter" radical

L7b.8 辣　*là* hot (spicy)
酸辣湯　*suān là tāng* hot and sour soup
辣白菜　*là bái cài* hot and sour Chinese cabbage (Sichuan)
辣子　*là zi* chili pepper
辣椒　*là jiāo* chili pepper
麻辣腰花　*má là yāo huā* fancy-cut pork kidney slices in chili and brown pepper sauce
辣醬　*là jiàng* hot sauce
辣油　*là yóu* oil flavored with chili peppers

L7b.10 辦　*bàn* to manage
辦麵　*bàn miàn* braised noodle

L7b.12 瓣　*bàn* petal
豆瓣醬　*dòu bàn jiàng* a spicy fermented bean sauce (Sichuan)

L7c 缶⊗　the "crock" radical

L7c.8 缾　*píng* bottle (alternate form of L6*5b)

L7c.14 罎　alternate form of L7c.18

L7c.18 罈　*tán* earthenware jar (also written as L3d.18)
罈子肉　*tán zi ròu* pork pieces simmered in earthenware jar (Shandong)

L7c.19 罐　*guàn* jar; can
罐兒蹄　*guàr tí* pig feet cooked in earthenware jar (Shandong)

L7d 束⊗　the "stabbing" element

L7d.2 刺　*cì* to stab, pierce
京都燒束參　*jīng dū shāo cì shēn* sea cucumber and pork in Peking-style bean sauce

糸
辛
缶
束
刨
甜
雜
艇
貓
豬
鴿
鵝

L7d.7 棘 *jí* thorn, spine
棘鬣魚 *jí lèi yú* porgy

L7* Miscellaneous Seven-Stroke Left Halves

L7*2 刨 *páo* to dig deeply (also used as popular form of T4a.14c 薄 *báo* thin)

刨片 *páo piàn* sliced pig's ear

L7*6 甜 *tián* sweet

甜酸全魚 *tián suān quán yú* sweet and sour whole fish
甜瓜 *tián guā* muskmelon
甜米酒 *tián mǐ jiǔ* or 甜酒釀 *tián jiǔ niàng* a kind of sweet rice wine
甜麵醬 *tián miàn jiàng* sweet and salty bean paste

L7*8 雜 see L10*8

L7*9a 艇 *tǐng* long, narrow boat

艇仔粥 *tǐng zi zhōu* congee with mixed seafood

L7*9b 貓 *māo* cat (see L3c.9b 猫)

L7*9c 豬 *zhū* pig (see L3c.9a 猪)

L7*13a 鴿 *gē* pigeon

L7*13b 鵝 *é* goose

L8 Eight-Stroke Left Halves

L8a 酉⊗ the "wine" radical
L8a.5 酥 *sū* flaky, crisp

香酥鶏塊　*xiāng sū jī kuài* (HÈUNG SÒU GĀI FAI) hong su chicken pieces (chicken pieces, marinated, steamed, and deep-fried)

豆沙酥餅　*dòu sā sū bǐng* deep-fried flaky buns, filled with sweet bean paste

鶏酥角　*jī sū jiǎo* (GAI SÒU GOK) flaky pastry turnover with chicken filling

元寶酥　*yuán bǎo sū* baked flaky pastries with bean-paste filling

酥魚　*sū yú* sour stewed fish

酥菜　*sū cài* sour hot pot (Shandong)

L8a.8a 酸　*suān* sour

酸菜　*suān cài* sour pickled vegetable

酸辣湯　*suān là tāng* hot and sour soup

酸筍衣　*suān sǔn yī* sour bamboo shoot

L8a.8b 醉　*zuì* drunken

醉蝦　*zuì xiā* shrimps marinated in wine (lit., "drunken shrimps")

醉燒紅蟳　*zuì shāo hóng xu* crab marinated in wine, then deep-fried (Fujian)

L8a.8c 酪　*lào* cream, puree

兩色酪　*liǎng sè lào* two-color cream (two sweet purees served together)

核桃酪　*hé tào lào* sweet walnut puree

L8a.8d 酵　*xiào* yeast

酵母粒　*xiào mǔ lì* yeast

L8a.9a 醋　*cù* vinegar

糖醋鶏球　*táng cù jī qiú* sweet and sour chicken morsels

醋椒魚　*cù jiāo yú* hot and sour fish soup (Beijing)

醋烹蝦段　*cù pēng xiā duàn* shrimp segments cooked in sweet and sour sauce

醋溜魚片　*cù liū yú piàn* fish slices with sweet and sour sauce

L8a.9b 醃　*yān* salted

醃肉　*yān ròu* salted pork

砂鍋醃鮮　*shā guō yān xiān* casserole of salted and fresh pork

L8a.19 釀　*niàng* fermented; stuffed

酉
金
豆
足
車
臣
乳
彩
野
教
瓜
賜
鶉
護

L8b 金⊗ the "gold" radical

L8b.2 針 *zhēn* needle
金針菜 *jīn zhēn cài* gold needle vegetable (dried tiger lily)

L8b.5a 鈎 *gōu* hook
金鈎魷魚絲 *jīn gōu yóu yú sī* shredded dried squid, stir-fried with pork
L8b.5b 鉗 *qián* claw (of crab or lobster)
L8b.5c 鈕 *niǔ* button
酒釀鈕扣圓 *jiǔ niàng niǔ kòu yuán* sweet dumplings in wine soup (Zhejiang)
L8b.5d 鉄 *tiě* iron (abbreviated form of L8b.14)

L8b.6 鈴 *líng* bell
炸響鈴 *zhá xiǎng líng* deep-fried ringing bell (stuffed bean curd skin or wonton, fried very crisp)
炸金鈴 *zhá jīn líng* deep-fried golden bells (crisp-fried wonton with walnut-coconut-sesame filling)

L8b.7 銀 *yín* silver
銀芽肉絲 *yín yá ròu sī* stir-fried bean sprouts and shredded pork
銀耳 *yín ěr* white tree fungus
銀針焗乳鴿 *yín zhēn jú rǔ gē* pigeon baked with shark fin (lit., "silver needles")
銀魚 *yín yú* whitebait
銀杏 *yín xìng* sweet almond
銀腦豆腐 *yín nǎo dòu fu* steamed pudding of pig brain and bean curd, served in soup (Taiwan)
銀針粉 *yín zhēn fěn* rice-flour vermicelli

L8b.8 銅 *tóng* copper
銅井巷素麵 *tóng jǐng xiàng sù miàn* copper-mine vegetarian noodles (with spiced sesame sauce; Sichuan)

L8b.10 錦 *jǐn* brocade
錦繡 *jǐn xiù* fancy embroidery
錦繡魚翅羹 *jǐn xiù yú chì gēng* fancy thick shark fin soup
錦雞 *jǐn jī* pheasant (usually written 山雞)

L8b.11 鎮 *zhèn* township

鎮江　*zhēn jiāng* Chenkiang (city in Jiangsu Province; noted for vinegar)

鎮江焗骨　*zhēn jiāng jú gǔ* spareribs deep-fried then baked with sweetened vinegar

L8b.12 鍋　*guō* (WOHK) frying pan, wok; pot

鍋貼　*guō tiē* scorch-fried, esp. scorch-fried ravioli (pot stickers)

鍋巴　*guō ba* crispy rice

火鍋　*huǒ guō* fire pot (Mongolian fondue)

砂鍋　*shā guō* earthenware pot, casserole

鍋燒鴨　*guō shāo yā* duck slices and vegetables in batter, fried in pancake form

鍋塌豆腐　*guō tā dòu fu* bean curd pan-fried in egg batter (Beijing)

棗泥鍋餅　*zǎo ní guō bǐng* pancakes filled with date paste

香蕉鍋炸　*xiāng jiāo guō zhá* deep-fried banana custard (Beijing)

L8b.14 鐵　*tiě* iron

鐵板牛排　*tiě bǎn niú pái* beef rib cooked on iron griddle

鐵鍋蛋　*tiě guō dàn* pie-form pork souffle (Fujian)

鐵觀音茶　*tiě guān yīn chá* (TIT GŪN YÀM CHÀH) iron goddess of mercy tea

鐵羅漢茶　*tiě luó hàn chá* (TIT LŌ HÒN CHÀH) iron arhat (Buddhist saint) tea

L8b.19 鑲　*xiāng* inlay; stuffed

鑲寶珠梨　*xiāng bǎo zhū lí* pears stuffed with sticky rice, steamed (Yunnan)

鑲萬年青　*xiāng wàn nián qīng* fancy platter of cabbage stalks garnished with mushroom and minced chicken

L8c 豆⊗　the "bean" radical

L8c.3 豇　*jiāng* cowpea

豇豆　*jiāng dòu* cowpea; black-eyed bean

L8c.5 豉　*chǐ* fermented black bean

豉汁　*chǐ zhī* black bean sauce

豉油　*chǐ yóu* soy sauce

L8c.10 頭　*tóu* head

L8

酉 金 [豆 足 車 臣 乳 彩 野 敎 瓠] 賜 鵠 護

獅子頭　*shī zi tóu* lion's head (large meatballs simmered with Chinese cabbage)

饅頭　*mán tou* steamed bread

頭檯　*tóu tái* appetizers

芋頭　*yù tou* taro; sweet potato

L8c.12 豌　*wān* green pea

豌豆　*wān dòu* green pea

豌豆黃　*wān dòu huáng* pea porridge

L8d 足⊗　the "foot" radical

L8d.9 蹄　*tí* hoof

蹄筋　*tí jīn* pork achilles tendon

馬蹄　*mǎ tí* water chestnut (lit., "horse hoof")

馬蹄糕　*mǎ tí gāo* (MÁH TÀIH GŌU) water chestnut pudding

蹄膀　*tí bǎng* pork shoulder

L8d.14 蹦　*bèng* jump

蹦肚仁　*bèng dǔ rén* pig tripe deep-fried, then stir-fried (Beijing)

L8e 車⊗　the "car" radical

L8e.4a 軟　*ruǎn* soft

軟炸　*ruǎn zhá* deep-fried in egg batter

軟筋　*ruǎn jīn* gluten puff; vegetarian steak

軟奔魚　*ruǎn bēn yú* fried whole fish with sweet and sour sauce (Guizhou)

L8e.4b 斬　*zhǎn* to chop off

斬魚圓　*zhǎn yú yuán* fish balls in soup (Zhejiang)

L8e.12 轉　*zhuǎn* to turn

生燒大轉彎　*shēng shāo dà zhuǎn wàn* stewed chicken wings (Sichuan)

L8f 臣⊗　the "minister" radical

L8f.8 頤之時棗糕　*yi zhi shí zǎo gāo* steamed cake with preserved fruits (Sichuan)

L8f.14 臨 *lín* to approach
四菇臨門 *sì gū lín mén* four kinds of mushroom in soup (Taiwan)

L8* Miscellaneous Eight-Stroke Left Halves

L8*1 乳 *rǔ* milk

腐乳 *fǔ rǔ* fermented bean curd; bean cheese
乳腐肉 *rǔ fǔ ròu* pork stewed with fermented bean curd
南乳 *nán rǔ* red fermented bean curd
乳酪 *rǔ lào* curds
乳扇 *rǔ shàn* a kind of yak milk cheese
乳豬 *rǔ zhū* suckling pig
乳鴿 *rǔ gē* squab

L8*3 彩 *cǎi* color; stage makeup

七彩魚塊 *qī cǎi yú kuài* seven-color fish chunks (with mixed shredded vegetables in thick sauce)

L8*4a 野 *yě* open country; wild (of animals)

野餐子鷄 *yě cān zǐ jī* picnic chicken (marinated boneless chicken and pickles, wrapped in lotus leaf and charcoal-grilled; Sichuan)
野鷄 *yě jī* pheasant
野鴨 *yě yā* wild duck
野豬 *yě zhū* wild boar

L8*4b 教 *jiào* to teach

教門菜 *jiào mén cài* Moslem cooking

L8*5 瓠 *hù* bottle gourd

瓠瓜 *hù guā* bottle gourd

酉
金
豆
足
車
臣
乳
彩
野
教
瓠
賜
鶉
護

L8*10 賜 *sì* to bestow (used as a pun for 四 four, as in next item)

賜喜雙發 *sì xǐ shuāng fā* appetizer course consisting of four plates, each containing two different foods (Taiwan)

L8*13 鵓 *bó* a type of pigeon

鵓鴣 *bó gu* a type of pigeon

L8*15 護 *hù* to protect

護國菜 *hù guó cài* sweet-potato leaves and straw mushrooms in thick sauce (Guangdong)

L9 Nine-Stroke Left Halves

L9a 𦍌⊗ the "ancient" element

L9a.4 散 *sàn* to scatter
散丹 *sàn dān* lamb tripe
散旦 *sàn dàn* lamb tripe
奶湯散丹 *nǎi tāng sàn dān* lamb tripe in thick soup (Beijing)

L9a.13 鵲 *què* magpie
鵲巢野雞絲 *què chǎo yě jī sī* shredded pheasant in "magpie nest" (deep-fried basket made of shredded vegetables)
鵲橋慶相逢 *què qiáo qìng xiāng féng* meeting at the magpie bridge celebration (steamed soup of pigeon and ham in winter melon; Guangdong)

L9* Miscellaneous Nine-Stroke Left Halves

L9*4a 乾 *gān* dry

乾煸牛肉絲 *gān bian niú ròu sī* dry-cooked shredded beef (Sichuan)
乾菜 *gān cài* dried cabbage

L9*4b 新 *xīn* fresh, new

新姜炒牛肉絲 *xīn jiáng chǎo niú ròu sī* shredded beef stir-fried with sprouting ginger

新加坡 *xīn jiā pō* Singapore

新風鷄 *xīn fēng jī* chicken cubes steamed on lotus leaves (Zhejiang)

L9*4c 就 *jiù* exact

就手 *jiù shǒu* pig's trotters

L9*6 群 *qún* nonstandard character used in the following compound

群翅 *qún chì* a type of shark fin

L9*8 靚 *jìng* to ornament

青蘿蔔 *jìng luó bo* a medium-sized white radish

L9*10 類 *lèi* category (in headings of sections of menus)

L9*13a 鶧 *ying* nonstandard character used in the following compound

鶧嘴龜 *ying zuǐ guī* a type of turtle

L9*13b 鶉 *ān* quail

鶉鶉 *ān chun* quail

L10 Ten-Stroke Left Halves

L10a 食⊗ the "eating" radical

L10a.5 飯 *fàn* cooked rice

炒飯 *chǎo fàn* fried rice

昔
乾
新
就
群
靚
類
鵤
鶴
〔食
革
剝
都
殼
雜
龍〕
鵤

L10a.6a 餃子　*jiǎo zi* Chinese ravioli (fried, steamed, or boiled)
水餃　*shuǐ jiǎo* boiled ravioli
蒸餃　*zhēng jiǎo* steamed ravioli
鍋貼餃子　*guō tiē jiǎo zi* scorch-fried ravioli; pot stickers
菠餃魷魚　*bō jiǎo yóu yú* squid with spinach-wrapped minced meat

L10a.6b 餅　see L10a.8
L10a.6c 飽　alternative form of E2b.4a 包 *bāo* steamed filled bun
L10a.6d 餌　*ěr* bait
餌飫　*ěr kuì* cakes of mashed boiled rice

L10a.8 餅　*bǐng* cake (pancake, flat bun, meat pattie)
煎蝦餅　*jiān xiā bǐng* slow-fried shrimp croquettes
燒餅　*shāo bǐng* griddle-fried flat bun (served with Monoglian barbecue)
蘿白餅　*luó bái bǐng* griddle-fried flat bun with shredded turnip filling

L10a.9a 餑　*bē* sweet pastry
L10a.9b 餚　see T2*7 肴

L10a.11a 餛　*hún* wonton
餛飩　*hún tún* wonton
餛飩大王　*hún tún dà wáng* wonton with vegetables in soup
L10a.11b 餡　*xiàn* stuffing of ground meat
餡餅　*xiàn bǐng* fried cakes with ground meat filling
L10a.11c 饃　*mó* steamed bread

L10a.14 饅　*mán* steamed bread
饅頭　*mán tou* steamed bread
饅首　*mán shǒu* steamed bread

L10b 革⊗　the "leather" radical

L10b.8 鞘　*qiào* scabbard
海鞘　*hǎi qiào* sea squirt

L10b.10 鞭　*biān* whip
牛鞭　*niú biān* ox penis
海狗鞭　*hǎi gǒu biān* seal penis

L10* Miscellaneous Ten-Stroke Left Halves

L10*2 剝 *bō* to peel

剝皮菊花心 *bō pí jú huā xīn* fried sliced boiled chicken with skin (lit., "peel skin chrysanthemum heart"; Jiangxi)

L10*4 都 *dū* capital; Peking (Beijing)

成都 *chéng dū* Chengtu (capital of Sichuan)

京都肉絲 *jīng dū ròu sī* shredded pork in fried bean paste (Beijing)

都三樣 *dū sān yàng* stewed lamb brain, eye, and bone marrow (Beijing)

L10*6 殼 *ké* shell, crust

蟹殼黃 *xiè ké huáng* meat-filled raised buns, pan-fried (Shanghai)

L10*8 雜 *zá* miscellaneous

雜碎 *zá sui* (JAAHP SÙI) chop suey ("odds and ends")
雜拌凉菜 *zá bàn liáng cài* cold mixed vegetables
清湯雜燴 *qīng tāng zá huì* fancy mixed ingredients in clear soup

L10*9 龍 *lóng* dragon

龍蝦 *lóng xiā* lobster
龍鬚菜 *lóng xū cài* asparagus (lit., "dragon beard vegetable")
龍鬚燕丸 *lóng xū yān wàn* dragon beard meatball soup (with meatballs rolled in shredded dried pork sheet to give hairy appearance; Fujian)
龍井茶 *lóng jǐng chá* dragon well tea (green)
龍眼 *lóng yǎn* longan (lit., "dragon eye")
龍爪菜 *lóng zhuǎ cài* fernbrake (lit., "dragon claw vegetable")
龍全魚 *lóng quán yú* deep-fried whole fish with pork stuffing (Fujian)
龍脷 or 龍利 *lóng lí* flounder, sole

昔乾新就群靚類鵝鶉食革剝都殼雜〔龍〕鵪

龍昇鳳舞　*lóng shēng fēng wǔ* dragon-phoenix dance
(fancy cold appetizer plate in shape of that scence)

L10*13 鶉　*chún* quail

鵪鶉　*ān chún* quail
鶉蛋　*chún dàn* quail egg

L11　Eleven-Stroke Left Halves

L11a 奚⊗

L11a.8 雞　*jī* chicken (alternate form of L11a.13)

L11a.13 鷄　*jī* chicken
鷄油　*jī yóu* chicken fat
鷄蛋　*jī dàn* chicken egg
田鷄　*tián jī* frog
鷄毛菜　*jī máo cài* brussel sprout or other cabbage sprout
鷄泡魚　*jī pào yú* blowfish (Jap. *fugu*)
鷄冠　*jī guān* cock's comb
鷄紅　*jī hóng* jellied chicken blood (Hakka, Guangdong)

L11b 馬⊗　the "horse" radical

L11b.6 駝　*tuó* camel
燒駝掌　*shāo tuó zhǎng* roast camel's foot

L11b.18 驢　*lǘ* donkey
驢打滾兒　*lǘ dǎ gǔr* rolling donkeys (boiled sticky-rice
flour dumplings rolled in bean-flour and nut coating)

L11c 夋⊗　See E11a

L11*　Miscellaneous Eleven-Stroke Left Halves

L11*13 鷓　*zhè* partridge

鷓鴣　*zhè gū* partridge

L12 Twelve-Stroke Left Halves

L12a 奐⊗ alternate form of L13a

L12*5 瓢 *piáo* bottle gourd

干瓢 *gān piáo* dried bottle gourd

L12*10 鹹 *xiān* salty (see U10b)

鹹菜 *xiān cài* salt-pickled vegetables

L12*11 歸 *guí* return

歸巢錦雞 *guí cháo jǐn jī* pheasant returns to nest (stir-fried shredded meat served over nest of seaweed [konbu]; Sichuan)

L13 Thirteen-Stroke Left Halves

L13a 魚⊗ the "fish" radical (many of the characters listed under this radical are nonstandard "fancy" versions of more common characters to which the "fish" radical has been added; in most cases, if the character denotes a species, it is usually combined with 魚 *yú* "fish", e.g., "squid" is normally written 魷魚 rather than simply 魷)

L13a.3 魟 *gōng* ray

L13a.4a 魷 *yóu* squid
L13a.4b 鯔 *chǐ* mackerel
L13a.4c 魪   KAAI flat fish
L13a.4d 鯋 *shā* shark
L13a.4e 黿 *yuán* turtle

L13a.5a 鮒 *fù* silver carp; perch
L13a.5b 鮭 *huì* sole
L13a.5c 鮓 *zhá* salt fish; jellyfish
L13a.5d 鮇 *wèi* barbel, swordfish

奚
馬
麥
鷉
隺
瓢
鹹
歸
[魚]
骨
鄂
點
麒
翻
影
歐

L13a.5e 魬 *bǎn* sole, flounder
L13a.5f 魽 *gan* yellowtail
L13a.5g 魴 *fǎng* bream
L13a.5h 鮃 *píng* sole

L13a.6a 鮮 *xiān* fresh
海鮮 *hǎi xiān* seafood
海鮮醬 *hǎi xiān jiàng* (HÓI SÌN JEUNG) hoisin sauce
三鮮湯 *sān xiān tāng* three fresh ingredient soup (e.g.,
    chicken, shrimp, and abalone)
鮮燉咸 *xiān dùn xián* fresh and salted pork stewed
    together
L13a.6b 鮭 *guī* salmon
L13a.6c 鮫 *jiāo* shark; mackerel
馬鮫魚 *mǎ jiāo yú* mackerel
L13a.6d 鮎 *nián* catfish
L13a.6e 鮐 *tái* globefish; mackerel
L13a.6f 鮥 WUH shad
L13a.6g 鮀 TÒH snakefish

L13a.7a 鮑 *bào* abalone
鮑魚菇 *bào yú gū* oyster mushroom (a variety of girolle)
L13a.7b 鯎 *zhe* dried fish
L13a.7c 鮚 *jié* oyster
L13a.7d 鮪 *wei* tuna; sturgeon
L13a.7e 鮨 *qí* fish paste
L13a.7f 鮋 YĀU bullhead
L13a.7g 鮞 *ér* roe

L13a.8a 鯉 *lǐ* carp
L13a.8b 鯡 *fei* herring
L13a.8c 鯇 *huǎn* grass carp
L13a.8d 鯆 *hui* sturgeon; catfish
L13a.8e 鮠 NGÀIH shad
L13a.8f 鮦 *tong* snakefish
L13a.8g 鯆 *pū* ray
L13a.8h 鯠 *lai* eel

L13a.9a 鯖 *qīng* mackerel
L13a.9b 鯟 *liàn* shad
L13a.9c 鯪 *líng* dace; carp
L13a.9d 鯬 *lǐ* snakehead mullet

L13a.9e 鰍 *qiū* loach (small mud-dwelling eel)
L13a.9f 鯰 *niàn* catfish
L13a.9g 鯨 *jīng* whale

L13a.10a 鯧 *chāng* pomfret
L13a.10b 鰂 *zé* cuttlefish
L13a.10c 鰌 *qiū* loach (small mud-dwelling eel)
L13a.10d 鯤 *kun* crucian carp
L13a.10e 鰈 *dié* sole
L13a.10f 鯛 *diāo* porgy, bream
L13a.10g 鰔 *xiān* croaker
L13a.10h 鯽 *ji* silver carp, bass
L13a.10i 鯣 *yì* bonito
L13a.10j 鰉 *huáng* sturgeon
L13a.10k 鯷 *tí* anchovy
L13a.10l 鰠 *sāu* carp; catfish

L13a.11a 鯿 *biān* freshwater bream
L13a.11b 鰣 *shí* shad
L13a.11c 鰩 *yáo* ray
L13a.11d 鰭 *qí* fish fin
L13a.11e 鰜 *jiān* sole
L13a.11f 鱄 *pū* ray

L13a.12a 鶬 *chāng* pomfret
L13a.12b 鰱 *lián* silver carp, catfish
白鰱 *bǎi lián* silver carp
L13a.12c 鱆 *zhāng* octopus
L13a.12d 鯔 *zi* gray mullet
L13a.12e 鱒 *zùn* trout
L13a.12f 鱄 *zhuan* fine fish
沙鱄魚 *shā zhuan yú* whiting
L13a.12g 鮔 *zhuī* nonstandard character used in following compound
油鮔魚 *yóu zhuī yú* smelt
L13a.12h 鰾 *biào* fish maw (airbag)
L13a.12i 鰛 *wēn* sardine
L13a.12j 鲂 *fǎng* bream

L13a.13a 鰽 *cáo* herring
鰽白 *cáo bái* white herring
盲鰽魚 *máng cáo yú* sea perch

奚
馬
麥
鷌
奅
瓢
鹹
歸
⌐魚
骨
鄂
點
麒
翻
影
歐

L13a.13b 鰳 *lè* shad; Chinese herring
L13a.13c 鱈 *xuě* cod
L13a.13d 鰙 DAAHP sole
L13a.13e 鳇 *huáng* sturgeon

L13a.14a 鰻 *mán* conger eel
L13a.14b 鲟 *xún* sturgeon
鲟骨 *xún gǔ* edible cartilage from head of large fish
L13a.14c 鳝 *shàn* small freshwater eel
清蒸青鳝 *qīng zhēng qīng shàn* steamed freshwater eel
L13a.14d 鰹 *jiān* bonito
L13a.14e 鰼 *xí* mudfish
L13a.14f 鱏 *xún* ray; sturgeon
L13a.14g 鱐 *sù* dried fish

L13a.15a 鳝 *shàn* freshwater eel
L13a.15b 鲚 *ji* mullet
L13a.15c 鳢 *lǐ* snakehead mullet
L13a.15d 鲙 *guì* chopped fish

L13a.16 鳣 *zhān* sturgeon; eel

L13a.18a 鲈 *lú* perch; sea bass
L13a.18b 鲚 *jì* anchovy

L13a.22 鱺 *lí* eel

L13b 骨⊗ the "bone" radical

L13b.14 髓 *suǐ* bone marrow
炒桂花脊髓 *chǎo guì huā jǐ suǐ* scrambled egg with pork
marrow (Guangdong)

L13b.15 體 *tǐ* body (also written 体)
乳猪全體 *rǔ zhū quán tǐ* roast whole suckling pig

L13* Miscellaneous Thirteen-Stroke Left Halves

L13*3 影 *yǐng* shadow, image

春竹雙影 *chún zhū shuāng yǐng* two shadows of spring
bamboo (stewed yellow asparagus and green kale;
Guangdong)

L13*4 鄂 *è* Hubei Province

鄂菜　*è cài* Hubei cuisine

L13*6 點 *diǎn* dot

點心　*diǎn xīn* (DÍM SÀM) pastry; Cantonese pastry
　　brunch
鹹點　*xián diǎn* salty dimsam
甜點　*tián diǎn* sweet dimsam

L13*8a 麒 *qí* male unicorn

麒麟　*qí lín* unicorn (the second character refers to the
　　female)
麒麟石斑　*qí lín shí bān* fancy sliced fish steamed with
　　ham and bamboo shoots

L13*8b 翻 *fān* to turn over

翻炸去刺葡萄魚　*fān zhá qù cì pú tao yú* deep-fried
　　whole fish with grape sweet and sour sauce (Anhui)

L15 Fifteen-Stroke Left Halves

L15*4 歐 *ōu* Europe

歐歐湯　*ōu ōu tāng* O-O soup (roughly, hot and sour soup
　　without the hotness and sourness)

T1 One-Stroke Tops

T1a ⊗ the "one" top

T1a.1 二 *èr* two
炒二冬　*chǎo èr dōng* stir-fried two winters (bamboo
　　shoot and dried mushroom)

二竹　*èr zhú* a type of bean curd skin

排骨二吃　*pái gǔ èr chī* spareribs eaten two ways (e.g., a plate with sweet and sour spareribs on one side and deep-fried spareribs on the other)

湖南二樣　*hú nán èr yàng* two Hunanese dishes served on one plate

二面黃　*èr miàn huáng* noodles pan-browned on both sides (lit., "two sides yellow")

T1a.2 三　*sān* three

涼拌三絲　*liáng bàn sān sī* shredded three ingredient cold plate

一雞三味　*yì jī sān wèi* one chicken cooked three ways

三丁包子　*sān dīng bāo zi* steamed dumplings stuffed with three diced ingredients (Yangzhou)

炒三冬　*chǎo sān dōng* stir-fried three winters (bamboo shoot, dried mushroom, and preserved cabbage)

三司會審　*sān sī huì shěn* pork liver, lung, and heart with pineapple and vegetables (Taiwan)

沙鍋三白　*shā guō sān bái* casserole of three white things (e.g., pork, pig tripe, and chitterlings; or abalone, asparagus, and chicken)

三洞橋軟燒大蒜鯰魚　*sān dòng qiáo ruǎn shāo dà suàn liàn yú* catfish braised with garlic and hot bean sauce (Sichuan)

三文魚　*sān wén yú* salmon

三線魚　*sān xiàn yú* silver bass

三錢魚　*sān qián yú* silver bass

三黎魚　*sān lí yú* hilsa herring

三汁麵　*sān zhī miàn* noodles with curry sauce

三邊腐竹　*sān biān fǔ zhú* a type of dried bean curd skin

三層樓　*sān céng lóu* three-story building (layers of different vegetables; Hunan)

T1a.3a 元　*yuán* primary; dollar

元宵　*yuán xiāo* New Year's dumplings (sweet sesame filling in glutinous rice-flour wrapping)

元蹄　*yuán tí* pig's feet

一元五毛　*yì yuán wǔ máo* $1.50

元寶肉　*yuán bǎo ròu* a part of leg of lamb

元魚　*yuán yú* turtle

元菜　*yuán cài* turtle
元茄　*yuán qié* eggplant (real eggplant, as opposed to
　　番茄 *fān qié* "barbarian eggplant" = tomato)
T1a.3b 云　*yún* to say; cloud (abbreviation of T9a.4b)

T1a.7 豆　*dòu* bean
豆腐　*dòu fu* bean curd
豆腐皮　*dòu fu pí* bean curd skin
豆皮　*dòu pí* bean curd skin
豆沙　*dòu sa* sweet bean paste
豆沙鍋餅　*dòu sa guō bīng* pancakes filled with sweet
　　bean paste
豆渣　*dòu zhā* bean curd dregs
豆花　*dòu huā* unset bean curd
豆瓣醬　*dòu bàn jiàng* chili bean paste (Sichuan)·
豆瓣魚　*dòu bàn yú* fish simmered in soy sauce and chili
　　bean paste
豆豉油　*dòu chǐ yóu* salt-free soy sauce
豆角　*dòu jiǎo* yard-long green beans
豆仔　*dòu zi* yard-long green beans
豆鷄　*dòu jī* vegetarian chicken (made from bean curd
　　skin)
豆魚　*dòu yú* bean sprouts and jellyfish skin, wrapped in
　　bean curd skin and pan-fried (Sichuan)
豆苗　*dòu miáo* pea shoots
豆枝　*dòu zhī* soybean stick
豆蔻　*dòu kòu* nutmeg

T2 Two-Stroke Tops

T2a 亠　the "hat" radical

T2a.1 ㇀　popular form of 七 *qī* seven

T2a.2a 六　*liù* six
六安茶　*liù ān chá* (LUHK ON CHÀH) luk on tea
T2a.2b 丷　popular form of 八 *bā* eight

一
艹
人
亼
厶
公
余
肴
眞

T2a.4a 市　*shì* market
市的　*shì dì* (SÍH DĪK) steak
上市　*shàng shì* for sale, available
T2a.4b 玄　*xuán* black
糟汁炒玄光　*zāo zhī chǎo xuán guāng* beef tripe fried
　　with wine lees

T2a.7 京　*jīng* capital; Peking (Beijing)
北京　*běi jīng* Peking
北京烤鴨　*běi jīng kǎo yā* Peking duck
京都肉絲　*jīng dū ròu sī* shredded pork in fried bean paste
　　(Beijing)
京菜　*jīng cài* Peking cuisine
京蘇菜　*jīng sū cài* Nanking-Soochow (Nanjing-Suzhou)
　　cuisine
京溜蝦鬆　*jīng liū xiā sōng* minced shrimp with Peking
　　sauce
京葱　*jīng cōng* leek

T2a.11a 毫　*háo* ten cents
T2a.11b 高　*gāo* high
高麗　*gāo li* Korea
高麗參　*gāo li shēn* ginseng
高麗菜　*gāo li cài* cabbage
高粱　*gāo liáng* sorghum
T2a.11c 烹　*pēng* to cook

T2a.13 裹　*guǒ* to bind
裹蒸糭　*guǒ zhēng jiòng* Chinese tamale

T2a.16 膏　*gāo* ointment, paste
醬油膏　*jiàng yóu gāo* bean paste
竹蓀肝膏湯　*zhú sūn gān gāo tāng* liver paste and
　　bamboo shoot soup (Sichuan)

T2a.19 甕菜　*wèng cài* water spinach (generally cooked
　　quickly with garlic and shrimp sauce; Guangdong)

T2b 亼　another form of the "man" radical (cf.
L2a)

T2b.1 个　*gè* classifier for miscellaneous things (simplified
form of L2a.10 個)

T2b.4 全　*quán* whole
糖醋全魚　*táng cù quán yú* sweet and sour whole fish
八寶全鴨　*bā bǎo quán yā* whole duck with eight-treasure stuffing
全家福　*quán jiā fú* happy family (mixed seafoods and vegetables)
爆全丁　*bào quán dīng* quick-fried mixed diced ingredients

T2b.5 合　*hé* to combine (also used as simplified form of T2b.10)
合桃　*hé tao* walnut
合桃鷄丁　*hé tao jī dīng* diced chicken with walnuts (Guangdong)
百合　*bǎi hé* lily
合時瓜菜類　*hé shí guā cài lèi* seasonal vegetable dishes

T2b.10 盒　*hé* box
冬菇盒　*dōng gū hé* stuffed black mushrooms
菜盒子　*cài hé zi* a type of filled fried ravioli or turnover

T2b.12 會　*huì* to meet (used in names of dishes in which precooked ingredients are mixed into something being cooked with a gravy)

T2c 仐⊗

T2c.4 年　*nián* year
年糕　*nián gāo* New Year rice-flour pasta

T2c.6 每　see T2d.7

T2c.7 每　*měi* each
每碟六毛　*měi dié liù máo* sixty cents per dish

T2d 台⊗

T2d.4 台灣　*tái wān* Taiwan
台北　*tái běi* Taipei

T2d.9 參　*shēn* short for 海參 *hǎi shēn* sea cucumber

一
丶
八
丷
厶
囗
公
尒
肴
眞

T2* Miscellaneous Two-Stroke Tops

T2*2 公 *gōng* public
公司 *gōng sī* company
公保 *gōng bǎo* nonstandard simplifed form of 宮保
T4b.9

T2*5 氽 *cuān* blanch, dip in hot liquid
油氽魷魚 *yóu cuān yóu yú* squid dipped in hot oil

T2*7 肴 *yáo* mixed
肴肉 *yáo ròu* jellied salt pork

T2*10 眞 alternate form of T8*3

T3 Three-Stroke Tops

T3a 圭 or 士 the "earth" and "gentleman" radicals (the difference between them is ignored here)

T3a.2 去 see U5r

T3a.4a 吉 *jí* lucky, auspicious
吉燒鰻魚 *jí shāo mán yú* see eel slices with pork filling, deep-fried (Fujian)
吉利蝦綉球 *jí lì xiā xiù qiú* shrimp balls rolled in chopped toasted bread and deep-fried (Guangdong)
吉利千層 *jí lì qiān céng* mock roast fowl (made of sheets of bean curd skin)
T3a.4b 赤 *chì* red (see U7j)

T3a.11a 喜 *xǐ* happiness
喜爆雙丁 *xǐ bào shuāng dīng* diced shrimp and chicken quick-fried with bean paste
T3a.11b 壹 fraud-proof form of — *yī* one

T3a.12 壽 *shòu* longevity
壽桃 *shòu táo* peach-shaped buns with sweet filling
壽眉茶 *shòu méi chá* a kind of black tea

T3a.14a 賣　*mài* to sell (used as a short from of the following item)

燒賣　*shāo mài* (SÌU MAAIH) open-ended steamed ravioli (Guangdong)

T3a.14b 壺　*hú* jug, teapot

一壺茶　*yì hú chá* a pot of tea

T3b 𡨄

T3b.11 煎　*jiān* to pan-fry slowly

煎麵　*jiān miàn* pan-browned noodles

油煎子鶏　*yóu jiān zǐ jī* pan-fried chicken

煎堆　*jiān duǐ* (JÌN DEÙI) balls of glutinous rice dough with sweet filling, deep-fried

煎茶　*jiān chá* a Japanese variety of green tea

T3b.12 慈　*cí* benevolent (used as simplified form of L6a.11b)

慈菇　*cí gū* arrowroot

糯米慈　*nuó mǐ cí* sweet-filled boiled sticky-rice flour dumplings

T3c 𡨄　see T4a

T3* Miscellaneous Three-Stroke Tops

T3*3 尖 *jiān* point

筍尖　*sǔn jiān* tip of bamboo shoot

T3*6a 奇 *qí* strange

奇花吐艷　*qí huā tǔ yàn* strange flowers in bloom (broccoli spears with crabmeat and crab cream)

T3*6b 盲 *máng* blind

盲鰽魚　*máng cáo yú* sea perch

T3*7 冠 *guàn* crown, cock's comb

T3*8 貢 *gòng* tribute (to an overlord)

貢丸湯　*gòng wàn tāng* fish ball soup
貢鴨　*gòng yā* pressed duck

T4 Four-Stroke Tops

T4a 艹 the "grass" radical

T4a.3a 芋　*yù* potato, tuber
芋頭　*yù tóu* taro
芋角　*yù jiǎo* (WÙH GOK) taro croquette (Guangdong)
家鄉炸芋蝦　*jiā xiāng zhà yù xiā* shrimp coated with
　　shredded potato, deep-fried
T4a.3b 芒　*máng* a kind of grass
芒果　*máng guǒ* mango

T4a.4a 花　*huā* flower
花卷　*huā juǎn* fancy-rolled steamed bread
腰花　*yāo huā* fancy-cut kidney slices
花生　*huā shēng* peanut
花椒　*huā jiāo* brown (Sichuan) pepper
花瓜　*huā guā* pickled cucumber
花素餃　*huā sù jiǎo* vegetarian ravioli
花枝　*huā zhī* cuttlefish
炸花枝丸　*zhá huā zhī wàn* deep-fried cuttlefish balls
　　(Taiwan)
菜花　*cài huā* cauliflower
花柳菜　*huā liǔ cài* broccoli
花菇　*huā gū* dried Chinese mushroom
T4a.4b 芝麻　*zhī má* sesame
芝麻油　*zhī má yóu* sesame oil
芝麻醬　*zhī má jiàng* sesame paste
芝麻如意　*zhī má rú yi* sesame cakes filled with bean
　　paste
芝加哥　*zhī jiā gē* (JI GÀ GŌ) Chicago
芝士　*zhī shì* cheese
T4a.4c 芥菜　*jiè cài* Chinese mustard green
芥末　*jiè mo* mustard
芥蘭 or 芥藍　*jiè lán* (GAAI LÀAHN) Chinese broccoli

芥蘭菜　*jiè lán cài* kohlrabi

T4a.4d 芹菜　*qín cài* celery

T4a.4e 芫荽　*yán suī* coriander leaf

T4a.4f 芙蓉　*fú róng* (FÙH YÙHNG) Chinese omlet (foo yung); egg-coated ingredients

芙蓉蟹　*fú róng xiè* crab foo yung

T4a.4g 茉　*mò* jasmine

茉芋　*mò yú* jelly made from a tuber (Jap. *konnyaku*)

茉芋燒鴨　*mò yú shāo yā* duck red-cooked with konnyaku (Sichuan)

T4a.4h 芯　*xīn* alternate form of U4h, used in following compound

菜芯　*cài xīn* flowering cabbage

T4a.4i 杬　Simplified form of T4a.12h

T4a.5a 芽　*yá* sprout

豆芽　*dòu yá* bean sprout

T4a.5b 苹　*píng* duckweed (popular form of T4a.18b)

苹果　*píng guo* apple

T4a.5c 茅　*máo* couch grass

茅苔酒　*máo tāi jiǔ* mau-tai brandy

香茅　*xiāng máo* lemon grass

T4a.5d 苤　*piě* kohlrabi

T4a.5e 甘　*gān* licorice root

T4a.5f 芭　*bā* banana

T4a.6a 茶　*chá* tea

五香茶葉蛋　*wǔ syāng chá yé dàn* five-spice tea-leaf eggs (boiled eggs with cracked shells, marinated in tea-leaf and spice mixture)

沙茶牛肉　*shā chá niú ròu* beef slices in satay sauce (esp. the Hunanese version, which uses powdered tea leaves)

茶瓜　*chá guā* tea melon (a kind of pickled gourd)

T4a.6b 苦　*kǔ* bitter

苦瓜　*kǔ guā* bitter melon

T4a.6c 茨　*cí* potato; tuber

甜茨　*tián cí* sweet potato

茨菇　*cí gū* arrowhead

五香茨仔角　*wǔ xiāng cí zǐ jiǎo* five-spice potato puffs

T4a.6d 茸　*róng* mince

鶏茸　*jī róng* minced chicken
金茸　*jīn róng* gold needle mushroom
T4a.6e 苔菜　*tái cài* moss; also a type of seaweed and a
　　type of fern
苔菜烤肉　*tái cài kǎo ròu* roast pork with deep-fried fern
　　leaves (Jiangsu-Zhejiang)
菜苔　*cài tái* broccoli
T4a.6f 英　*yīng* hero; English
英鯸　*yīng yóu* dried squid
英德茶　*yīng dé chá* a kind of black tea

T4a.7a 草　*cǎo* grass
草菇 or 草菰　*cǎo gū* straw mushroom
草頭　*cǎo tóu* clover, trefoil
草鶏　*cǎo jī* hen
草魚　*cǎo yú* river carp
草果　*cǎo guǒ* cardamom
草莓　*cǎo méi* strawberry
T4a.7b 茄　*qié* eggplant; tomato
茄子　*qié zi* eggplant
茄瓜　*qié guā* Chinese (long, thin) eggplant
番茄　*fān qié* tomato (lit., "barbarian eggplant")
茄泥　*qié ní* mashed eggplant
茄汁蝦仁　*qié zhī xiā rén* shelled shrimps in tomato sauce
T4a.7c 華　*huá* splendid, elegant; China
中華　*zhōng huá* China
T4a.7d 苟杞　nonstandard variant of L4a.7c 枸杞 *gǒu qí*
　　boxthorn
T4a.7e 荳　WÙHN celery

T4a.8a 菜　*cài* vegetable; cuisine; dish
菜花　*cài huā* cauliflower
菜心　*cài xīn* flowering cabbage
菜遠　*cài yuǎn* bok choi stems
菜瓜　*cài guā* cucumber
菜蔬　*cài shū* vegetable
菜果　*cài guǒ* kohlrabi
菜膽　*cài dàn* heart of Chinese mustard green
京菜　*jīng cài* Peking cuisine
菜捲　*cài juǎn* stuffed cabbage rolls
菜甫煎蛋　*cài fǔ jiān dàn* omlet with salted radish
　　(Taiwan)

T4a.8b 荷　*hé* lotus
鮮荷蒸鴿　*xiān hé zhēng gē* pigeon steamed in lotus leaf
荷葉鴨子　*hé yè yā zi* duck pieces steamed in lotus leaves
荷蘭豆　*hé làn dòu* pea pods (lit., "Holland beans")
荷包蛋　*hé bāo dàn* eggs fried in crescent shape, with soy
　　sauce and vinegar
T4a.8c 萍果　*píng guo* apple
T4a.8d 茴香　*huí xiāng* fennel
小茴　*xiǎo huí* fennel
茴香菜　*huí xiāng cài* fennel root
大茴　*dà huí* anise
T4a.8e 莧菜　*xiàn cài* a spinach-like vegetable
T4a.8f 堇　*jǐn* an edible fern
T4a.8g 萊豆　*lái dòu* string bean
T4a.8h 荳　*dòu* (see 豆 T1a.7)
荳角　*dòu jiǎo* string bean
T4a.8i 茼蒿菜　*tóng hāo cài* chrysanthemum greens

T4a.9a 菠菜　*bō cài* spinach
菠蘿　*bō luó* pineapple
菠菜餅　*bō cài bǐng* deep-fried spinach fritters
T4a.9b 菊　*jú* chrysanthemum
菊花茶　*jú huā chá* chrysanthemum flower tea
菊花魚羹鍋　*jú huā yú gēng guō* chrysanthemum flower
　　fish-stock hot pot (a fondue containing fish, chicken,
　　pork kidney, and vegetables; Sichuan)
炒菊紅　*chǎo jú hóng* stir-fried duck gizzards (Shanghai)
T4a.9c 荔枝　*lì zhī* lichee
荔芋　*lì yù* yam
荔茸　*lì róng* minced yam
T4a.9d 荸薺　*pí qí* water chestnut
T4a.9e 菱角　*líng jiao* water caltrops
T4a.9f 韮　*jiǔ* Chinese chive
韮菜水餃　*jiǔ cài shuǐ jiǎo* boiled ravioli with pork and
　　chive filling
T4a.9g 菌　*jùn* fresh mushroom
菌菜　*jùn cài* celery
T4a.9h 菰　Nonstandard variant of T4a.10c 菇 *gū*
　　mushroom
T4a.9i 蓯　*jiòng* a type of mushroom; Chinese tamale (an
　　alternate form of L6a.9a)

鶏蓯　*jī jiòng* a kind of mushroom that grows in Yunnan

T4a.9j 菓　*guǒ* fruit (usually written U9c 果)

粉菓　*fěn guǒ* ravioli with rice-flour skin

荣菓　*cài guǒ* kohlrabi

菓汁琵琶鴨　*guǒ zhī pí pá yā* crisp duck in fruit sauce (Guangdong)

T4a.9k 第　*tí* sprout

白汁老第扒翅　*bái zhī lǎo tí pá chì* shark fin braised with chicken and ham (Shanghai)

T4a.9l 苺　*méi* strawberry

T4a.9m 黄　*huáng* yellow (see U13a)

T4a.10a 葱　*cōng* scallion, green onion

洋葱　*yáng cōng* (round) onion

京葱　*jīng cōng* leek

葱頭　*cōng tóu* shallot

葱油餅　*cōng yóu bǐng* scallion pancake

葱爆羊肉片　*cōng bào yáng ròu piàn* lamb slices quick-fried with scallions (Beijing)

葱烤魚　*cōng kǎo yú* whole fish baked with scallions

T4a.10b 蒜　*suàn* garlic

蒜泥白肉　*suàn ní bái ròu* cold boiled pork with garlic puree (Beijing, Sichuan)

大蒜干貝　*dà suàn gān bèi* scallops with whole garlic cloves in spicy sauce (Sichuan)

青蒜　*qīng suàn* garlic leaves; leek

蒜苗　*suàn miáo* garlic shoots

T4a.10c 菇　*gū* mushroom

冬菇　*dōng gū* dried black mushroom

蘑菇　*mó gū* fresh mushroom

T4a.10d 葉　*yè* leaf

荷葉　*hé yè* lotus leaf

百葉　*bǎi yè* third stomach of cow

T4a.10e 葵　*kuí* sunflower

葵花　*kuí huā* sunflower

山葵　*shān kuí* horseradish

葵花鶏　*kuí huā jī* alternating slices of chicken and green vegetable, arranged in sunflower shape (Guangdong)

湯蒸葵花魚　*tāng zhēng kuí huā yú* fancy steamed fish slices with gravy

T4a.10f 萬　*wàn* ten thousand

T4a.10g 莖　*jīng* stalk
莖椰菜　*jīng yé cài* broccoli
T4a.10h 茸　*róng* mince (see T4a.6d)
T4a.10i 蘿　*luó* radish, turnip (alternate form of T4a.21)

T4a.11a 蓮　*lián* lotus root
蓮子　*lián zi* lotus seed
蓮蓉粽　*lián róng jiòng* Chinese tamale filled with lotus
　　seed paste
T4a.11b 蓋　*gài* to cover; lid
釀焗蟹蓋　*niàng jú xiè gài* baked stuffed crab shell
　　(Guangdong, Shanghai)
鷄片蓋飯　*jī piàn gài fàn* boiled rice topped with stir-fried
　　chicken slices
T4a.11c 落　*lào* to fall
落花生　*lào huā shēng* peanut
T4a.11d 蒙　*méng* to wrap; Mongolia
鷄蒙三色　*jī méng sān sè* three ingredients wrapped in
　　chicken slices (Sichuan)
蒙古　*méng gǔ* Mongolia
蒙古牛肉　*méng gǔ niú ròu* Mongolian beef (quick-fried
　　with scallions)
T4a.11e 葡　*pú* grape; Portugal
葡國　*pú guo* Portugal
葡國鷄　*pú guo jī* Portuguese chicken (with a creamy
　　curry sauce; Hong Kong)
葡汁焗四蔬　*pú zhī jú sì shū* four vegetables baked in
　　Portuguese sauce (same flavoring as in preceding dish)
葡萄　*pú tao* grape
T4a.11f 葫　*hú* bottle gourd
葫蘆　*hú lú* green gourd
葫蘆八寶鴨　*hú lú bā bǎo yā* stuffed boneless duck in
　　gourd shape
T4a.11g 蒲　*pú* rushes from which mats are woven
蒲瓜　*pú guā* smooth melon
T4a.11h 葷　*hūn* diet that includes meat and fish
葷菜　*hūn cài* nonvegetarian food
T4a.11i 蔗　*zhè* sugar cane
T4a.11j 蔌　*sù* vegetables
蔌菜　*sù cài* vegetarian dishes
T4a.11k 蔴　*má* see E3a.8 麻

丬宀圭木山口夕夂孚炎孟雀熊

T4a.11l 葯　*yào* see T4a.18c 藥

T4a.12a 蒸　*zhēng* to steam
蒸餃　*zhēng jiǎo* steamed ravioli
蒸鍋　*zhēng guō* steamer pot
T4a.12b 蔬　*shū* vegetables
蔬菜　*shū cài* vegetable dishes
T4a.12c 萵苣　*wō jù* lettuce
萵筍　*wō sǔn* lettuce
T4a.12d 葠　*shēn* alternate form of T2d.9
海葠　*hǎi shēn* sea cucumber
人葠　*rén shēn* ginseng
T4a.12e 蓀　*sūn* a kind of aromatic grass (fancy alternate
　　for T6a.5 笋 or T6a.8a 筍 *sǔn* bamboo shoot)
T4a.12f 純菜　*chún cài* water shield (*Brasenia purpuria*)
T4a.12g 蓴菜　*chún cài* water shield (*Brasenia purpuria*)
T4a.12h 橄　*gǎn* olive

T4a.13a 蕓豆　*yún dòu* long string bean
T4a.13b 蕃　*fán* abundant (used as variant of T7*6 番)
T4a.13c 蔻　*kòu* nutmeg
肉蔻　*ròu kòu* nutmeg
豆蔻　*dòu kòu* nutmeg
蔻仁　*kòu rén* cardamom
T4a.13d 蔭　*yìn* shade
蔭汁蚵　*yìn zhī hé* oysters stewed with black beans and
　　scallions (Taiwan)
T4a.13e 葒　*hóng* to flourish
雪裡葒　*xuě li hóng* red-in-snow (pickled *Brassica cernua*;
　　usually written with L7a.3 紅, though T4a.13e is the
　　original form)

T4a.14a 薰　*xūn* to smoke (meat or fish)
薰鷄　*xūn jī* smoked chicken
薰魚　*xūn yú* smoked fish; deep-fried marinated fish
　　steaks, served cold (Sichuan)
T4a.14b 燕　*yàn* swallow
燕窩　*yàn wō* swallow's nest
燕菜　*yàn cài* bird's nest (or such substitutes as agar-agar)
燕皮　*yàn pí* dried pork sheet (Fujian)
肉燕　*ròu yàn* dumplings (pork and shrimp filling
　　wrapped in dried pork sheet) in soup (Fujian)

T4a.14c 薄　*báo* thin
薄餅　*báo bǐng* thin pancake (such as is served with
　　Peking duck)
薄餅料　*báo bǐng liào* fancy stew served with thin pan-
　　cakes and assorted condiments (Amoy festival dish)
T4a.14d 薩　*sà* boddhisattva (Buddhist saint who forgoes
　　nirvana to remain on earth helping others)
薩門魚　*sà mén yú* salmon
薩其馬　*sà qí mǎ* fried dough strips with sesame, sugar,
　　and raisins (usually written with L3b.4a)
T4a.14e 薏　*yì* pearl barley
薏米　*yì mǐ* pearl barley

T4a.15a 薑　*jiāng* ginger
糖薑　*táng jiāng* sugar-preserved ginger
T4a.15b 薺　*jì* shepherd's purse (or other green vege-
　　table); *jí* caltrop, water chestnut
T4a.15c 蕎　*qiáo* buckwheat
蕎麵　*qiáo miàn* buckwheat noodles
蕎頭　*qiáo tóu* pickled scallion heads (eaten with pre-
　　served eggs or cold meats)
蕗蕎　*lù qiáo* bukeri garlic

T4a.16a 薯　*shǔ* potato; tuber
番薯　*fān shǔ* sweet potato
T4a.16b 藕　*ǒu* lotus root

T4a.17a 蘑　*mó* mushroom
蘑菇　*mó gū* mushroom
T4a.17b 藏　*cáng* to hide
蟹裡藏珠　*xiè li cáng zhū* pearls hidden in crab (steamed
　　crab with quail eggs inside the shell; Beijing)

T4a.18a 蘇　*sū* fancy alternate form of L8a.5; Soochow
　　(Suzhou)
蘇州　*sū zhōu* Soochow
江蘇　*jiāng su* Kiangsu
蘇造丸子　*sū zào wán zi* fragrant fried meatball soup
　　(Beijing)
蘇梅醬　*sū méi jiàng* plum sauce
蘇梅蝦　*sū méi xiā* shrimp with ground pork and plum
　　sauce

山 (radical column on left)
宀
丰
木
山
口
夕
夂
孚
吞
灸
孟
雀
熊

T4a.18b 蘋 *píng* apple
蘋果 *píng guo* apple
蘋果巴西 *píng guo bā xī* toffee apple
T4a.18c 藥 *yào* medicine
山藥 *shān yào* yucca
酒藥 *jiǔ yào* wine ball
T4a.18d 蘆 *lú* reed, gourd
蘆笋 or 蘆筍 *lú sǔn* asparagus
胡蘆 *hú lú* green gourd
T4a.18e 藠頭 *jiao tóu* a kind of shallot (Yunnan)

T4a.19a 蘭 *lán* orchid
蘭菜 *lán cài* Chinese broccoli
芥蘭 *jiè lán* Chinese broccoli
蘭州 *lán zhōu* Lanchow
蘭州醬肉 *lán zhōu jiàng ròu* Lanchow-style lamb stewed
　　in bean paste
蘭花 *lán huā* orchid
蘭花豆 *lán huā dòu* a cold bean dish
蘭花酥 *lán huā sū* orchid-shaped sweet flaky pastry
香蘭 *xiāng lán* vanilla
T4a.19b 藿 *huò* leaf of bean plant
炸藿香 *zhá huò xiāng* bean leaf, filled with sweet bean
　　paste and deep-fried (Shandong)

T4a.20 蘿 *luó* radish, turnip
蘿蔔 *luó bo* radish, turnip
蘿白 *luó bái* long white radish (Jap. *daikon*)
蘿蔔酥餅 *luó bo sū bǐng* deep-fried flaky pastry filled
　　with shredded pork and giant radish
胡蘿蔔 *hú luó bo* carrot (lit., "barbarian giant radish")

T4b ⌂ the "roof" radical

T4b.2 宁 see T4b.12b

T4b.4a 安 *ān* peace
安徽 *ān huī* Anhwei
六安茶 *liù ān chá* (LUHK ÒN CHÀH) a type of black
　　tea
T4b.4b 宋 *sòng* Song dynasty; common Chinese
　　surname

宋嫂麵　*sòng sǎo miàn* noodles with diced fish sauce (Sichuan)

T4b.5a 宝　*bǎo* treasure (simplified form of T4b.20 寶)
T4b.5b 宗　*zōng* ancestor
左宗棠鷄　*zuǒ zōng táng jī* General Zuo Zong Tang's chicken (diced chicken, batter-fried, then stir-fried with chili peppers; Hunan; General Zuo is regarded by many Chinese the way that General Sherman is regarded in Georgia)

T4b.7a 家　*jiā* home
家常豆腐　*jiā cháng dòu fu* home-style bean curd (fried bean curd slices, stir-fried with meat, vegetables, and hot bean sauce; Sichuan, Hunan)
家鄉豆腐　*jiā xiāng dòu fu* home-style bean curd
全家福　*quán jiā fú* happy family (mixed seafoods and vegetables in clear gravy)
家鄉扒鴨　*jiā xiāng pá yā* country-style stir-fried duck pieces
家庭貴州鷄　*jiā tíng guì zhou jī* home-style Kweichow chicken (small chunks of boneless chicken stir-fried with diced chili peppers)
T4b.7b 宣威　*quān wēi* town in Yunnan, celebrated for its ham
宣腿　*quān tuǐ* Quanwei ham

T4b.8 客　*kè* guest
客人　*kè ren* guest; portion
客家　*kè jiā* Hakka
客菜　*kè cài* Hakka cuisine
客飯　*kè fàn* table d'hote, prix fixe (a set dinner consisting of a set number of dishes, soup, and rice)

T4b.9 宮　*gōng* palace
宮保鷄丁　*gōng bǎo jī dīng* diced chicken stir-fried with charred chili peppers and peanuts (Sichuan)
宮燕　*gōng yàn* whole bird's nest

T4b.10 塞　*sāi* to stuff
茄子塞肉　*qié zi sāi ròu* eggplants stuffed with meat

T4b.11 富　*fù* wealthy

富貴火腿　*fù guì huǒ tuǐ* rich man's ham (ham baked with brown sugar in clay, eaten with bread, the name parodies "beggar's chicken"; Hunan)

T4b.12a 蜜　*mì* honey

蜜橘　*mì jú* tangerine

蜜柑　*mì gān* tangerine

蜜浸　*mì jìn* honey-soaked; in sweet syrup

蜜脯　*mì fǔ* sugar-preserved fruit

蜜瓜　*mì guā* honeydew melon

蜜錢　*mì qián* preserves, sweetmeats

蜜錢蕃薯　*mì qián fán shǔ* candied sweet potatoes

T4b.12b 寧波　*níng po* Ningpo (city in Zhejiang Province)

寧波湯團　*níng po tāng tuán* rice-flour dumplings with sesame filling

T4b.15 賽　*sài* compete, excel

賽螃蟹　*sài páng xie* mock crab foo yung (made with thin-sliced fish; Shantung)

賽蟹黃　*sài xiè huáng* mock crab roe (made from steamed fish and egg yolk)

T4b.20 寶　*bǎo* treasure

八寶鴨　*bā bǎo yā* eight-treasure duck (whole roast duck, boned and stuffed with sticky rice and diced meats and vegetables)

八寶飯　*bā bǎo fàn* eight-treasure sticky-rice pudding

寶塔花捲　*bǎo tǎ huā juǎn* treasure tower steamed rolled buns (with raisin and pork-fat filling; Zhejiang)

寶島串燒蝦　*bǎo dǎo chuàn shāo xiā* treasure island skewered grilled prawns (Taiwan)

T4c 青
⊗

T4c.5a 青　*qīng* green, blue

青豆　*qīng dòu* green pea

青椒　*qīng jiāo* green pepper

青菜　*qīng cài* bok choy (a type of cabbage, called 白菜 by the Cantonese)

炸青絲肉　*zhá qīng sī ròu* pork medallions coated with shredded cabbage and deep-fried

青江菜　*qīng jiāng cài* flowering cabbage

青梗菜　*qīng gěng cài* green cabbage
青瓜　*qīng guā* cucumber
青葱　*qīng cōng* leek
青菜花　*qīng cài huā* broccoli (lit., "green cauliflower")
青魚　*qīng yú* herring, mackerel
青花魚　*qīng huā yú* mackerel
青衣　*qīng yī* bream; bastard carp
青口　*qīng kǒu* mussel
青島　*qīng dǎo* Tsingtao (a city in Shandong province, after which a celebrated brand of beer is named)
青島啤酒　*qīng dǎo pí jiǔ* Tsingtao beer
T4c.5b 青　alternate form of T4c.5a

T4c.7 素　*sù* plain; vegetarian
素什錦　*sù shí jǐn* stir-fried fancy vegetarian ingredients
素火腿　*sù huǒ tuǐ* vegetarian ham (made from bean curd skin)
素烤鴨　*sù kǎo yā* vegetarian roast duck
素方　*sù fāng* deep-fried pie with vegetable filling wrapped in bean curd skin

T4d 木　the "tree radical" (cf. L4a)

T4d.4a 杏仁　*xìng rén* almond
杏仁鷄塊　*xìng rén jī kuài* chicken pieces with almonds
杏仁豆腐　*xìng rén dòu fu* almond curd (a sweet)
杏子　*xìng zi* apricot
T4d.4b 李　*lǐ* a common surname
李鴻章什碎　*lǐ hóng zhāng shí suì* original chop suey (popularly believed to have first been prepared for the Ching minister Lǐ Hóng Zhāng, 1823–1901, though the dish is actually much older)

T4e 山　the "mountain" radical

T4e.6 岩　*yán* cliff
岩鯉　*yán lǐ* a type of freshwater carp (Sichuan)

T4e.8 崧　*sōng* a mountain in Henan (nonstandard form of T10*8 嵩)
黃糖崧糕　*huáng táng sōng gāo* steamed cake filled with brown sugar (Guangdong)

七彩崧　*qī cǎi sōng* stir-fried diced meats and vegetables, wrapped in lettuce leaves

T4f 吕 the "mouth" radical (cf. L4c)

T4f.4 吴 alternate form of T4f.6

T4f.6 吳 *wú* Soochow (Suzhou)
吳山酥油餅　*wú shān sū yóu bǐng* Soochow deep-fried pies
吳家湯圓　*wú jiā tāng yuán* deep-fried glutinous rice ravioli with eight different fillings (some sweet, some salty)
吳淞蟹羹　*wú sōng xiè gēng* soft-shell crab chowder (named after a suburb of Shanghai)

T4g 夕 the "evening" radical

T4g.4a 名　*míng* name; famous
名茶　*míng chá* famous varieties of tea
名菜　*míng cài* specialty of the house
T4g.4b 多　*duō* many
多士　*duō sī* (DŌ SÌH) toast
蝦多士　*xiā duō sī* (HĀ DÒ SÌH) shrimp toast

T4h 冬

T4h.2 冬　*dōng* winter
冬菇　*dōng gū* dried black mushroom
兩冬　*liǎng dōng* two winters (bamboo shoot and black mushroom)
冬筍　*dōng sǔn* winter bamboo shoots
冬菜　*dōng cài* shredded preserved cabbage
三冬　*sān dōng* three winters (bamboo shoot, black mushroom, and preserved cabbage)
冬瓜　*dōng guā* winter melon
火腿冬瓜湯　*huǒ tuǐ dōng guā tāng* ham and winter melon soup
冬粉　*dōng fěn* peastarch noodles, bean threads

T4h.4 各　*gè* each, every
各式炒麵　*gè shì chǎo miàn* every variety of fried noodles

T4* Miscellaneous Four-Stroke Tops

T4*4a 孚 *fú* drumstick

清燉鶏孚 *qīng dùn jī fú* chicken drumsticks, coated with ground pork, deep-fried, then simmered in soup (Jiangsu)

T4*4b 吞 *tūn* to swallow whole

雲吞 *yún tūn* wonton (also written with L10a.11a)
鳳吞花菇 *fēng tūn huā gū* phoenix swallows mushrooms whole (stewed chicken stuffed with whole mushrooms)

T4*4c 炙 *jiǔ* to cauterize with moxa

蜜炙火腿 *mì jiǔ huǒ tuǐ* honey-glazed ham

T4*6 孟 *méng* a family name; Mencius

孟買葱 *méng mǎi cōng* shallot

T4*8 雀 *què* sparrow

雀巢鶏丁 *què cháo jī dīng* sparrow's nest diced chicked (fried diced chicken and vegetables in "nest" of deep-fried shredded potato)
素燒黄雀 *sù shāo huáng què* vegetarian braised orioles (bean curd skin with mushroom and bamboo shoot stuffing; Jiangsu-Zhejiang)
雀肉 *què ròu* liver paté

T4*11 熊 *xióng* bear

紅燒熊掌 *hóng shāo xióng zhǎng* red-cooked bear paw

T5 Five-Stroke Tops

T5a 曼 the "sun" radical (cf. L5b)

T5a.1 旦 *dàn* alternative form for T5d.6a 蛋

冒
壶
禾
卫
灸
岳
春]
背
盆
蛊
粲

T5a.3 旱　*hàn* drought
旱蒸回鍋肉　*hàn zhēng huí guō ròu* twice-cooked pork (made with steamed pork; Sichuan)

T5a.4 昇　*shêng* a zucchini-like squash

T5a.5 星　*xīng* star
星州 or 星洲　*xīng zhōu* Singapore
星臨軒凉拌牛肉　*xīng lín xuān liáng bàn niú ròu* cold sliced boiled beef with hot and sour sauce (Sichuan)

T5a.10 晶　*jīng* crystal
水晶鷄　*shuǐ jīng jī* jellied chicken

T5a.11 冕　*miǎn* crown
冕頂餃　*miǎn dǐng jiǎo* crown-shaped fancy ravioli

T5b 󰀀 the "standing" radical)

T5b.7 章　*zhāng* chapter
章魚　*zhāng yú* octopus

T5b.8 童　*tóng* child
童子鷄　*tóng zǐ jī* Henan-style stewed chicken

T5c 禾 the "grain" radical (cf. L5e)

T5c.3 季　*jì* season
季菜　*jì cài* seasonal vegetable
四季豆　*sì jì dòu* string bean (lit., "four-season bean")

T5c.5 香　*xiāng* fragrance
香酥鴨　*xiāng sū yā* (HÈUNG SÒU NGÁAP) hong soo duck (spiced duck, steamed, then deep-fried until crisp)
五香花生　*wǔ xiāng huā shēng* peanuts cooked with five-spice powder
香港　*xiāng gǎng* (HÈUNG GÓNG) Hong Kong
香茶　*xiāng chá* jasmine tea
香片　*xiāng piàn* jasmine tea
香花鮑魚　*xiāng huā bào yú* abalone with jasmine petals (Sichuan)
香菜　*xiāng cài* coriander leaf
香草　*xiāng cǎo* Chinese coriander

香蕉　*xiāng jiāo* banana
香瓜　*xiāng guā* muskmelon
香頭　*xiāng tóu* wild onion
香杧　*xiāng máng* mango
香蘭　*xiāng lán* vanilla
香茅　*xiāng máo* lemon grass
香菇　*xiāng gū* dried mushroom
香菌　*xiāng jùn* dried black mushroom
香肉　*xiāng ròu* dog meat

T5d 卫

T5d.6a 蛋　*dàn* egg
蛋花湯　*dàn huā tāng* egg drop soup
蛋黃　*dàn huáng* egg yolk
蛋清　*dàn qīng* egg white
皮蛋　*pí dàn* black preserved egg
蛋包　*dàn bāo* omlet
蛋夾　*dàn jiā* omlet
蛋皮春捲　*dàn pí chūn juǎn* egg roll
蛋捲　*dàn juǎn* original egg roll (thin sheet of fried egg
　　batter, with filling, rolled up jelly-roll fashion)
T5d.6b 蚤　nonstandard variant of T5d.6a

T5* Miscellaneous Five-Stroke Tops

T5*4a 炙 *zhī* to broil

蜜炙雲腿　*mì zhī yún tuǐ* ham stewed with rock sugar
　　(Guangdong)

T5*4b 岳 *yuè* part of the names of the five sacred
mountains

岳陽牛柳　*yuè yáng niú liù* sliced beef fillet in hot sauce,
　　with watercress (Hunan; see also L3e.16a)

T5*5a 春 *chūn* spring

春捲　*chūn juǎn* spring roll

春餅　*chūn bǐng* thin pancakes
春雨一聲雷　*chūn yǔ ì shēng lèi* thunder in the spring rain
(fancy name for 鍋巴湯 *guō bā tāng* crispy rice soup)
小長春　*xiǎo cháng chūn* steamed spring rolls with pork
sheet wrapper (Fujian)

T5*5b 背　*bèi* back

T5*6a 益　*yì* to improve

益血炒蜇柳　*yì xiě chǎo zhé liǔ* jellyfish and seaweed stir-
fried with medicinal herbs (lit., "improve blood stir-
fried jellyfish willow")

T5*6b 盅　*zhōng* cup

冬瓜盅　*dōng guā zhōng* mixed ingredients and soup
simmered inside whole winter melon (Guangdong)

T5*7 紮　*zhá* to tie

紮裏肉　*zhá lǐ ròu* deep-fried pork chunks stewed with
white radish in sweet and sour gravy (Fujian)

T6 Six-Stroke Tops

T6a 竹　the "bamboo" radical

T6a.4 笑　*xiào* laugh
笑口棗　*xiào kǒu zǎo* a type of deep-fried raised dough
pastry

T6a.5a 笋　*sǔn* bamboo shoot
T6a.5b 笙　*shēng* panpipes
竹笙　*zhú shēng* bamboo fungus

T6a.8a 筍　*sǔn* bamboo shoot
筍衣　*sǔn yī* shell of bamboo shoot
酸筍衣　*suān sǔn yī* pickled bamboo shoot shell
筍雞　*sǔn jī* young chicken
T6a.8b 筋　*jīn* muscle; tendon

麵筋　*miàn jīn* vegetarian steak (a deep-fried puffy dough); wheat gluten puffs

蹄筋　*tí jīn* pig's Achilles tendon

T6a.8c 筒　*tóng* tube

滾筒排骨　*gǔn tóng pái gǔ* vegetables rolled up in thin pork slice, deep-fried

T6a.8d 箝　*xián* crab claw

T6a.11 節　*jié* section; season

冬節圓　*dōng jié yuán* deep-fried sweet dough balls (Zhejiang)

節瓜　*jié guā* hairy melon

T6a.15 簽　*qiān* bamboo slips (used in divination)

簽餅　*qiān bǐng* fortune cookie

T6a.17a 籠　*lóng* basket; bamboo steamer

小籠包　*xiǎo lóng bāo* small meat-filled buns, steamed in bamboo steaming basket

T6a.17b 籃　*lán* basket

花籃冷盤　*huā lán léng pán* a kind of fancy appetizer plate

T6b ⊗ the "crooked" radical

T6b.4 罗　*luó* white radish, turnip (nonstandard form of T4a.20)

T6b.9 蜀　*shǔ* Szechuan (Sichuan)

蜀米　*shǔ mǐ* corn

T6b.15 羅　*luó* thin silk; used in transcribing foreign names

羅漢　*luó hàn* arhat (Buddhist saint)

羅漢齋　*luó hàn zhāi* arhat's feast (mixed fancy vegetarian ingredients)

羅漢朝佛　*luó hàn cháo fó* arhats visiting Buddha (a fancy vegetarian cold appetizer plate)

羅漢扒大鴨　*luó hàn pá dà yā* duck braised with fancy mixed vegetables

羅勒　*luó lè* sweet basil

羅定豆豉鷄　*luó dìng dòu chǐ jī* chicken braised with black bean sauce

竹
四
此
羊
穴
尚
失
点
脊
帶
貴
巢
發

T6c 此

T6c.4 柴 *chái* firewood
柴杷鴨 *chái ba yā* duck strips and shredded vegetables, tied into bundles and batter-fried
柴魚 *chái yú* dried cod
洋柴蘇 *yáng chái sū* basil

T6c.7 紫 *zǐ* purple
紫菜 *zǐ cài* seaweed (Jap. *nori*)
紫米稀飯 *zǐ mǐ xī fàn* red-rice porridge with preserved fruits (Yunnan)
紫蓋肉 *zǐ gài ròu* red-cooked pork, sliced and batter-fried (lit., "purple lid meat"; Yunnan)
紫堇 *zǐ jǐn* an edible fern

T6d 羊 the "sheep" radical

T6d.3 美 *měi* beauty; America
美味 *měi wèi* fine flavor

T6d.4a 姜 *jiāng* ginger
T6d.4b 羔 *gāo* lamb
羔蟹 *gāo xiè* soft-shell crab

T6d.13 羹 *gēng* thick soup; chowder
魚羹 *yú gēng* fish chowder

T6e 穴 the "hole" radical

T6e.3 空 *kōng* empty
空心菜 *kōng xīn cài* water convulvulus (a green)

T6e.12 窝 *wō* nest (also used as substitute for 鍋 *guō* pan)
燕窝 *yàn wō* bird's nest
鳳窩白鰻 *fēng wō bái mán* phoenix-nest eel (stir-fried eel pieces served over nest of deep-fried bean threads; Sichuan)
窩麵 *wō mián* noodles with soup in tureen
酥皮窩鴨 *sū pí wō yā* deep-fried stuffed duck
窩燒鴨 *wō shāo yā* pressed duck
免治牛肉窩米 *miǎn zhì niú ròu wō mǐ* minced beef with rice vermicelli in soup

T6f 宀
⊗

T6f.8 掌 *zhǎng* foot, paw
蠔油鴨掌 *háo yóu yā zhǎng* duck feet in oyster sauce
掌中四寶 *zhǎng zhōng sì bǎo* four treasures wrapped in duck feet (Fujian)
紅燒熊掌 *hóng shāo xióng zhǎng* red-cooked bear paw

T6f.10 當 *dāng* ought
當歸 *dāng guī* ligusticum (a medicinal root)

T6g 关
⊗

T6g.4 卷 *juǎn* roll (see L3a.10a)
卷子肉 *juǎn zi ròu* beef shank

T6g.13 鯗 *xiǎng* dried fish

T6* Miscellaneous Six-Stroke Tops

T6*4 点 *diǎn* dot (See L12*6)

T6*5 脊 *jí* back

脊髓 *jí suǐ* spinal cord

T6*7 帶 *dài* belt

帶子 *dài zi* scallop
帶絲 *dài sī* a type of seaweed
帶魚 *dài yú* a kind of eel; scabbard fish
裙帶菜 *qún dài cài* a type of seaweed (lit., "apron string vegetable"; Jap. *wakame*)

T6*8 貴 *guì* honorable; imperial

貴妃雞翅 *guì fēi jī chì* imperial concubine chicken wings (simmered in sweet and salty gravy; Shanghai)
貴州 *guì zhōu* Kweichow
貴州牛肉 *guì zhōu niú ròu* Kweichow orange-flavor beef

T6*9 巢 *cháo* nest

雀巢八珍 *què cháo bā zhēn* eight treasures in magpie's nest (fancy ingredients in thick gravy, served in deep-fried basket made of shredded potato)

T6*12 發 *fā* to rise (dough); to soften (dried ingredients) in water

發菜 *fā cài* black moss (usually written with T10a.5)

T7 Seven-Stroke Tops

T7a 覀 the "west" radical

T7a.4 栗 *lì* chestnut
栗子燒鷄塊 *lì zi shāo jī kuài* chicken pieces stewed with chestnuts

T7a.6 粟 *sù* grain; millet
粟米 *sù mǐ* corn, maize

T7* Miscellaneous Seven-Stroke Tops

T7*4a 唇 *chún* lip

鳳絲魚唇 *fèng sī yú chún* fish lips with chicken shreds (Guangdong)

T7*4b 梨 *lí* pear

鳳梨 *fèng lí* pineapple (lit., "phoenix pear")

T7*4c 臭 *chòu* to stink or *xiù* odor

臭豆腐 *chòu dòu fu* stinking bean curd (a type of fermented bean curd; Jiangsu, Zhejiang)

T7*4d 热 *rè* hot (temperature) (abbreviated form of T12*4)

T7*6a 番 *fān* barbarian

番茄 *fān qié* tomato
番瓜 *fān guā* pumpkin
番荔枝 *fān lì zhī* custard apple (lit., "barbarian lichee")
番椒 *fān jiāo* bell pepper
番薯 *fān shǔ* sweet potato

T7*6b 盘 *pán* plate (simplified form of T13*6)

T7*6c 蜇 *zhé* jellyfish

T7*6d 袈 *jiā* Buddhist monk's robe

袈裟酥鱼排 *jiā shā sū yú pǎi* fish slices wrapped in net-fat and deep-fried

T7*7a 枣 *zǎo* date

枣泥锅饼 *zǎo ní guō bǐng* pancakes filled with date paste
软脆豆沙枣 *ruǎn cuì dòu sa zǎo* sweet potato and sticky-rice balls, filled with sweet bean paste, deep-fried (Hangzhou)

T7*7b 蒙 see T4a.11d

T7*13a 鲨 *shā* shark

T7*13b 鸳 *yuān* male mandarin duck

鸳鸯 *yuān yāng* mandarin duck; couple in love (the second character refers to the female mandarin duck; used in names of dishes where one ingredient is cooked in two different ways)
鸳鸯鸡 *yuān yāng jī* frog

T8 Eight-Stroke Tops

T8a 隹 the "sparrow" radical

T8a.3 隻 *zhī* classifier for counting birds

T8a.4a 焦 *jiāo* scorched
焦圈 *jiāo quǎn* Chinese donuts (Beijing)
焦拼青椒 *jiāo bàn qīng jiāo* pan-roasted green peppers with black beans, served cold (Sichuan)
焦鹽圈子 *jiāo yán quǎn zi* pan-fried pork chitterlings (Shanghai)

T8a.4b 集會 *jí huì* meeting
八珍大集會 *bā zhēn dà jí huì* eight fancy ingredients in thick soup

T8b 羽 the "wing" radical

T8b.8 翠 *cuì* green jade
翠皮魚 *cuì pí yú* crispy skin fish (a pun on L5a.9b)

T8b.12 翼 *yì* wing

T8* Miscellaneous Eight-Stroke Tops

T8*3 真 *zhēn* true, real

真珠 *zhēn zhū* pearl
真珠魚球 *zhēn zhū yú qiú* fish balls with ginko nuts

T8*4 無 *wú* not

無花果 *wú huā guǒ* fig (lit., "flowerless fruit")
干貝無黃蛋 *gān bèi wú huáng dàn* scallops in steamed egg-white custard (Hunan)
無錫 *wú xí* Wusih (city in Jiangsu Province)

T8*5a 骨 *gǔ* bone

排骨 *pái gǔ* spareribs
香骨酥雞 *xiāng gǔ sū jī* fragrant bone flaky chicken (deep-fried marinated chicken)

骨髓　*gǔ suǐ* bone marrow

T8*5b 琵　*pí* Chinese lute

琵琶　*pí pá* Chinese lute
琵琶魚　*pí pá yú* ray (fish)
琵琶豆腐　*pí pá dòu fu* balls of bean curd, pork, and shrimp, with crabmeat sauce
琵琶鴨　*pí pá yā* crispy barbecued duck with fruits (Guangdong)
琵琶菓　*pí pá guǒ* loquat

T8*5c 普　*pǔ* universal

普洱　*pǔ ěr* place in Yunnan after which a celebrated black tea is named
普洱茶　*pǔ ěr chá* (PU YÍ CHÀH) poo nei tea

T8*7 腐　*fǔ* to curdle, rot

豆腐　*dòu fu* bean curd
腐乳　*fǔ rǔ* fermented beancurd
腐竹　*fǔ zhú* stick-form dried bean curd skin
腐衣　*fǔ yī* extra thin bean curd skin
腐皮　*fǔ pí* extra thin bean curd skin
腐衣黃魚　*fǔ yī huáng yú* yellow croaker wrapped in thin bean curd skin and deep-fried

T8*8 翡　*fěi* emerald

翡翠鷄片　*fěi cuì jī piàn* emerald and green jade chicken slices (steamed minced chicken, sliced, arranged in floral pattern, and served with gravy; Zhejiang)

T9 Nine-Stroke Tops

T9a 雨　the "rain" radical

T9a.4a 雪　*xuě* snow
雪豆　*xuě dòu* snow peas; Chinese peapods
雪裏紅　*xuě li hóng* red-in-snow (salty pickled mustard green)
雪裡紅　*xuě li hóng* red-in-snow

隹 羽 真 無 骨 琵 普 腐 翡 〔雷 魚 里 煮 塩 黎 餐〕

雪菜　*xuě cài* red-in-snow

雪筍包子　*xuě sǔn bāo zi* steamed buns, filled with salted greens, bamboo shoot, and pork

雪花銀耳　*xuě huā yín ěr* silver tree fungus in egg-white custard

雪花鷄腿　*xuě huā jī tuǐ* chicken legs deep-fried in egg-white and bread-crumb batter

雪山　*xuě shān* soufflé (lit., "snow mountain")

T9a.4b 雲　*yún* cloud; Yunnan; Yunnan ham; wonton

雲南　*yún nán* Yunnan

雲腿　*yún tuǐ* Yunnan ham

雲片　*yún piàn* slices of Yunnan ham; steamed shelled quail eggs

雲白肉　*yún bái ròu* thin-sliced boiled pork with garlic sauce (Sichuan)

雲耳　*yún ěr* cloud ear (white tree fungus)

雲吞　*yún tūn* wonton

雲龍園毛肚火鍋　*yún lóng yuán máo dǔ huǒ guō* beef and tripe fondue (Sichuan)

雲丹　*yún dān* sea urchin sauce (Taiwan)

T9a.6 雷　*lèi* thunder

春雨一聲雷　*chūn yǔ ì shēng lèi* thunder in the spring rain (fancy name for 鍋巴湯 *guō bā tāng* crispy rice soup)

T9a.9 霉　*méi* mold

霉乾菜　*méi gān cài* fermented red-in-snow (pickled mustard green)

T9a.15 霸王　*bà wáng* leader among feudal lords

霸王燉鴨　*bà wáng dùn yā* fancy stewed stuffed duck

T9a.16 露　*lù* mist (also a pun on U12b 鹵 *lǔ* gravy)

露笋　*lù sūn* asparagus

玫瑰露　*méi guì lù* a rose-flavored brandy

杏仁露　*xìng ren lù* almond cream

T9b 魚 ⊗

T9b.1 鱼　simplified form of T9b.4

T9b.3 魚　alternate form of T9b.4

T9b.4 魚　*yú* fish

魚翅　*yú chì* shark fin

魚香茄子　*yú xiāng qié zi* fish flavor eggplant (eggplant pieces in chili and garlic sauce, which goes well with fish; Sichuan)

魚肚　*yú dǔ* fish stomach (actually, airbag of large fish)

魚子 or 魚仔　*yú zi* fish roe

魚潑水　*yú pō shuǐ* fish tails

魚禿肺　*yú tū fèi* fish liver and intestines steamed with egg (Shanghai)

T9b.9 魯　*lǔ* Shandong

T9c 黑 ⊗

T9c.4 黑　*hēi* black

黑芥　*hēi jiè* pickled mustard root (Yunnan)

黑菜　*hēi cài* a Hunanese pickle

T9c.7 墨　*mò* ink

墨魚　*mò yú* cuttlefish

T9* Miscellaneous Nine-Stroke Tops

T9*4 煮　*zhǔ* to boil

T9*6 塩　*yán* salt

塩水鶏　*yán shuǐ jī* salt-boiled chicken

塩焗鶏　*yán jú jī* chicken baked in salt (Hakka)

T9*7 黎　*lí* black

黎巴燒肉　*lí bā shāo ròu* Fukien-style thrice-cooked pork (Fujian)

T9*10 餐　*cān* meal

餐廳　*cān tīng* restaurant

野餐　*yě cān* picnic

午餐　*wǔ cān* lunch

保
碧
蠶
喫
腎
傲
熱
將
魚
燙
盤
鷔
鷹
點
擘
鸞
鬱
雙
蟹
響
甕
鹽

T10 Ten-Stroke Tops

T10a 髟⊗ the "hair" radical

T10a.5 髮 *fā* hair
髮菜 *fā cài* hair vegetable (dried black moss)

T10a.8 鬆 *sōng* loose; minced, powdered
豆腐肉鬆 *dòu fu ròu sōng* bean curd stir-fried with ground pork
肉鬆 *ròu sōng* pork concentrate (pork cooked dry until reduced to a near powder)

T10* Miscellaneous Ten-Stroke Tops

T10*4 煲 *bào* to simmer in casserole

煲仔豆腐 *bào zi dòu fu* bean curd casserole
煲飯 *bào fàn* rice and meat pieces cooked together in casserole

T10*6 碧 *bì* green

碧古魚 *bì gǔ yú* pickerel
碧綠釀仙掌 *bì lǜ niàng xiān zhǎng* green stuffed fairy feet (boneless duck feet stuffed with green vegetable; Guangdong)
碧螺春茶 *bì luó chūn chá* a kind of green tea

T10*17 蠶 *cán* silkworm

蠶豆 *cán dòu* broad bean; lima bean

T11 Eleven-Stroke Tops

T11*4 喫 *kā* nonstandard character used in following compound

喫喱 *kā lí* curry

T11*5 腎　*shèn* kidney

T12 Twelve-Stroke Tops

T12a 敞̸

T12a.13　鱉　*biē* turtle

T12a.18　鼈　*biē* turtle

T12* Miscellaneous Twelve-Stroke Tops

T12*4 熱　*rè* hot (temperature)

熱盤　*rè pán* assorted hot appetizers
薑汁熱碗鷄　*jiāng zhī rè wǎn jī* chicken steamed with
　ginger juice in serving bowl (Sichuan)

T13 Thirteen-Stroke Tops

T13a 將̸

T13a.5　漿　*jiāng* soybean milk
豆腐漿　*dòu fu jiāng* soybean milk

T13a.8　醬　*jiàng* sauce; bean paste (Jap. *miso*)
醬油　*jiàng yóu* soy sauce
芝麻醬　*zhī má jiàng* sesame paste
醬爆鷄丁　*jiàng bào jī dīng* diced chicken quick-fried with
　bean paste
醬菜　*jiàng cài* vegetables pickled in soy sauce or bean
　paste
醬瓜　*jiàng guā* cucumber strips pickled in bean paste

T13b 魚̸　the "fish" radical (see T9b)

T13* Miscellaneous Thirteen-Stroke Tops

T13*4 燙　*tàng* scald

髟
保
碧
蠶
喋
腎
敝
熱
將
魚
[
燙
盤
鰵
鷹
點
擘
鱟
鬱
雙
蟹
響
甕
鹽

鷄肉燙麵餃　*jī ròu tàng miàn jiǎo* steamed chicken and pork filled ravioli, made with hot water dough (Hangzhou)

T13*6 盤 *pán* tray, plate

拼盤　*pīn pán* assorted appetizer plate

T13*13a 鰵 *mín* cod

T13*13b 鷹 *yīng* hawk

翔鷹拼盤　*xiāng yīng pīn pán* cold appetizers arranged in form of soaring hawk

T15–T22 Tops of Fifteen-Strokes or More

T15*4a 點 alternative form of L13*6

T15*4b 擘 *bò* to split

擘酥鮮奶撻　*bò sū xiān nǎi dà* tarts filled with milk pudding

T15*13 鱟 *hòu* king crab

T15*17 鬱 *yù* tulip; luxuriant

冬菇鬱鷄　*dōng gū yù jī* fancy steamed chicken with black mushrooms

T16*3 雙 *shuāng* pair

一雙筷子　*yì shuāng kuài zi* one pair of chopsticks

雙冬鷄片　*shuāng dōng jī piàn* two-winter chicken slices (chicken slices with bamboo shoots and dried mushrooms)

生炒雙脆　*shēng chǎo shuāng cuì* stir-fried pig tripe and dried squid (Hakka)

T16*6 蟹 *xiè* crab

芙蓉蟹 *fú róng xiè* crab foo yung
蟹黃 *xiè huáng* crab roe
羔蟹 *gāo xiè* soft-shell crab

T16*10 響 *xiǎng* ring, resound

響鈴 *xiǎng líng* ringing bell (stuffed bean curd skin or
wonton, deep-fried until very crisp)
響皮 *xiǎng pí* deep-fried pig skin
響螺 *xiǎng luó* snail

T17*5 甕 *wèng* jar

甕菜 *wèng cài* water spinach

T22*6 鹽 *yān* salt (see T9*6)

E2 Two-Stroke Enclosures

E2a 左⊗

E2a.3 左 *zuǒ* left
左口魚 *zuǒ kǒu yú* flounder
左宗棠鷄 *zuǒ zōng táng jī* General Zuo's chicken
(chicken chunks with red peppers, ginger, and garlic;
Hunan)

E2a.4 布 *bù* cloth
布袋鷄 *bù dài jī* steamed stuffed chicken (Shandong)
布甸 *bù diàn* pudding
布丁 *bù dīng* pudding

E2* Miscellaneous Two-Strokes Enclosures

E2*4 可 *kě* be able

可口可樂 *kě kǒu kě lè* Coca-Cola
可可 *kě kě* cocoa

ナ
可
司
虫
原
广
几
之
太
叉
式
冈
包

E2*5 司　*sī* to manage

公司　*gōng sī* company
三司會審　*sān sī huì shěn* pork liver, heart, and lung with pineapple and vegetables (Taiwan)

E2*7 虱　*shī* louse
虱目魚　*shī mù yú* milkfish (lit., "louse-eye fish")

E2*9 原　*yuán* origin
原晒豉　*yuán shài shì* ground brown-bean sauce
原汁鮑魚　*yuán zhī bào yú* abalone in its own juices

E3 Three-Stroke Enclosures

E3a 广

E3a.8 麻　*má* sesame; numb (especially numbness induced by brown pepper)
麻油　*má yóu* sesame oil
椒麻鷄　*jiāo má jī* cold chicken in chili and brown pepper sauce
麻醬　*má jiàng* sesame paste
麻婆豆腐　*má po dòu fu* Ma Po bean curd (bean curd cubes in spicy thick gravy with ground pork; Sichuan)
麻雀　*má què* sparrow; ma jong

E3a.9 唐　*táng* Tang dynasty, 618–907 A.D.
唐式龍蝦　*táng shì lóng xiā* lobster Cantonese
唐人街　*táng rén jiē* Chinatown

E3a.10 鹿　*lù* deer
清燉鹿沖　*qīng dùn lù chūng* clear-stewed deer penis
炸鹿尾　*zhá lù wěi* mock deer tail (deep-fried sausage; Beijing)
鹿角菜　*lù jiǎo cài* a kind of mushroom (lit., "antler vegetable")
鹿茸　*lù róng* antlers of young deer (used medicinally)

E3a.12a 腐　see T8*7
E3a.12b 廈門　*xià mén* Amoy
廈門炒米粉　*xià mén chǎo mǐ fěn* Amoy-style fried rice-flour noodles (flavored with curry powder)

E3a.13a 廣　*guǎng* wide
廣東　*guǎng dōng* Canton Province
廣州　*guǎng zhōu* Canton City
廣西　*guǎng xī* Kwangsi
E3a.13b 麂　*jǐ* a small animal of the deer family

E3a.14 磨　*mó* mushroom
磨襠　*mó dāng* lamb tenderloin
磨原豉　*mó yuán chǐ* mushroom-flavored soy sauce

E3a.18 盧　*lú* hut
盧江燒賣　*lú jiāng shāo mài* steamed small dumplings
　　made of walnut, sugar, and bread crumbs

E3b 几

E3b.3 甩　*shuǎi* to flip, throw
甩水　*shuǎi shuǐ* fish tail

E3b.8 風　*fēng* wind
風鷄　*fēng jī* salt-cured chicken
風沙芋　*fēng shā yù* sliced yam with sugar (Swatow)

E3b.14 鳳　*fèng* phoenix (fancy name for chicken)
鳳凰　*fèng huáng* phoenix
鳳尾蝦　*fèng wěi xiā* batter-fried butterfly shrimp
鳳尾燕窩　*fèng wěi yàn wō* phoenix-tail bird's nest (bird's
　　nest with fancy sauce)
鳳尾魚　*fèng wěi yú* long-tailed anchovy
鳳爪　*fèng zhǎo* chicken feet
鳳足　*fèng zú* chicken feet
鳳城野鷄捲　*fèng chéng yě jī juǎn* mock pheasant rolls
　　(sausage and pork fat wrapped in bean curd skin,
　　deep-fried; Guangdong)
鳳梨　*fèng lí* pineapple (lit., "phoenix pear")

E3c 辶 see E4c

E3* Miscellaneous Three-Stroke Enclosures

E3*1a 太　*tài* large, great

太陽　*tài yáng* sun

ナ
可
司
虱
原
广
几
辶
太
叉
式
回
包

太陽餅　*tài yáng bǐng* sun cake (meat-filled flaky bun;
　　Fujian)

太極　*tài jí* great antipodes (i.e., yin and yang; used in
　　names of dishes involving contrasting colors, esp. in
　　the form of the yin-yang symbol; the same characters
　　also appear in "tai chi chuan," Chinese "shadow
　　boxing")

太極粟米湯　*tài jí sù mǐ tāng* corn and green pea soups
　　served together in the form of the yin-yang symbol

太史豆腐　*tài shǐ dòu fu* court historian bean curd (cakes
　　of bean curd steamed with chopped fish meat, then
　　deep-fried)

太爺鶏　*tài yé jī* ancestor's chicken (a type of smoked
　　chicken)

E3*1b 叉　*chā* fork

叉燒　*chā shāu* (CHÀ SÌU) roast pork tenderloin

E3*3 式　*shì* style

中式煎豬排　*jōng shì jiān zhū pái* Chinese-style fried pork
　　chops

E3*4a 回　*huí* return (see E4a.4a)

E3*4b 包　*bāo* wrap; steamed filled bun

叉燒包　*chā shāo bāo* (CHÀ SÌU BÀAU) roast pork
　　steamed bun

小籠包　*xiǎo lóng bāo* small meat-filled pastries,
　　served in bamboo steaming basket

包心菜　*bāo xīn cài* round cabbage

包菜　*bāo cài* round cabbage

包燒魚　*bāo shāo yú* stuffed fish, wrapped in net fat, pan-
　　fried (Sichuan)

炸蝦包　*zhá xiā bāo* shrimp toast

紙包鶏片　*zhǐ bāo jī piàn* paper-wrapped chicken slices,
　　deep-fried

包種茶　*bāo zhǒng chá* pouchong tea

E4 Four-Stroke Enclosures

E4a ⊗

E4a.3 团 *yuán* circle (popular form of E4a.12)

E4a.4a 回 *huí* return
回鍋肉 *huí guō ròu* twice-cooked pork (lit., "return-pot meat"; boiled pork, sliced, then stir-fried with vegetables and spicy bean paste; Sichuan)
回春香鹽蝦 *huí chūn xiāng yán xiā* large and small shrimps, one kind prepared with salty flavor, the other with fragrant spices

E4a.4b 园 *yuán* dollar

E4a.9a 國 *guó* country
國泰 *guó tài* Cathay
國藩鷄球 *guó fán jī qiú* General Zhang's chicken (named after a Hunanese hero; chicken curls in hot sauce)

E4a.9b 圈 *quān* ring
洋芋炸圈餅 *yáng yù zhá quān bǐng* mashed-potato donuts (Shanghai)
圈子 *quān zi* chitterling (pig's small intestine)

E4a.10 團 *tuán* round; dumpling
寧波湯團 *níng pō tāng tuán* Ningpo sesame-filled rice-flour boiled dumplings

E4a.12 圓 *yuán* circle, round; dollar
肉圓湯 *ròu yuán tāng* meatball soup
圓菜 *yúan cài* turtle
圓竹 *yúan zhù* stick-form dried bean curd skin

E4b 尸 ⊗

E4b.4 尾 *wěi* tail; classifier for counting fish
牛尾 *niú wěi* oxtail
甜酸豬尾 *tián suān zhū wěi* sweet and sour braised pig tails (Guangdong)

E4b.5 屁股 *pì gu* buttock

E4b.7a 屈 *qū* to bend; *jū* (as alternate form of L4b.11c) to stew precooked ingredients together
家鄉屈鷄 *jiā xiāng jū jī* home-style stewed chicken in thick gravy

口尸辶或尸疒豸气翅䒑越鳥門鼎夒

E4b.7b 展 *zhǎn* to spread

鳳凰展翅 *fèng huáng zhǎn chì* phoenix spreading its
wings (a fancy cold appetizer plate, with ingredients
arranged in that form)

E4b.9 犀 *xī* rhinoceros

犀埔鰱魚 *xī pǔ lián yú* deep-fried catfish cooked in hot
bean sauce (Sichuan)

E4b.14 層 *céng* layer; story of a building; tier of a
steamer pot

千層糕 *qiān céng gāo* thousand-layer cake (flaky pastry)

三層塔 *sān céng tǎ* three-story pagoda (for example,
fried vegetables, covered with mushrooms and topped
with quail eggs)

E4c 辶

E4c.6 迫 *pò* to press

蘿蔔迫牛腩 *luó bo pò niú nǎn* turnip and beef stew

E4c.8a 通 *tōng* to reach, communicate

通菜 *tōng cài* a spinach-like vegetable

通天排翅 *tōng tiān pǎi chì* reach-heaven shark fin
(steamed, served with thick brown sauce; Beijing)

E4c.8b 這厘 *zhè lí* jelly

E4c.9 透明 *tòu míng* transparent

透明鷄 *tòu míng jī* cellophane-wrapped chicken slices

E4c.12 過 *guò* pass

過橋麵 *guò qiáo miàn* cross-the-bridge noodles (noodles,
soup, and side fishes, served separately and mixed by
the diners; Yunnan)

過橋丸子 *guò qiáo wán zi* meatballs with sweet and sour
dipping sauce

E4c.16 邊豆 *biān dòu* green bean

E4* Miscellaneous Four-Stroke Enclosures

E4*5 或 *huò* or

E5 Five-Stroke Enclosures

E5a 戶⊗ the "door" radical

E5a.6 扁 *biǎn* flat
扁豆 *biǎn dòu* string bean; lentil
扁尖 *biǎn jiān* dried bamboo shoot tips
扁魚 *biǎn yú* bream
扁鮫 *biǎn jiāo* monkfish, angelfish

E5a.8 扇 *shàn* fan
鮮菇川蝦扇 *xiān gū chuān xiā shàn* mushrooms and fan-cut shrimps in soup (Guangdong)
煎釀蝦扇 *jiān niàng xiā shuān* grilled stuffed fan-cut shrimps (Guangdong)

E5b 广⊗ the "sick" radical)

E5b.4 疙瘩 *gē da* pimple
面疙瘩 *miàn gē da* dumplings in soup

E5b.11 瘦肉 *shòu ròu* lean meat

E5* Miscellaneous Five-Stroke Enclosures

E5*6a 廹 *pò* to press (see E4c.6)

E5*6b 气 *qì* steam (see L3b.5a)

E5*8 翅 *chì* wing

魚翅 *yú chì* shark fin

E6 Six-Stroke Enclosures

E6a 癶⊗ see T6g

卩口尸辶或戶广廴氣翅夨[越鳥門鼎夋

E7 Seven-Stroke Enclosures

E7*5 越 *yuè* to cross (a boundary)

越南 *yuè nán* Vietnam

E9 Nine-Stroke Enclosures

E9a 鳥

E9a.4a 島 *dǎo* island
青島 *qīng dǎo* Tsingtao (city in Shandong Province; brand of beer)
寶島串燒蝦 *bǎo dǎo chuàn shāo xiā* treasure island grilled skewered prawns (Taiwan)
E9a.4b 鳥 *niǎo* bird
鳥蛤 *niǎo gé* cockle

E10 Ten-Stroke Enclosures

E10a 門 the "gate" enclosure

E10a.4a 開 *kāi* to open
開烏炖乳鴿 *kāi wū dùn rǔ gē* sea cucumbers steamed with pigeons (Fujian)
開口笑 *kāi kǒu xiào* a donut-like sweet pastry (lit., "open mouth laughing")
開陽 or 開洋 *kāi yáng* dried shrimp
E10a.4b 閏 *rùn* having excess
豬閏 *zhū rùn* pork liver

E10a.6a 閘 *zhá* gate
大閘蟹 *dà zhá xiè* a variety of crab somewhat like Dungeness (Shanghai)
E10a.6b 閩江 *mín jiāng* Min River (Fujian)
閩菜 *mín cài* Fukien (Fujian) cuisine

E10* Miscellaneous Ten-Stroke Enclosures

E10*6 鼎 *dǐng* large bronze tripod; ruling troika

鼎湖 *dǐng hú* replacement of old by new dynasty
鼎湖上素 *dǐng hú shàng sù* steamed garnished mushrooms

E11 Eleven-Stroke Enclosures

E11a 麥⊗ the "wheat" radical, (also written as left half 麦⊗).

E11a.4 麩 *fū* rice bran dough
烤麩 *kǎo fū* red-cooked deep-fried bran dough (Shanghai)
麩皮饅頭 *fū pì mán tou* whole-wheat steamed buns

E11a.6 麵 *miàn* wheat; noodles (see E11a.10)

E11a.7 麴米 *qū mǐ* malt

E11a.10 麵 *miàn* wheat; noodles
炒麵 *chǎo miàn* fried noodles
麵包 *miàn bāo* bread
麵筋 *miàn jīn* vegetarian steak (made of gluten dough)
麵餃 *miàn jiǎo* ravioli (= 餃子 *jiǎo zi*)
麵線 *miàn xiàn* wheat-flour vermicelli

U1 Indivisible One-Stroke Characters

U1a ━ *yì* one

一品 *yì pǐn* first class
一鷄三味 *yì jī sān wèi* one chicken cooked three ways
一二三四五排骨 *yī èr sān sì wǔ pái gǔ* 1-2-3-4-5 spareribs (stewed in a sweet and sour sauce whose ingredients are in the ratio of 1-2-3-4-5)

U1b ▎ *yī* one (variant of U1a used when the characters are handwritten in columns, not rows)

一
宁
丁
人
七
亠
大
干
上
下
千
九
刀
士
土
丫
才

U2 Indivisible Two-Stroke Characters

U2a 十 *shí* ten

素十香菜　*sù shí xiāng cài* ten-variety vegetarian dish

炒十錦　*chǎo shí jǐn* stir-fried ten ingredients (makes pun with L2a.2b 什錦)

十香菜　*shí xiāng cài* an Yunnanese variety of carrot

U2b 丁 *dīng* to dice

醬爆鶏丁　*jiàng bào jī dīng* diced chicken, quick-fried with bean paste

丁香　*dīng xiāng* clove

U2c 人 *rén* person

人蔘　*rén shēn* ginseng

U2d 七 *qī* seven

七彩魚塊　*qī cǎi yú kuài* seven-decoration fish chunks

七鰓魚　*qī sāi yú* lamprey (lit., "seven-gill fish")

U2e 亠 *liù* six (popular alternate to T2a.2a)

U3 Indivisible Three-Stroke Characters

U3a 大 *dà* large

大滷麵 or 大魯麵　*dà lǔ miàn* noodles in thick soup with fried meats, vegetables, and egg

什錦大品鍋　*shí jǐn dà pǐn guō* soup with many ingredients, steamed in bowl (Guizhou)

大地　*dà dì* dried bream

大地炒鴿鬆　*dà dì chǎo gē sōng* minced pigeon stir-fried with dried bream (Guandgong)

大魚　*dà yú* grass carp

大茴　*dà huí* anise

大料　*dà liào* large fennel

大菜　*dà cài* agar-agar (gelatin made from a seaweed)
大豆　*dà dòu* soybean
大米　*dà mǐ* pearl rice
大良　*dà liàng* Taliang (a county in Guangdong Province)
大良炒鮮奶　*dà liàng chǎo xiān nǎi* fried milk (stir-fried
　　egg-white and milk mixture, served over deep-fried
　　rice-flour noodles; Daliang County, Guangdong)

U3b 干　*gān* dry

干貝　*gān bèi* dried scallop (sometimes used even for fresh
　　scallop)
豆腐干　*dòu fu gān* pressed bean curd
干絲　*gān sī* shredded pressed or dried bean curd
干煸四季豆　*gān bian sì jì dòu* dry-cooked string beans
　　(deep-fried string beans, stir-fried with seasonings
　　until liquid has evaporated; Sichuan)
生煎干肉包　*shēng jiān gān ròu bāo* pan-fried meat-filled
　　flaky pastry (Shanghai)

U3c 上　*shàng* up; superior; to climb

上海　*shàng hǎi* Shanghai
上湯　*shàng tāng* consommé
螞蟻上樹　*mǎ yǐ shàng shū* ants climbing a tree (deep-fried
　　bean threads with spicy minced pork sauce; Sichuan)

U3d 下　*xià* down; to descend

下巴　*xià bā* fish cheeks (Shanghai)

U3e 千　*qiān* thousand
千層糕　*qiān céng gāo* thousand-layer cake (flaky pastry)
千層鴨　*qiān céng yā* pressed duck
千層肚　*qiān céng dǔ* third stomach of cow
千張　*qiān zhāng* bean curd pressed into thin sheets

U3f 九　*jiǔ* nine

九孔　*jiǔ kǔng* abalone

一
十
丁
人
七
大
干
上
下
千
[九
刀
士
丫
才

九龍　*jiǔ lóng* (**GÁU LÙHNG**) Kowloon
九層塔　*jiǔ céng tǎ* sweet basil

U3g 刀 *dāo* knife

刀削麵　*dāo xuè miàn* hand-cut noodles
刀魚　*dāo yú* swordfish
刀豆　*dāo dòu* string bean

U3h 士 *shì* gentleman, officer

士的　*shì dì* (**SÌH TÌK**) steak
芝士　*zhī shì* cheese

U3i 土 *tǔ* earth

土魷　*tǔ yóu* dried squid

U3j 丫 *yā* branching upward

丫芝竹　*yā zhī zhú* artichoke

U3k 才 *cài* vegetable (nonstandard alternate of T4a.8a)

U4 Indivisible Four-Stroke Characters

U4a 木 *mù* wood

木耳　*mù ěr* wood ears (tree fungus)
木樨肉　*mù xū ròu* moo shoo pork (shredded pork stir-fried with gold needle vegetable, other vegetables, and beaten egg, served with pancakes)
木須肉絲　*mù xū ròu sī* moo shoo pork
木瓜　*mù guā* papaya
湘木鴨　*xiāng mù yā* Hunan-style smoked duck

U4b 山 *shān* mountain

山東　*shān dōng* Shantung Province

山東白菜 *shān dōng bái cài* celery cabbage
山東湯 *shān dōng tāng* soup with several shredded
　ingredients
山西 *shān xī* Shanhsi Province
山瑞 *shān ruì* turtle
山鷄 *shān jī* pheasant
山楂 *shān zhā* boxthorn
山藥 or 山葯 *shān yào* yam; yucca
山芋 *shān yù* sweet potato
山竹子 *shān zhú zi* mangosteen (lichee-like fruit with
　hard purple shell)
山葵 *shān kuí* horseradish
山竹卷 *shān zhú juǎn* meatballs wrapped in bean curd
　skin

U4c 火 *huǒ* fire

火鍋 *huǒ guō* fire pot (fondue)
火腿 *huǒ tuǐ* ham
火鷄 *huǒ jī* turkey
火鴨 *huǒ yā* (FÓ NGÁAP) spit-roasted duck
火肉 *huǒ ròu* (FÓ YUHK) spit-roasted pig
火把魚翅 *huǒ bǎ yú chì* torch shark fin (shark fin, sliced
　chicken, and shark skin, tied with gourd shaving into
　torch shape and steamed; Taiwan)

U4d 毛 *máo* fur; ten cents

毛豆 *máo dòu* soy beans in pods (Jap. *edamame*)
毛肚 *máo dǔ* third stomach of cow
文毛 *jiǔ máo* ninety cents
毛牛肉 *máo niú ròu* strips of beef simmered with spices
　(Sichuan)
毛筍 *máo sǔn* spring bamboo shoot
毛峯茶 *máo fēng chá* a kind of green tea (lit., "fur
　peak")

U4e 牛 *niú* cow

牛肉 *niú ròu* beef
牛奶 *niú nǎi* (cow's) milk

木山火毛牛手口心丸子文天王井斗爪夫戈尤升午厶六廿

木山火毛牛手口心丸子文天王井斗爪夫戈尤升午厶六廿

雪豆牛肉片　*xuě dòu niú ròu piàn* beef slices with snow peas

牛蛙　*niú wā* bullfrog

牛蛙鰱魚　*niú wā lián yú* silver carp fried in shape of bullfrog

U4f 手 *shǒu* hand

手撕鷄　*shǒu sī jī* hand-shredded chicken

抄手　*chāo shǒu* Szechuan-style wonton

豬手　*zhū shǒu* pig's trotters

U4g 口 *kǒu* mouth

口蘑　*kǒu mó* kalgan mushrooms

口毛菇　*kǒu máo gū* a type of mushroom

開口笑　*kāi kǒu xiào* sweet raised donut-like pastry (lit., "open mouth smile")

口袋豆腐　*kǒu dài dòu fu* deep-fried bean curd balls

U4h 心 *xīn* heart

菜心　*cài xīn* bok choi hearts

點心　*diǎn xīn* (DÍM SÀM) dimsum (pastries and small dishes as brunch)

U4i 丸 *wàn* ball, meatball

乾炸丸子　*gān zhá wàn zi* deep-fried meatballs without sauce

雙丸湯　*shuāng wàn tāng* meatball and fishball soup

U4j 子 *zǐ* child (often used as a diminutive suffix)

子鷄　*zǐ jī* chicken

子母會　*zǐ mǔ huì* child and mother meet (deep-fried pigeon with pigeon-egg sauce; Sichuan)

子母蝦　*zǐ mǔ xiā* large and small shrimps

U4k 文 *wén* literature, culture; *jiǔ* nine (non-standard alternative to U3f)

文旦 *wén dàn* pomelo

文山鶏丁 *wén shān jī dīng* chicken cubes fried with chili peppers (Jiangxi)

文昌鶏 *wén chāng jī* boneless chicken and chicken liver in spicy sauce

川炸文武肉 *chuān zhá wén wǔ ròu* scholar and soldier pork (two kinds of deep-fried marinated pork slices; Fujian)

文蛤 *wén gé* clam

U4l 天 *tiān* heaven

天津 *tiān jing* Tientsin

天津麵 *tiān jīng miàn* noodles in soup with crab foo yung

天津白菜 *tiān jīng bái cài* celery cabbage

天官賜福 *tiān guān sì fú* gods bestow fortune (a vegetarian appetizer assortment served on five plates)

U4m 王 *wáng* king

王牙白 *wáng yá bái* Chinese cabbage

U4n 井 *jǐng* well, mine

龍井茶 *lóng jǐng chá* longching green tea

銅井巷素麵 *tóng jǐng xiàng sù miàn* copper-mine vegetarian noodles (with spiced sesame sauce; Sichuan)

U4o 斗 *dǒu* peck (unit of volume)

斗糕 *dǒu gāo* steamed pudding made of glutinous rice with sweet filling

U4p 爪 *zhǎo* claw; foot of chicken, etc.

鳳爪湯鮑片 *fēng zhǎo tāng bào piàn* chicken and abalone slices in soup

木
山
火
毛
牛
手
口
心
丸
子
文
天
王
井
斗
爪
夫
戈
尤
升
午
太
厶
六
廿

U4q 夫 *fū* husband

夫妻肺片 *fū qī fèi piàn* cold sliced beef and kidney (Sichuan)

U4r 戈 *gē* spear

戈乍 *gē zhà* custard
戈揸 *gē zhā* custard
鷄子戈揸 *jī zi gē zhā* pudding of egg and chicken gizzard, cut into strips and deep-fried

U4s 尤 *yóu* cuttlefish (see L13a.4a)

炒雙尤 *chǎo shuāng yóu* stir-fried cuttlefish and squid

U4t 升 *shēng* to rise

升瓜 *shēng guā* a zucchini-like vegetable

U4u 午 *wǔ* noon

午餐 *wǔ cān* lunch

U4v 太 see E3*1

U4w 厶 older form of U3c

U4x 六 *liù* six (see T2a.2a)

U4y 廿 alternate form of 二十 *èr shi* twenty

U5 Five-Stroke Indivisible Characters

U5a 水 *shuǐ* water

水餃 *shuǐ jiǎo* boiled ravioli
水晶鷄 *shuǐ jīng jī* jellied chicken (lit., "water crystal chicken")

水潸肉　*shuǐ hǔ ròu* water's edge pork (named after a
　　famous Ming dynasty novel; pork slices, stir-fried in
　　peppery oil, served on bed of bean sprouts; Sichuan)
水魚　*shuǐ yú* turtle
水貝　*shuǐ bèi* scallop
水母　*shuǐ mǔ* jellyfish
水芹菜　*shuǐ qín cài* parsley
水果　*shuǐ guǒ* fresh fruit
水菜　*shuǐ cài* watercress; trefoil
水底雲霞　*shuǐ dǐ yún xiá* clouds at the bottom of the
　　water (a five ingredient soup)
水仙茶　*shuǐ xiān chá* (SÉUI SÌN CHÀ) daffodil tea

U5b 五 *wǔ* five

五香粉　*wǔ xiāng fěn* five-spice powder (made of star
　　anise, clove, cinnamon, fennel, and brown pepper)
五香牛肉　*wǔ xiāng niú ròu* five-spice beef (cold
　　appetizer)
五柳全魚　*wǔ liǔ quán yú* five-willow whole fish (whole
　　fish with sweet and sour sauce containing five
　　shredded vegetables)
五彩 or 五綵　*wǔ cài* multi-colored (lit., "five
　　decorations")
五花肉　*wǔ huā ròu* pork rib meat
五花南　*wǔ huā nàn* flank meat
五星苹果鶏　*wǔ xīng píng guo jī* apples stuffed with
　　chicken meat, steamed (Beijing)

U5c 生 *shēng* raw, fresh

花生　*huā shēng* peanut
生菜蝦仁　*shēng cài xiā rén* shrimps with green
　　vegetable
生炒墨魚　*chēng chǎo mò yú* stir-fried squid and
　　vegetables
生菜　*shēng cài* lettuce
生菜包　*shēng cài bāo* stir-fried diced ingredients,
　　wrapped in lettuce leaves and eaten like tacos
生根　*shēng gēn* deep-fried gluten dough

水五生玉瓜中片方甘月平末巴本禾丘日去屯正

水五[生玉瓜中片方甘月平末巴本]禾丘日去屯正

生抽　*shēng chōu* light soy sauce
生馬麵　*shēng mǎ miàn* fresh noodles with fried meat and vegetables in thick soup

U5d 玉 *yù* jade

玉米　*yù mǐ* corn
玉蜀黍　*yù shú shǔ* corn
玉筍　*yù sǔn* baby corncobs
玉樹珊瑚　*yù shù shān hú* jade tree coral (crabmeat sauce served on parboiled Chinese broccoli)
玉蘭片　*yù lán piàn* dried sliced bamboo shoot
玉溪醬油　*yù xī jiàng yóu* fragrant sweet soy sauce
玉沿仙班　*yù zhǎo xiān bān* mock fried grouper (made of taro root)

U5e 瓜 *guā* melon, squash

黃瓜　*huáng guā* cucumber
冬瓜　*dōng guā* winter melon
瓜菜什錦　*guā cài shí jǐn* fancy mixed vegetables
香瓜　*xiāng guā* muskmelon
水瓜　*shuǐ guā* watermelon
西瓜　*xī guā* watermelon
木瓜　*mù guā* papaya
海瓜子　*hǎi guā zi* small clam
瓜皮蝦　*guā pí xiā* cucumber, jellyfish skin, and dried shrimp in vinegar dressing

U5f 中 *zhōng* middle; China

中國　*zhōng guo* China
中式　*zhōng shì* Chinese style

U5g 片 *piàn* slice

片兒川　*piàn er chuān* flat noodles with pickled pork and red-in-snow in soup (Hangzhou)
香片　*xiāng piàn* jasmine tea

U5h 方 *fāng* direction; square

火方　*huǒ fāng* ham
烤方　*kǎo fāng* pork rib with skin on, spit-roasted
烤素方　*kǎo sù fāng* vegetarian Peking duck (Hunan)
炸爆方　*zhá bào fāng* deep-fried eel with sweet garlic and
　　ginger sauce (Shanghai)

U5i 甘 *gān* sweet

甘草　*gān cǎo* licorice root
甘蔗　*gān zhè* sugar cane
甘藍菜　*gān lán cài* kale

U5j 月 *yuè* moon

月餅　*yuè bǐng* (YUHT BÉNG) moon cake (round, flat,
　　thick flaky pastry, with either sweet or salty filling;
　　Guangdong)
五仁月　*wǔ rén yuè* moon cake with five-nut sweet filling
月母鷄湯　*yuè mǔ jī tāng* chicken, bamboo shoot, and
　　wood ear soup (Sichuan)

U5k 平 *píng* level

北平　*běi píng* Peiping (Nationalist name for Beijing)
平津菜　*píng jīn cài* Peiping-Tientsin cuisine

U5l 末 *mò* tip, powder

肉末　*ròu mò* minced pork

U5m 巴 *bā* crust

鍋巴　*guō bā* crispy rice
巴菌　*bā qùn* a kind of pine mushroom

U5n 本 *běn* this

本店　*běn diàn* this shop; house special
本樓　*běn lóu* this shop; house special

水
生
玉
瓜
中
片
方
甘
月
平
末
巴
本
禾
丘
日
去
屯
正

U5o 禾 *hé* grain, cereal

禾黍 *hé shǔ* millet

U5p 丘 *qiū* mound

丘三燉鷄汁 *qiū sān dùn jī zhī* stewed chicken (Sichuan)

U5q 日 *rì* sun, day

日月紫菜捲 *rì yuè zǐ cài juǎn* sun-moon seaweed rolls (salted egg yolk and pork rolled up in seaweed sheets; Taiwan)

U5r 去 *qù* to go; remove

去骨鴨 *qù gǔ yā* boneless duck

U5s 屯 *tún* to accumulate

芋屯 *yù tún* steamed taro pudding

U5t 正 *zhèng* appropriate, pure

正宗 *zhèng zōng* orthodox, authentic

U6 Stroke Indivisible Characters

U6a 白 *bái* white

白菜 *bái cài* (BAAHK CHOI) bok choi (Chinese cabbage)

白果 *bái guǒ* gingko nut

白切鷄 *bái qiē jī* white-cut chicken (chicken poached in fragrant soup stock, served cold)

白斬鷄 *bái zhǎn jī* white-cut chicken

白瓜 *bái guā* white cucumber

白花 *bái huā* croaker (fish)

白修魚 *bái xiū yú* dace (fish)

白薯 *bái shǔ* sweet potato

白玉藏珍　*bái yù zàng zhēn* treasures of the white jade vault (winter melon stuffed with crabmeat and vegetables, steamed)

白脫　*bái tuō* butter

白汁　*bái zhī* white sauce

蔴糖甜鍋白　*má táng tiān guō bái* boneless pork ribs stuffed with sweet bean paste and steamed with sticky rice, sesame, and sugar (Shanghai)

白雲猪手　*bái yún zhū shǒu* white cloud pig's trotters (pickled in sweet vinegar; Guangdong)

白煮魚　*bái zhǔ yú* whole fish cooked in soup with ham and chicken meat (Anhui)

白灼蝦　*bái shāo xiā* (BAAHK CHEUK HĀ) scalded shrimps with dipping sauce

U6b 四　*sì* four

四川　*sì chuān* Szechuan

四色疏菜　*sì sè sū cài* four parboiled vegetables

白油四件　*bái yóu sì jiàn* chicken liver and gizzard, bamboo shoot, and mushroom, in white sauce

四季豆　*sì jì dòu* string bean (lit., "four-season bean")

四季豆腐　*sì jì dòu fu* stuffed dried bean curd (Anhui)

燴鴨四寶　*huì yā sì bǎo* duck's feet, intestine, stomach, and tongue, in thick sauce (Beijing)

四喜蘋果　*sì xǐ píng guo* four-happiness apples (stuffed with sticky rice and dried fruit and nuts, steamed)

U6c 皮　*pí* skin

豆腐皮　*dòu fu pí* bean curd skin

脆皮鷄　*cuì pí jī* crisp-skin deep-fried chicken

拌皮絲　*bàn pí sī* shredded pigskin salad

皮蛋　*pí dàn* preserved egg

U6d 石　*shí* rock

石斑魚　*shí bān yú* grouper

石鷄　*shí jī* a kind of frog

石耳　*shí ěr* rock mushroom

石榴　*shí liú* pomegranate

石榴鶏　*shí liú jī* pomegranate chicken (chicken slices and vegetables, wrapped in cellophane and deep-fried)

石螺　*shí luó* small land snails

U6e 米 *mǐ* uncooked rice; rice-flour noodles

米粉　*mǐ fěn* rice-flour vermicelli

大米　*dà mǐ* pearl rice

米熏鶏　*mǐ xūn jī* chicken smoked over sawdust-rice mixture

蝦米　*xiā mǐ* dried shrimp

姜米　*jiāng mǐ* ginger cut into rice-grain-sized pieces

U6f 羊 *yáng* sheep, lamb, goat

羊糕　*yáng gāo* jellied mutton

炸羊尾　*zhá yáng wěi* batter-fried balls of sweet bean paste (Beijing)

羊腿　*yáng tuǐ* leg of lamb

U6g 耳 *ěr* ear

葱油白耳絲　*cōng yóu bái ěr sī* shredded pig's ear in scallion sauce

木耳　*mù ěr* wood ear, tree fungus

耳環尤魚　*ěr huán yóu yú* squid "earrings"

U6h 田 *tián* rice paddy

田鶏　*tián jī* frog

田腿　*tián tuǐ* frog legs

U6i 古 *gǔ* ancient (occasionally used as non-standard abbreviation for T4a.10b 菇 *gū* mushroom)

古鹵肉　*gǔ lǔ ròu* sweet and sour pork

古渝笋鶏　*gǔ yú sǔn jī* old Chungking young chicken (marinated, deep-fried, then stewed; Sichuan)

U6j 瓦 *wǎ* tile

瓦塊魚　*wǎ kuài yú* sweet and sour fish chunks

U6k 衣 *yī* coat

豆腐衣　*dòu fu yī* bean curd skin

U6l 目 *mù* eye

目魚　*mù yú* cod
比目魚　*bǐ mù yú* sole
虱目魚　*shī mù yú* milkfish (lit., "louse eye fish")

U6m 虫 *chóng* insect

虫草鴨子　*chóng cǎo yā zi* steamed duck with a medicinal
　herb in soup

U6n 甲 *jiǎ* armor (also used as nonstandard
　abbreviation of L6*13 鴨 *yā* duck)

甲魚　*jiǎ yú* turtle

U6o 申 *shēn* a Chinese family name

申江豆腐　*shēn jiāng dòu fu* deep-fried bean curd with
　crab and vegetables

U6p 占 *zhàn* to occupy

占補魚　*zhàn bǔ yú* whitefish

U6q 及 *jí* to attain

及第　*jí dài* pork liver, kidney, heart, etc.

U6r 只 *zhǐ* classifier for counting miscellaneous
　things

白
四
皮
石
米
羊
耳
田
古
瓦
衣
目
虫
甲
申
占
及
只
[老
氷
朱
冬

U6s 老 *lǎo* old

老抽　*lǎo chōu* thick soy sauce
老酒　*lǎo jiǔ* wine and liquor

U6t 氷 *bīng* ice (see L2b.5b)

U6u 朱 *zhū* red (esp. of ink)

朱古力　*zhū gǔ lì* chocolate

U6v 冬 *dōng* winter (see T4*2)

U7 Seven-Stroke Indivisible Characters

U7a 西 *xī* west

西湖　*xī hú* West Lake (famous sight in Hangzhou)
西湖全魚　*xī hú quán yú* poached whole fish with sweet
　　and sour sauce (Hangzhou)
西瓜　*xī guā* watermelon
西洋菜　*xī yáng cài* watercress
西菜　*xī cài* watercress
西芹　*xī qín* celery
西檸　*xī níng* lemon
西蘭　*xī lán* broccoli
西米　*xī mǐ* tapioca
西谷米　*xī gǔ mǐ* tapioca
西施蛋　*xī shī dàn* beaten fresh eggs, fried with preserved
　　eggs, red ginger, and scallion (named after a legendary
　　beautiful woman)
西施舌　*xī shī shé* razor clams

U7b 百 *bǎi* hundred

百葉 or 百頁　*bǎi yè* (BAAK YIHP) third stomach of
　　cow; bean curd skin (lit., "hundred leaves")

百合　*bǎi hé* lily buds

紅棗百合湯　*hóng zǎo bǎi hé tāng* sweet soup with red
dates and lily buds (Shanghai)

百花酥鶉蛋　*bǎi huā sū chún dàn* shrimp toast with a
quail egg in each piece (Guangdong)

百酥肥鴨　*bǎi sū féi yā* steamed boneless duck coated
with mashed taro and deep-fried

U7c 肉　*ròu* (YUHK) meat (pork if not otherwise specified)

牛肉　*niú ròu* beef

回鍋肉　*huí guō ròu* twice-cooked pork

火肉　*huǒ ròu* (FÓ YUHK) spit-roasted pig (Guangdong)

肉桂　*ròu guì* cinnamon

U7d 夾　*jiā* to sandwich, squeeze between chopsticks, etc.

炸蟹夾　*zhá xiè jiā* meat slices filled with crabmeat, deep-
fried

夾心肉　*jiā xīn ròu* pork shoulder meat

夾沙肉　*jiā shā ròu* fatty pork with sweet bean-paste
filling, stewed (Sichuan)

蛋夾　*dàn jiā* meat-filled omlet

清蒸三夾魚　*qīng zhēng sān jiā yú* steamed fish filled with
alternating slices of three ingredients

U7e 舌　*shé* tongue

滷豬舌　*lǔ zhū shé* cold stewed pork tongue

紅燒牛舌頭　*hóng shāo niú shé tou* red-cooked whole
beef tongue

西施舌　*xī shī shé* razor clam

舌鰨　SÌHT DAAHP sole

U7f 出　*chū* to leave; to remove

出骨鴨　*chū gǔ yā* boneless duck

西
百
肉
夾
舌
出
血
母
成
赤
糸

U7g 血 *xiě* blood

血腸 *xiě cháng* blood sausage

U7h 母 *mǔ* mother

母鷄 *mǔ jī* hen
子母會 *zǐ mǔ huì* mother and child meet (deep-fried
  pigeon with pigeon-egg sauce; Sichuan)

U7i 成 *chéng* become

成都 *chéng dū* Chengtu (capital of Sichuan)
成都子鷄 *chéng dū zǐ jī* chicken pieces on bone, quick-
  fried, then simmered in spicy sauce
成麥舟波 *chéng mài dān bō* corn boiled with beaten egg
  and served with mashed potato and garnish (Taiwan)
成吉斯汗 *chéng jí sī hàn* Genghis Khan
成吉斯汗烤羊肉 *chéng jí sī hàn kǎo yáng ròu* Genghis
  Khan lamb (thin slices cooked on convex griddle)

U7j 赤 *chì* red

赤璧會商 *chì bì huì shāng* red disk conference (shrimp
  cakes and steamed egg whites with meat and vegetables
  in soup; Taiwan)
赤線 *chì xiàn* red snapper

U7k 糸 *sī* thread (see L7a.7a)

U8 Eight-Stroke Indivisible Characters

U8a 金 *jīn* (GÀM) gold

金針菜 *jīn zhēn cài* gold needle vegetable (dried tiger lily)
金針菇 *jīn zhēn gū* needle mushroom
金茸 *jīn róng* needle mushroom
金華 *jīn huá* Kinhwa (place in Zhejiang Province,
  famous for its ham)

金華玉樹鷄　*jīn huá yù shù jī* Kinhwa jade tree chicken (ham slices sandwiched between chicken slices, on bed of greens)

金腿　*jīn tuǐ* Kinhwa ham

炸金花　*zhá jīn huā* deep-fried stuffed bean curd puffs

金橘　*jīn jú* (GÀM GWĀT) kumquat

金笋　*jīn sǔn* carrot

金瓜　*jīn guā* pumpkin

金槍魚　*jīn qiāng yú* tuna (lit., "gold spear fish")

金錢牛排　*jīn qián niú pǎi* gold coin steak (medallions of beef)

金銀絲　*jīn yín sī* gold and silver threads (shredded carrot and white radish)

金銀肝　*jīn yín gān* pork liver stuffed with fat, steamed (Guangdong)

金玉滿堂　*jīn yù mǎn táng* hall filled with gold and jade (fried bean curd in thick gravy; Guangdong)

U8b 長 *cháng* long

長沙　*cháng shā* Changsha (capital of Hunan Province)

長沙牛柳　*cháng shā niú liǔ* sliced beef and vegetables in hot sauce (Hunan)

長魚　*cháng yú* eel

長城　*cháng chéng* Great Wall of China

長江　*cháng jiāng* Yangtze River

長豇豆　*cháng jiang dòu* long green beans

U8c 貝 *bèi* mollusc, scallop

干貝　*gān bèi* dried scallop (sometimes also used for fresh scallop)

乾貝蘿蔔湯　*gān bèi luó bo tāng* dried scallop and turnip soup (Hunan)

U8d 武 *wǔ* warrior

武定壯涼鷄　*wǔ dìng zhuàng liáng jī* cold steamed spiced chicken (Yunnan)

武漢　*wǔ hàn* Wuhan (capital of Hubei Province)

金
長
貝
武
里
色
車
克
幸
甫
两

U8e 里 *Lǐ* Chinese mile

里脊 or 里吉 *lǐ jǐ* pork tenderloin
鷄里爆 *jī lǐ bào* quick-fried chicken meat and pig
stomach (Shandong)

U8f 色 *sè* color

四色蔬菜 *sì sè sū cài* four kinds of parboiled vegetables
三色拼盤 *sān sè pīn pán* three-variety cold appetizer
plate

U8g 車 *chē* car, vehicle

車厘 *chē lǐ* cherry

U8h 克 *kè* gram

克鐸魚 *kè duó yú* haddock

U8i 幸 *xìng* good fortune

幸福雙 *xìng fú shuāng* steamed cake with sweet filling
(Guangdong)

U8j 甫 *fǔ* abbreviation of L5a.8b

甫魚 *fǔ yú* flat fish; skate ray

U8k 两 *liǎng* two (see U9d)

U9 Nine-Stroke Indivisible Characters

U9a 東 *dōng* east

廣東 *guǎng dōng* Canton Province
東江菜 *dōng jiāng cài* cuisine of eastern Guangdong
Province
東坡肉 *dōng bō ròu* Tong-Po steamed pork (named after
a celebrated poet)

東安　*dōng ān* a county in Hunan Province

東安鷄　*dōng ān jī* chicken pieces stewed in spicy gravy (Hunan)

U9b 虎　*hǔ* tiger

虎皮　*hǔ pí* tiger skin (used in names of dishes that have a striped appearance, e.g., the following item)

虎皮扣肉　*hǔ pí kòu ròu* tiger skin thrice-cooked pork (served with the slices arranged so that fat and rind alternate)

熗虎尾　*qiàng hǔ wěi* quick-poached eels

U9c 果　*guǒ* fruit, nut

白果　*bái guǒ* gingko nut

蘋果　*píng guo* apple

果皮　*guǒ pí* tangerine peel

水果　*shuǐ guǒ* fresh fruit

U9d 兩　*liǎng* two, both

兩冬　*liǎng dōng* two winters (black mushroom and bamboo shoot)

兩吃大蝦　*liǎng chī dà xiā* large prawns cooked two ways (e.g., half of them deep-fried, the other half stir-fried with sauce)

兩面黃　*liǎng miàn huáng* noodles or bean curd pan-browned with scallions and garlic (lit., "both sides yellow"; Hunan, Sichuan, Shanghai)

U9e 角　*jiǎo* corner; triangle or square; croquette

芋角　*yù jiǎo* (WUH GOK) deep-fried taro croquette

鹹水角　*xián shuǐ jiǎo* (HÀAHM SÉUI GOK) sticky-rice dough with meat and vegetable filling, deep-fried

U9f 串　*chuàn* to string (beads), skewer

葱串排骨　*cōng chuàn pái gǔ* spareribs stuffed with scallion segments

U9g 兒 *ér* child; *-r* diminutive suffix (as in 蝦仁兒 *xiā rér* shelled shrimp; often written 儿 in such cases)

U9h 呂 *lǚ* one of the classical musical notes

呂宋　*lǚ sòng* Luzon
呂宋翅　*lǚ sòng chì* a type of shark fin from the Philippines

U9i 美 *měi* beautiful (see T6d.3)

U10 Ten-Stroke Indivisible Characters

U10a 南 *nán* south

南瓜　*nán guā* pumpkin or other winter squash
南乳　*nán rǔ* red fermented bean curd
南京　*nán jīng* Nanking
湖南　*hú nán* Hunan
河南　*hé nán* Henan
雲南　*yún nán* Yunnan
海南　*hǎi nán* Hainan
越南　*yuè nán* Vietnam
南安鴨　*nán ān yā* pressed duck
南塘鷄頭肉湯　*nán táng jī tóu ròu tāng* prickly water lily seeds cooked in syrup

U10b 咸 *xián* salty (also written L10*12 鹹)

咸水角　*xián shuǐ jiǎo* (HÀAHM SÉUI GOK) sticky-rice dough with meat and vegetable filling, deep-fried
咸蛋　*xián dàn* preserved egg
咸燒白　*xián shāo bái* steamed pork slices and pickled vegetable (a version of L3a.4a 扣肉; Sichuan)

U10c 重 *chóng* heavy

重慶　*chóng qìng* Chungking (former capital of Sichuan Province)

重油酥餅　*chóng yóu sū bǐng* flat buns with pork fat and sesame filling (Shanghai)

U10d 面 *miàn* face, surface; noodles (as abbreviated form of E11a.10)

兩面黃　*liǎng miàn huáng* noodles or bean curd pan-browned on both sides

U10e 兔 *miǎn* to avoid

免治　*miǎn zhì* minced
免治牛肉飯　*miǎn zhì niú ròu fàn* minced beef with rice (Guangdong)

U10f 姜 *jiāng* ginger (see T4a.15a)

U10g 羌 *jiāng* ginger (see T4a.15a)

U11 Eleven-Stroke Indivisible Characters

U11a 馬 *mǎ* horse

馬蹄　*mǎ tí* water chestnut (lit., "horse hoof")
馬蹄糕　*mǎ tí gāo* (MÁH TÀIH GŌH) water chestnut pudding
馬鈴薯　*mǎ líng shǔ* potato (lit., "horse bell tuber")
馬鈴茨　*mǎ líng cí* potato
馬豆糕　*mǎ dòu gāo* jellied lentil pudding
馬仔　*mǎ zǐ* Chinese "popcorn"
馬鮫魚　*mǎ jiāo yú* mackerel
馬友魚　*mǎ yǒu yú* sturgeon
馬安橋　*mǎ ān qiáo* a kind of eel
馬鞍橋燒肉　*mǎ ān qiáo shāo ròu* pork rib stewed with eel and garlic
馬蓮肉　*mǎ lián ròu* pork boiled with spices (Beijing)
馬寶子麵　*mǎ bǎo zǐ miàn* noodles with lamb (Lanzhou)
馬牙肉　*mǎ yá ròu* spareribs steamed in the form of horse's teeth (Shandong)
馬來　*mǎ lái* Malaya

[馬
麥
爽
兔
鬼
烏
鹵
黃
島
鳥
粵
象]

馬來亞　　*mǎ lái yǎ* Malaya
馬來糕　　*mǎ lái gāo* sweet flaky pastry (＝千層糕 *qiān cēng gāo*)
馬拉糕　　*mǎ lá gāo* sponge cake

U11b 麥　*mài* wheat

麥油　　*mài jiǔ* beer
麥魚　　*mài yú* squid

U11c 爽　*shuǎng* clear, happy

爽口牛丸　　*shuǎng kǒu niú wàn* beef meatball soup (Guangdong)

U11d 兔　*tù* rabbit

糊辣兔丁　　*hú là tù dīng* diced rabbit in gravy of charred chili peppers (Sichuan)

U11e 鬼　*guǐ* devil

油炸鬼　　*yóu zhá guǐ* deep-fried dough strips (alternate name for 油條 *yóu tiáo*)

U12 Twelve-Stroke Indivisible Characters

U12a 烏　*wū* crow

烏龍茶　　*wū lóng chá* Oolong tea
烏賊魚　　*wū zéi yú* cuttlefish
烏龍吐珠　　*wū lóng tǔ zhū* crow and dragon spit pearls (sea cucumber braised with quail eggs)
烏魚　　*wū yú* snakehead mullet
烏參　　*wū shēn* a type of sea cucumber

U12b 鹵　*lǔ* gravy; Shantung (Shandong)

鹵味　　*lǔ wèi* spiced stewed pig's offal

U13 Thirteen-Stroke Indivisible Characters

U13a 黃 *huáng* yellow; egg yolk

蟹黃　*xiè huáng* crab eggs
黃瓜　*huáng guā* cucumber
黃豆　*huáng dòu* soybean
黃芽白　*huáng yá bái* celery cabbage
黃山藥　*huáng shān yào* a long thin tuber (Jap. *yamaimo*)
黃花　*huáng huā* dried licorice buds
黃油　*huáng yóu* butter

U13b 島 *dǎo* island (see E9a.4a)

U13c 鳥 *niǎo* bird (see E9a. 4b)

U14 Fourteen-Stroke Indivisible Characters

U14a 粵 *yuè* Canton Province (Guangdong)

U14b 象 *xiàng* elephant

象牙鲅魚　*xiàng yá bu yú* elephant tusk fish (fish slices with spring bamboo shoot sauce; Zhejiang)
紅燒象鼻　*hóng shāo xiàng bí* red-cooked elephant trunk

Index of English Names

This Index lists selected dishes, ingredients, and cooking methods according to English names users of this book are likely to know, which are in many cases not names that are used in the Glossary. Therefore, do not be disconcerted when you look up "hundred-year eggs" in the Index, are referred to U6c, and then find no entry under U6c that says "hundred-year eggs": it is easy to guess that the entry "preserved eggs" is what you are looking for. In view of the diverse spellings of Chinese names found on English-language menus, it is impossible to list all the variant spellings of, say, 'moo shu pork,' though I have tried to include the more common spellings. If you don't find what you're looking for under the spelling that you know, run your eyes up and down the page in search of possible alternate spellings.